COOKING
WITH THE
MASTERS OF
FOOD & WINE

Front and back cover photographs by Robert N. Fish
Food styling by Susan Devaty
Editorial direction by Fred Hernandez
Editorial assistance by Nadine Guarrera

Each of the photographs is copyright © by the person who
has graciously consented to its use:

Peter Aaron, page: 188 bottom. *Franklin Avery*, page: 216. *Batista Moon Studio*, pages: 180, 181.
John Brennan, pages: 34, 35, 36. *Jim Britt*, page: 156. *Bruce Brown*, page: 38.
Rick Browne, pages: 6, 7, 20, 29, 33, 40 (all), 41 (all), 49, 51, 52, 54, 67, 74, 81, 88, 92, 93, 110,
125, 167, 168, 184, 199. *Ed Carey*, page: 157. *Molly Chappellet*, page: 189 right.
Naomi Duguid/Asia Access, page: 108. *Faith Echtermeyer*, page: 98.
Robert Fish, pages: Front & back cover, 16, 47, 90, 227. *Frankie Frankeny*, page: 58, 59.
Richard Gillette, page: 207. *Carol Gillot*, page: 86. *Gayle Gleason*, page: 198.
Lynn Grace, pages: 196, 197. *Richard Gorman*, page: 135. *Jacques Guillard/ Scope*, page: 243.
Michel Guillard, page: 237. *Helmut Horn*, pages: 3, 43, 113, 139, 143, 166, 203.
Kevin Hyde/Photographers of People, Ltd., page: 132. *Thomas Lea*, page: 189 left.
Fred Lyon, page: 188 top. *Peter Michael Winery*, pages: 204, 242. *Richard Mitchell*, page: 64.
Richard Morgenstein, page: 80. *Jim Patton*, page: 187. *Todd Pickering*, page: 212.
Randall Photography, page: 155. *Douglas Sandberg*, pages: 178, 186. *Saur Visum*, page: 240.
Patrick Tregenza, pages: 26, 97, 100, 102, 103, 173.

The author and publisher expressly disclaim any responsibility for any liability,
loss or risk, personal or otherwise, that is incurred as a consequence, directly
or indirectly, of the use and application of any of the contents of this book.

Library of Congress Cataloging-in-Publication Data

Fish, Kathleen DeVanna
    Cooking With The Masters of Food & Wine
    Kathleen DeVanna Fish
        p. 256 cm.
    ISBN 1-883214-14-9

1. Cookery, International. 2. Cooking Festivals. 3. Food and Wine.
4. Wineries. 5. Famous Chefs.

97-071558   CIP

Includes indexes
Autobiography page

Published by Bon Vivant Press
an imprint of The Millennium Publishing Group
PO Box 1994
Monterey, CA 93942

Printed in Singapore

COOKING
WITH THE
MASTERS OF
FOOD & WINE

Kathleen DeVanna Fish

BON
VIVANT

Table of Contents

The Chefs

The Wineries

United States

France

Germany

Italy

Portugal

Cooking with the Masters of Food & Wine

For more than a decade, the world's finest chefs and winemakers have gathered every year at the coast of California's incomparable Carmel Highlands to share their appreciation of food and wine with a select group of participants. Now, for the first time ever, their stellar recipes and exquisite wine pairings are available to everyone.

The Masters of Food & Wine event unites Michelin two-star and three-star chefs from throughout the world with the most notable wine masters.

For a week every year, the culinary masters present exhibition cooking demonstrations, prepare elegant caviar luncheons and impeccable dinners, participate in mushroom hunting tours and share their cooking secrets with one another. The wine masters from throughout Europe and the United States have a unique opportunity to introduce their best vintages and recommendations — and many of them present exquisite recipes from their wineries' kitchens. The event culminates with a black-tie grand finale dinner, complete with white-gloved servers.

It's truly a world-class gastronomic event, a living reference of contemporary culinary trends. And now you can sample the cuisine of the stars of food and wine.

This beautiful book is your ticket to the global gourmet gala. It presents top-of-the line recipes of 63 world-renowned chefs and winemakers. The 175 signature recipes are often accompanied by the experts' wine selections, as well as mouth-watering photographs that preview the flavors of The Masters of Food & Wine.

The chefs take us on a delectable journey around the world, offering dynamic menus for all occasions and tastes. This unique cookbook traverses a wide range of culinary and ethnic food traditions, resulting in a captivating array of creative, yet simple and clean dishes.

Julia Child, for example, prepares Monterey Bay Sole Food Stew, Roy Yamaguchi offers Seared Ahi with an Island-Style Passion Fruit Shrimp Salsa and Todd English prepares Risotto with Wild Mushrooms and Asparagus.

Joyce Goldstein offers a tempting Mediterranean meal, while Lisa and Anthony Damiano present their Provencal inspirations. Lidia Bastianich introduces her innovative Northern Italian fare and Larry Forgione presents highlights of his New American cuisine.

Norman Van Aken prepares Rhum and Pepper Painted Fish, Nancy Oakes offers Maple-Cured Pork Loin with White Corn, Matanzas Creek Winery presents Lavender-Roasted Lamb and Susan Spicer cooks a Vegetable Gratin with Polenta and Smoked Tomato Butter.

For dessert, Bruno Feldeisen prepares Chocolate Croissant Pudding and Gale Gand offers Plum Crostata.

And that's just a sampling.

The recipes have been adapted for the home cook, using contemporary ingredients in an easy-to-use format that includes preparation and cooking times. Some of the recipes are simple. Some are more complex. But each of them is exquisite.

This book gives you the opportunity to get to know the chefs. You'll learn how they started cooking and developed their approaches to cuisine, as well as where they cook and what some of their special accomplishments are.

The wines included in *Cooking with the Masters of Food & Wine* provide a practical reference to the best the world's vineyards have to offer. The selected wines represent the United States, France, Germany, Italy and Portugal.

American wines include such stars as J Wine Company, Bernardus Winery, Chalone, Chappellet Vineyard, Chateau Montelena Winery, Duckhorn Vineyards and Pahlmeyer.

France is represented by Champagne Taittinger and Le Domaines Barons de Rothschild, to name just two. German wines include Georg Breuer, and Italian wines include Marchesi Antinori, and Portuguese wines include Graham's Port and Blandy's Madeira.

Until now, participation in The Masters of Food & Wine event was available to a select few. Those who have been fortunate to attend will want to collect the best recipes the past decade has produced. Those who have never participated can now share in the knowledge, creativity and celebration of our modern gastronomic heritage.

Experience for yourself the recipes, flavors and artful presentations that have had the international media singing the praises of this spectacular event for more than ten years.

Prepare to be tempted.

On The Menu

Appetizers

Crab Cakes with Tartar Sauce - *Nancy Oakes, 116*
Everest Tarte Flambé - *Jean Joho, 95*
Grilled Foie Gras with Fig Chutney - *Michael Ginor, 79*
Mushrooms à la Russe - *Lisa and Anthony Damiano, 57*
Peppered Oysters - *Diana Kennedy, 102*
Roasted Oysters - *Todd English, 65*
Saint Tropez Terrine - *Michel Richard, 130*
Sautéed Foie Gras with Balsamic Sauce - *Michael Ginor, 79*
Seared Ahi with Island-Style Passion Fruit Shrimp Salsa - *Roy Yamaguchi, 176*
Seared Foie Gras with Sautéed Turnips and Tamarind Glaze - *Traci Des Jardins, 59*
Shrimp Pampusky with Orange Vodka Sauce - *Lisa and Anthony Damiano, 56*
Smoked Salmon and Caviar Tart - *Lisa and Anthony Damiano, 57*
Smoked Steelhead with Fennel and Green Olive Tapenade - *J Wine Company, 201*
Star-Anise-Cured Salmon with Arugula - *J Wine Company, 201*

Breads & Pastry

Country Ham, Cheese and Scallion Biscuits - *Larry Forgione, 75*
Harvest Focaccia - *Michael Chiarello, 45*
Kugelhopf - *Gerard Bechler, 32*
Rosemary Sourdough Flatbread - *Cuvaison Winery, 194*
Rustic Bread - *Nancy Silverton, 141*

Soups

Brodetto - *Michael Chiarello, 46*
Fresh Tomato Soup with Tomato and Basil Salad - *Guenter Seeger, 132*
Garlic Soup - *Susan Spicer, 145*
Monterey Bay Sole Food Stew - *Julia Child, 50*
Shrimp and Corn Soup - *Jan Birnbaum, 35*
Soup of Potato with Porcini Mascarpone en Brodo with Shaved Truffles and Parmigiano - *Todd English, 67*
Tomato and Red Pepper Soup - *Spottswoode Vineyard & Winery, 226*
Vegetable Soup with Fennel - *Lidia Bastianich, 30*

Salads and Dressings

Charlotte of Asparagus and Maine Crabmeat with Leek Vinaigrette - *Craig Shelton, 135*
Cucumber and Wakame Sunomono - *Nobuyuki Matsuhisa, 110*
Fire Roasted Ahi Tuna Tenderloin with Chopped Vegetable Salad and Ginger Glaze - *Bradley Ogden, 121*
Grilled Duck Salad with Endive - *Jeremiah Tower, 157*
Herb Spiced Venison Salad - *Charles Palmer, 123*
Romaine, Gorgonzola and Walnut Salad with Garlic Croutons - *Silver Oak Cellars, 222*
Rouget Filets in Herb Crust with Blood Orange Confit and Frisée Salad - *Guenter Seeger, 133*
Seared Shrimp Salad with Feta Cheese and Candied Garlic - *Roy Yamaguchi, 175*
Stone Crab Salad with Pickled Japanese Relish and Ginger - *Mark Militello, 113*
Tabbouleh of Maine Lobster with Cilantro Pesto - *Brian Whitmer, 172*

Pasta & Grains

Corn and Mushroom Ravioli with Mushroom Coulis - *Patrick Clark, 55*
Creamy Wild Mushroom Polenta - *Bradley Ogden, 120*
Fettuccine with Grilled Artichokes - *Michael Chiarello, 45*
Mahogany Rice - *Ridge Vineyards, 217*
Ravioli Filled with Rock Shrimp and Scallops - *J Wine Company, 202*
Ravioli Filled with Beans and Leeks - *Roberto Donna, 61*
Oriental Lobster Ravioli with Sun-dried Tomato and Smoky Chili Sauce - *Susur Lee, 109*
Red Table Wine Risotto - *Pahlmeyer, 213*
Risotto with Artichokes - *Marcella Hazan, 92*
Risotto with Squab - *Lidia Bastianich, 31*
Risotto with Wild Mushrooms and Asparagus - *Todd English, 65*
Spaghetti with Shrimp and Porcini - *Giuliano Hazan, 89*

Main Courses

Bastilla-Moroccan Chicken and Filo Pie - *Joyce Goldstein, 81*
Cannelloni of Lamb and Eggplant - *Brian Whitmer, 168*
Cassoulet of Lentils with Lamb, Sausage and Pork - *Fred Halpert, 86*
Cilantro Marinated Prawns with Cauliflower Tahini - *Monique Andrée Barbeau, 22*
Grilled Chicken Breast, Drunken Black Beans, Smoked Tomato Ranchero - *Dean Fearing, 69*
Marinated Lamb Sandwich with Spicy Aïoli - *Todd English, 66*
New Mexico Sausage and Chile Relleno Soufflé - *Bruce Aidells, 18*

Seafood

Creole Spiny Lobster with Fresh Conch - *Mark Militello, 114*
Curried Sea Scallops with Dungeness Crab Wontons - *Brian Whitmer, 170*
Fresh Sardine Filets on Basil Potatoes, Black Olives, Tomato-Rosemary Vinaigrette - *Cal Stamenov, 153*
Halibut with Avocado Butter - *Sarah's Vineyard, 220*
Herb-Crusted Prawns, Warm Mushroom Potato Salad, Truffle Essence - *Monique Andrée Barbeau, 27*
Lobster in Rosé Champagne Aspic - *Champagne Taittinger, 232*
Onion Bass with Hearts of Palm and Boniato - *Dawn Sieber, 137*
Oven-Roasted Salmon with Hazelnut Crust - *Monique Andrée Barbeau, 24*
Red Chile Crusted Sea Bass with Roasted Clams, Mussels, Calamari Risotto - *Mark Kiffin, 106*
Rhum & Pepper Painted Fish with Habañero-Mango Mojo - *Norman Van Aken, 160*
Roasted Halibut with Potato Purée and Mushroom Ragu - *Roberto Donna, 62*
Roasted Lobster with Ginger and Alsace Gewürztraminer - *Jean Joho, 96*
Salmon in Winter - *Madeleine Kamman, 99*
Pacific Salmon with Pencil Asparagus and Morels - *Brian Whitmer, 169*
Sardines "A Day in Nice" - *Joachim Splichal, 148*
Santa Barbara Shrimp with Spicy Lemon Garlic Sauce - *Nobuyuki Matsuhisa, 111*
Seared Ulua and Szechuan-Style Shrimp with Chinese Peas and Green Onions - *Roy Yamaguchi, 177*
Seattle's Pike Place Salmon Sausage - *Bruce Aidells, 20*
Shrimps in Pumpkin-Seed Sauce - *Diana Kennedy, 104*

Poultry & Game

Grilled Chicken and Turkey Sausage with Sun-Dried Tomatoes - *Bruce Aidells, 19*
Grilled Rabbit with Mustard Sauce - *Sarah's Vineyard, 220*
Roasted Breast of Chicken, Fava Beans, Grilled Portobella Mushrooms and Tarragon - *Fred Halpert, 87*
Roasted Quail with Dried Cherry Herb Stuffing - *Peter Michael Winery, 215*
Sautéed Breast of Chicken with Bacon, Mushrooms and Wilted Spinach - *Larry Forgione, 75*
Stove Top Duck - *Julia Child, 51*
Venison Chops Montelena - *Chateau Montelena Winery, 192*
Venison Sausage - *Bruce Aidells, 18*
Venison Wrapped in Pancetta with Turnips, Butternut Squash and Black Truffles - *Cal Stamenov, 151*

Meat

Chile Cured Beef - *Wendy Brodie, 39*
Filet Mignon in Pastry - *Chateau Pichon Longueville, 235*
Grilled Lamb Brochettes with Moroccan Spices - *Joyce Goldstein, 83*
Grilled Marinated Leg of Lamb - *Spottswoode Vineyard & Winery, 226*
Lavender Roasted Lamb - *Matanzas Creek Winery, 208*
Maple-Cured Pork Loin with Cider Sauce - *Nancy Oakes, 119*
Mesquite Grilled Pork Loin - *Ridge Vineyards, 217*
Roasted Rack of Lamb with Stuffed Tomatoes and Potato Risotto - *Cal Stamenov, 151*

Vegetables & Side Dishes

Braised Leeks with Black Truffles and Balsamic Vinaigrette - *Alessandro Stratta, 154*
Broccoli, Shiitake and Goat Cheese - *Laura Chenel, 42*
Caramelized Plantain Mash en Relleno - *Norman Van Aken, 164*
Corn Hominy Cakes with the Season's Best Vegetables and Smoky Onion Vinaigrette - *Jan Birnbaum, 37*
Gratin of Fennel - *Fred Halpert, 85*
Sautéed Japanese Mushrooms with Yuzu Dressing - *Nobuyuki Matsuhisa, 111*
Vegetable Gratin with Polenta and Smoked Tomato Butter - *Susan Spicer, 146*
Vegetable Tagine - *Joyce Goldstein, 84*

Sauces & Condiments

Asian Dipping Sauce - *Nancy Oakes, 116*
Caramel Citrus Sauce - *Wendy Brodie, 39*
Fig Chutney - *Michael Ginor, 79*
Fire-Roasted Tomato Chipotle Salsa - *Mark Kiffin, 107*
Ginger Glaze - *Bradley Ogden, 121*
Picante Dried Red Chile Rub - *Mark Kiffin, 106*

Final Temptations

Carta Da Musica - *Giuliano Bugialli, 41*
Chocolate Cake - *Graham's Port, 253*
Chocolate Crème Brûlée - *Bruno Feldeisen, 73*
Chocolate Croissant Pudding - *Bruno Feldeisen, 73*
Chocolate Hazelnut Bar with Raspberry Sauce - *Michel Richard, 129*
Chocolate Pine Nut Torte with Caramel Citrus Sauce - *Wendy Brodie, 39*
Chocolate Sour Cream Marble Cake - *Gale Gand, 77*
Cuban Bread Brûlée with Añejo Espresso Caramel - *Norman Van Aken, 165*
Earl Grey Tea Chocolate Truffles - *Anne Parker Johnson, 124*
Key Lime Natilla en Tortilla - *Norman Van Aken, 161*
Pecan Puff Pastry with Chocolate Sauce and Sabayon - *Jeremiah Tower, 158*
Plum Crostata - *Gale Gand, 77*
Tower of the Islands - *Dawn Sieber, 138*
Upside Down Chocolate Soufflés with Chocolate Spaghetti and
Bittersweet Chocolate Sorbet - *François Payard, 127*
White Chocolate Banana Cream Pie - *Nancy Oakes, 117*

Masters of Food & Wine: The First Decade

The idea that led to the highly successful Masters of Food & Wine took shape over the Atlantic Ocean in 1984.

During one of his frequent transatlantic flights, Helmut Horn, a businessman and president of Coastal Hotel Group, wondered how he could link the rich traditions of European cooking with the burgeoning cuisine of the United States.

The answer: an international summit of the best cooks and winemakers.

Horn's background provided him with the associations necessary to realize this ambitious plan. His years of international hostelry management gave him access to some of the world's great chefs and winemakers. Significantly, the 747 in which he was flying was under the management of his long-time friend, Frank Beckman, executive vice president of Lufthansa German Airlines.

When he arrived in Frankfurt, Germany, Horn decided to further pursue the idea. He contacted another close friend, German wine expert and author Bernhard Breuer, a man intimately involved with the fine wines and cuisine of Germany and the fourth generation Breuer to run Scholl and Hillebrand wine company.

Horn's enthusiasm for the idea seemed to be contagious. The next step was to find a spot where the ground-breaking event could take root.

A site was selected — the spectacular Highlands Inn on the Pacific Ocean's rugged Carmel Highlands coast and the flagship of the Coastal Hotel Group

properties. Horn felt confident that the resort's management team contained the collective talent and dedication necessary to bring to fruition this extraordinary and difficult undertaking. He also felt certain that the dramatic setting of Highlands Inn was just right for the prestigious international event he envisioned.

Although scores of people helped get the event on its feet, the responsibility of transforming the initial concept into reality was put primarily in the hands of three people: David Fink, then Highlands Inn food and beverage director and now general manager; Gabriela Knubis of Knubis Communications, who was handling the hotel's public relations; and, in Germany, Horn's friend and advisor, Bernhard Breuer. Also among the founding figures were Mario Scheuermann, writer/consultant, Hamburg, Germany; Bernd Philippi of Weingut Koehler-Ruprecht, Rheinpfalz, Germany; Josef Viehauser of Le Carnard, Hamburg, Germany, and Chef Joachim Splichal.

While Fink coordinated the logistics and countless details involved in presenting the event at the hotel, Knubis worked closely with him in creating the program and bringing the event to the attention of the public. Meanwhile, in Germany, Breuer began talking to chefs and winemakers, the finest in that country and among the best in the world, convincing them to travel halfway around the world to display their talents on the California coast.

Providing the vital transatlantic link to the event was Lufthansa German Airlines. Drawing upon a reputation as one of the finest airlines in the world, Lufthansa's management decided that support for the event would further the company's own goals in conveying and showcasing the quality of fine German wine and cuisine.

When the event debuted in 1987, it was applauded by the media, the participating chefs and winemakers, and the audience, for its sophistication and accessibility. Then, as now, cooking classes, luncheons, dinners, culinary tours and wine seminars formed the core format.

In the third year, a new player joined the team. Chef Brian Whitmer, recently from New York's famed Montrachet restaurant and Tavern-On-the-Green, and formerly a protégé of Bradley Ogden, became executive chef at Highlands Inn. His influence advanced the entire food operation at the resort, adding a new dimension to the Masters of Food & Wine. And, because of the success of the event's first years, it was decided to expand the scope, to include Italy, France and Canada, as well as Germany and the United States. It had become a truly international exposition of the best food and wine the world has to offer.

In 1994, Lufthansa was joined by its alliance partner, United Airlines, as co-sponsor of the prestigious event and serving as official airline of the Masters within the United States.

Highlands Inn appointed Cal Stamenov to the post of executive chef in 1995. Stamenov brought experience acquired in the European tradition, under some of the world's most prestigious chefs, among them Masa Kobaishi, Jean-Louis Palladin, Alain Ducasse, Pierre Gagnaire and Michel Richard. With preparations well underway for the ninth Masters of Food & Wine, Stamenov joined in with enthusiasm.

As the prestige and reputation of the Masters spread throughout the industry and to food and wine connoisseurs across the world, it attracted many of the profession's most notable names. The roster of visiting chefs and winemakers who have participated in the first decade reads like a virtual Who's Who of international gastronomy.

Throughout the ten years of its existence, the Masters of Food & Wine has offered an extraordinary forum where the world's culinary and wine stars cook for one another and for fortunate audience members.

And, as it begins its second decade, the Masters of Food & Wine has become a living reference of contemporary culinary trends — a global gourmet gala.

As one writer, David Hay of Gourmet Traveller, says, "This must be one of the most exciting food and wine festivals in the world . . . It takes supreme talent, magically orchestrated dining adventures and a fairy tale seascape location and weaves them into an event full of culinary brilliance, yet it never loses touch with the basic premise that food and wine should be fun."

Helmut Horn
President and Founding Shareholder
Coastal Hotel Group

Helmut Horn is the visionary who first conceived of the Masters of Food & Wine. His revolutionary concept was to bring together Europe's rich epicurean traditions and the excitement of America's contemporary culinary scene.

His idea came to fruition in 1987, when the first Masters of Food & Wine was presented at Highlands Inn.

"In offering the Masters of Food & Wine, our interest is not only to educate and heighten awareness of the culinary arts, but to deepen the enjoyment of that happy love affair," he said.

Horn joined Horizon Hotels (a predecessor of Coastal Hotel Group) as president in 1985. His early hotel experiences include various food and beverage positions at the Ritz Hotel-Paris, Waldorf Astoria-New York, Hilton Hotels-Chicago and Denver, leading to the position of food & beverage director at the Fairmont Hotel in Dallas.

In 1974, he joined Hyatt International Corp. as operations coordinator for the entire Far East and Australia, based in Hong Kong. He was the opening general manager of Hyatt International United Nations Plaza Hotel in New York.

In 1981, he joined Dunfey (now Omni) Hotels as group director and vice president in charge of the six Dunfey Classic Hotels. He later advanced to vice president of Omni's Midwestern region and general manager of the Ambassador East in Chicago.

A native of Germany, he graduated from the School of Commerce and Economics in Nordhorn, and the Hotel Administration School in Heidelberg, Germany.

Mark Jensen
Wine Director, Sommelier and Cellar Master
Highlands Inn

Mark Jensen's job is one about which many people might fantasize. When Jensen isn't busy overseeing the 27,000-bottle inventory or making recommendations from the 1,200 selections on Pacific's Edge Restaurant's venerable wine list, he is actively engaged in planning the next series of tastings at the Masters of Food & Wine event.

As Wine Director of the prestigious Highlands Inn since 1985, pairing the finest vintages of the great domaines and estates from around the world with the cuisine of gastronomy's elite corps is all in a day's work. Now into the second decade of this one-of-a-kind event, Jensen's work more than qualifies him to lend his expertise to the pairing suggestions included in *Cooking with the Masters of Food & Wine.*

With a colorful background embracing a wide range of experience and study — from carpentry to photography to chiropractic medicine — it was serendipity that steered Jensen to a career in wine. As a college student, his professional course took a pivotal turn when, as a guest at a perfectly executed five-course dinner complemented by as many outstanding wines, he became captivated by the remarkable alchemy that results when beautiful food is combined with exquisite wine.

Gabriela Knubis
Knubis Communications

Gabriela Knubis helped bring the Masters of Food & Wine to the attention of international culinary circles. Handling public relations for Highlands Inn, she worked closely with David Fink in creating the event's program and developing a format for maximum effectiveness.

"It has been a personal and professional pleasure to assist in bringing this visionary idea to international prominence," she says.

Knubis began her public relations/journalism training at the University of Wisconsin-Milwaukee. In 1978, she joined the publicity department of Warner Bros. Records in Burbank, leading eventually to her appointment as manager of national college artist development. Moving to Monterey in 1983, she directed comprehensive public relations programs, including the grand opening of the Monterey Sheraton Hotel.

From 1986-87, she was public relations director at the renowned Highlands Inn. In 1987, Gabriela and Jess Knubis founded Knubis Communications. The firm specializes in graphic design and creative advertising strategy, as well as media relations, public awareness campaigns, special events and communications for clients throughout the world.

David B. Fink
Vice President and General Manager
Highlands Inn

David Fink was at the right place at the right time when planning began for the Masters of Food & Wine in 1985. Fink was given the task of creating the event and coordinating the complicated logistics and countless details.

He immediately grasped the global significance of the project. "Each year for six days, we are given a wonderful opportunity to experience the flavors of the world in one incomparable setting," he said. "Michelin star chefs and celebrated winemakers from continents away gather here to share their talents. To all of us, they speak a common language, presenting food and wine as a bridge between diverse cultures and nations."

A founding member of the Monterey Peninsula Chapter of the American Institute of Wine and Food, Fink today is Vice President and General Manager of the 142-room Highlands Inn.

A graduate of Roanoke College in Virginia, Fink joined the hotel's management team in 1984. Subsequently he was promoted to food and beverage director, followed by 2½ years as executive assistant general manager. He also has consulted for the hotel's management company, Coastal Hotel Group, at the company's other properties in the United States.

Highlands Inn, nestled on the scenic coastal cliffs of the Carmel Highlands at the gateway to Big Sur, is a member of Small Luxury Hotels of the World, a unique collection of finely appointed, individually owned hotels dedicated to maintaining exceptionally high standards of service.

"The Monterey Peninsula is a worldwide travel destination and Highlands Inn today is recognized among the premier properties, not only here, but on the entire West Coast," he says. "I consider it to an honor to be a participant in the inn's long tradition of excellence."

Bruce Aidells

AIDELLS SAUSAGE COMPANY • SAN LEANDRO, CALIFORNIA

"I first started making sausages when I was living in London, working as a cancer researcher," remembers Aidells. "After a few months subsisting on a diet of pub food and bangers, I decided to make my own sausage. It took me most of the night to stuff all I'd made. But the next day when I fried them up and sat down to a hearty and delicious meal for the first time in months, I was hooked."

Bruce Aidells' sausage-making career evolved when he returned to the United States. While doing research in Berkeley, he began making sausage and pâté and selling it to local restaurants. By 1983, word of Aidells' unique brand of hand-crafted sausage had spread throughout the San Francisco Bay Area. His charcuterie was a staple on the menus of the Bay Area's top restaurants and consumer demand was swelling. His reputation as a master of seasonings was unchallenged.

Aidells continues to develop new varieties of sausage at home, where he collaborates with his wife, Nancy Oakes, chef/owner of San Francisco's popular Boulevard Restaurant. Aidells is the author of seven cookbooks as well as a regular contributor to numerous magazines and newspapers and a speaker panelist and teacher throughout the United States.

Today, his following has reached national proportions. More than 25 varieties of sausage and cured meats are available at specialty stores and on restaurant menus nationwide.

Aidells' imagination is deliciously showcased here with his recipes for Venison Sausage, New Mexico Sausage and Chile Relleno Soufflé, Grilled Chicken and Turkey Sausage with Sun-Dried Tomatoes served on Tuscan Beans with Goat Cheese and Seattle's Pike Place Salmon Sausage.

VENISON SAUSAGE

Yields 4 lbs.

Preparation Time: 20 Minutes (note marinating time)
© Hot Links & Country Flavors

1½ lbs. venison shoulder	4 tsps. kosher salt
1 lb. pork butt	2 tsps. coarsely ground black pepper
¾ lb. pork back fat	1 tsp. fresh rosemary or ½ tsp. dried
½ lb. slab bacon, rind removed	2 Tbsps. brandy
1 tsp. garlic, minced	3 Tbsps. dry red wine
1 tsp. shallots, minced	Medium hog casings
2 tsp. minced juniper berries	

Cut the venison shoulder, pork butt, pork back fat and bacon into 2-inch strips. In a large bowl, mix the meat, fat and all the remaining ingredients except the casings. Cover and place in the refrigerator to marinate overnight.

The next day, grind the mixture through a ¼-inch plate. Add any juices remaining in the bowl. Knead to blend all the ingredients thoroughly. Stuff into hog casings and tie into 6-inch links.

Dry the sausage, uncovered, in the refrigerator overnight before grilling or pan-frying. Will keep for 3 days refrigerated or 2 months frozen. ✳

NEW MEXICO SAUSAGE AND CHILE RELLENO SOUFFLÉ

Serves 4

Preparation Time: 30 Minutes • Pre-heat oven to 350°
© Flying Sausages

⅓ lb. Jack cheese, cut into ½ x 3-inch strips	½ tsp. salt
2 cans, 4 oz. each, whole, fire-roasted green chiles, drained	Pinch of nutmeg
	4 large eggs, separated
	2 additional egg whites
¾ lb. Aidells New Mexico Chicken and Turkey Sausage, chopped	2 cups milk
	1 cup tomato salsa
	2 Tbsps. cilantro, chopped
½ cup flour	8 corn tortillas, warmed
	2 cups refried or black beans, cooked

Grease a medium-size baking dish. Insert a strip of cheese into each chile and layer them in the dish. Sprinkle with chopped sausage.

In a food processor, combine the flour, salt and nutmeg with the egg yolks and milk. Mix until smooth. Beat the egg whites until they form firm peaks. Fold the yolk mixture into the whites until no white areas remain. Spoon the egg mixture over the chiles and bake 12 to 15 minutes or until a toothpick inserted into the center comes out clean.

Serve soufflé with salsa, cilantro and warm corn tortillas. Garnish with cooked beans. ✳

GRILLED CHICKEN AND TURKEY SAUSAGE WITH SUN-DRIED TOMATOES SERVED ON TUSCAN BEANS WITH GOAT CHEESE

Serves 4 to 6

Preparation Time: 45 Minutes (note soaking time)
© Flying Sausages

2 cups dried white beans, rinsed and picked over	4 links Aidells Chicken and Turkey Sausage with Sun-dried Tomatoes
4 cups chicken broth	
4 large garlic cloves, chopped	
¼ cup olive oil	2 Tbsps. fresh lemon juice
1 tsp. sage, fresh, chopped or 2 tsps. dried	½ cup goat cheese, sliced
½ tsp. salt	½ tsp. Herbs de Provence

In a large bowl, soak the beans overnight in cold water to cover. Place beans in a medium-sized saucepan with chicken broth to cover. Bring to boil over high heat. Add the chopped garlic, olive oil, sage and salt. Simmer for 30 minutes or until beans are tender. Cover and set aside.

Grill the sausages over medium heat, turning frequently. Sausages are done when firm, about 5 to 7 minutes. Remove from grill and keep warm.

Stir lemon juice into beans before serving.

Place the beans on a serving platter. Top with sliced goat cheese and sprinkle with herbs.

Serve with grilled sausages. ✳

TRADE SECRET: *A good substitution for this dish is the Aidells Andouille, Turkey with Fresh Herbs or Fresh Chicken Apple Sausage.*

SEATTLE'S PIKE PLACE SALMON SAUSAGE

Yields 2 to 3 lbs.

Preparation Time: 45 Minutes (note refrigeration time)
© Hot Links & Country Flavors

1½ lbs. fresh salmon,
  boned, skinned
1 egg white,
  well chilled
1⅓ cups heavy cream,
  well chilled
2 Tbsps. kosher salt
½ tsp. finely ground
  white pepper
1 tsp. sweet Hungarian
  paprika
¼ tsp. freshly grated
  nutmeg
½ cup fresh parsley,
  finely chopped

¼ cup mushrooms,
  chopped
1 cup scallops, cut
  into ½-inch chunks
¼ cup fresh shrimp
  or lobster, cut
  into ¼-inch pieces
3 Tbsps. Pernod
½ tsp. fennel seed
3 Tbsps. green onion,
  scallions or chives,
  minced
2 Tbsps. fresh tarragon
  or chervil
  Sheep casings
  (optional)

Place the food processor bowl and metal blade into the freezer for at least 30 minutes before beginning. Cut about 1 lb. of the salmon into ¾-inch chunks, the remainder into ¼-inch pieces. Freeze the larger pieces for 15 minutes and refrigerate the others for the same amount of time.

In the food processor, using the metal blade, process the partially frozen large chunks of salmon until smooth. With the motor running, gradually add the egg white until it is incorporated. Then pour in the cream in a steady stream until blended. Add the salt, pepper, paprika and nutmeg.

Transfer the salmon purée to a bowl and stir in the small salmon chunks along with the parsley, mushrooms, scallops and the shrimp or lobster meat. Add the Pernod, fennel seed, green onion and tarragon or chervil. Stir well.

Make small balls of the mixture and poach in simmering water for 5 minutes. Adjust the salt, pepper and other seasonings to taste.

Stuff the mixture into sheep casings (not hog, they are too coarse) and tie into 5-inch links. Alternatively, spread the sausage on lightly oiled plastic wrap and roll into a long cylinder, approximately 1-inch in diameter. Tie the ends with string.

Bring a large pot of lightly salted water to a boil. Add the sausage and adjust the heat to just below a simmer, about 180°. Poach the links 15 minutes before slicing. Enjoy hot, or serve cold. ✳

 TRADE SECRET: *The linked sausages can be reheated by poaching for 5 to 7 minutes in 180°F. water. This sausage keeps 2 to 3 days refrigerated, but does not freeze well.*

Monique Andrée Barbeau

FULLERS • SEATTLE, WASHINGTON

Wary of stereotypes, Barbeau has described her cuisine as "Americanized Northwest gourmet with French techniques, Pacific Rim influences and some rustic touches." Meet Monique Andrée Barbeau, head chef at Fullers, a four-star Seattle restaurant.

At the age of 19, she left her hometown of Vancouver for New York to attend the Culinary Institute of America. Thereafter, she worked for three New York City four-star restaurants: The Quilted Giraffe, Le Bernardin and Chanterelle.

One of the reigning queens of Northwestern cookery, Barbeau is a constant winner of awards, stars and accolades. In 1994 she won the James Beard Award as best Northwest chef (an honor she shared with Tom Douglas). She is one of 26 nationally prominent chefs — and the only Northwest chef — to cook with Julia Child in Child's newest PBS series, *"In Julia's Kitchen"*.

We are delighted to include her recipes for Cilantro Marinated Prawns with Cauliflower Tahini and Curried Lentils, Oven-Roasted Salmon with a Hazelnut Crust and Onion Tomato Vinaigrette with Herbed Morel Barley, and Herb-Crusted Prawns with a Warm Mushroom Potato Salad and Truffle Essence.

CILANTRO MARINATED PRAWNS WITH CAULIFLOWER TAHINI AND CURRIED LENTILS

Serves 4

Preparation Time: 45 Minutes (note marinating time)

Prawn and Tahini Ingredients:

16 prawns, peeled, deveined	1½ tsps. garlic, chopped
1 cup mint leaves, picked, washed	2 oz. tahini paste
	1½ tsps. cumin
1 cup cilantro, picked, washed	¼ tsp. sambal
	1½ lemons, juiced
1 cup olive oil	1 tsp. water
¼ cauliflower, cut into florets	Salt and pepper to taste

Lentil Ingredients:

2 tsps. olive oil	2 Tbsps. curry powder
½ onion, diced	1 cup French green lentils
1 Tbsp. garlic, minced	
1 Tbsp. ginger, grated	3 cups chicken stock
1 small jalapeño, minced	2 Tbsps. butter, cold, cubed
1 tsp. ground cinnamon	3 Tbsps. cilantro, chopped
2 bay leaves	

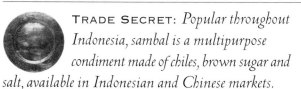 **TRADE SECRET:** *Popular throughout Indonesia, sambal is a multipurpose condiment made of chiles, brown sugar and salt, available in Indonesian and Chinese markets.*

FOR THE PRAWNS: Combine the mint, cilantro and oil in a blender and purée until smooth. Pour into a container and add the prawns. Let marinate overnight.

FOR THE TAHINI: Bring 4 cups of salted water to a boil. Add the cauliflower and cook until tender. Plunge into a bowl of ice water. Drain well.

In a blender, purée the garlic, tahini paste, cumin, sambal, lemon juice and water until it has a smooth, paste-like consistency. More water may need to be added. Season with salt and pepper. The tahini can be made a day in advance.

FOR THE LENTILS: In a saucepan, heat the oil over medium heat. Add the onion, garlic, ginger and jalapeño, and cook until the onions become translucent, about 3 to 5 minutes. Add the spices and incorporate well. Add the lentils and stock, and bring to a boil. Lower heat and simmer for 6 to 8 minutes. Remove the lentils from the heat and swirl in the butter. If there is too much liquid, drain the lentils before adding the butter. Stir in the cilantro.

Remove the shrimp from the marinade and drain. In a sauté pan with a slight coating of oil, cook the prawns over medium-high heat until flesh turns pink, approximately 2 minutes. Remove from heat.

To serve, spoon curried lentils onto individual serving plates. Place a dollop of cauliflower tahini on top of the lentils. Top with 4 shrimp on each plate. ✳

OVEN-ROASTED SALMON WITH A HAZELNUT CRUST AND ONION TOMATO VINAIGRETTE WITH HERBED MOREL BARLEY

Serves 6

Preparation Time: 1³/4 Hours (note refrigeration time)
Pre-heat oven to 350°

Morel Barley Ingredients:

4 Tbsps. oil	³/4 cup Pinot Noir
¹/2 cup onion, diced	wine
1 cup barley	¹/4 cup fresh herbs,
2 to 2¹/2 cups chicken	chopped
stock	1 tsp. each salt
1 large shallot, minced	and pepper
2 cups morel	
mushrooms, cleaned,	
quartered lengthwise	

Onion Tomato Vinaigrette Ingredients:

6 onions,	¹/4 cup sun-dried
Walla Walla	tomatoes
preferably; reserve	1 cup olive oil
2 onions, finely	4 tomatoes, peeled,
diced	seeded, chopped
Olive oil,	1 lemon, juiced,
to coat onions	optional
³/4 cup sherry vinegar	Salt and pepper
	to taste

FOR THE MOREL BARLEY: In a medium-size saucepan heat 2 Tbsps. oil and gently sweat the onion until soft and translucent. Add the barley and stir until well coated. Add the chicken stock and bring to a boil. Cover with a tight-fitting lid and bake for approximately 30 minutes.

In a sauté pan over medium-high heat, sauté the minced shallot in 2 Tbsps. oil. Add the morels and cook for 3 minutes, stirring often. Add the red wine and let reduce until dry.

Remove the barley from the oven and stir in the cooked morels. Toss in the fresh herbs and season with salt and pepper. Hold warm.

FOR THE VINAIGRETTE: Cut the 4 onions in quarters and lightly coat in oil. Place in a pan and cover with aluminum foil. Bake for 20 minutes or until tender.

In a blender, purée the cooked onions with the vinegar until smooth. Add the sun-dried tomatoes and, with the machine still running, slowly pour in the oil. Transfer the liquid to a bowl. Mix in the onions and fresh tomatoes. Add the lemon juice if desired and season with salt and pepper.

This vinaigrette can be served at room temperature or slightly heated. Reserve.

Hazelnut Crust Salmon Ingredients:

¾ cup hazelnuts

1 egg yolk

2 Tbsps. water

6 salmon filets,
 5 oz. each

¼ cup flour, seasoned
 with salt and
 pepper

2 to 3 Tbsps. oil

FOR THE SALMON: Roast the hazelnuts on a cookie sheet for approximately 10 to 12 minutes or until the skins crack. Remove from the oven. While still warm, rub the hazelnuts together, removing as much of the bitter, dark skin as possible. In a food processor fitted with a metal blade, process the nuts until smooth. Transfer to a shallow dish.

In a bowl, make an egg wash by whisking together the egg yolk and water.

Dredge the salmon filets in seasoned flour. Dip the top side of each filet in the egg wash and coat generously with the ground hazelnuts.

Lightly pat down the coating. Place in the refrigerator for 20 minutes before cooking.

In a sauté pan, heat the oil. Gently place the salmon in the pan, crust side down. Agitate the pan slightly so the fish will not stick to the pan. Cook for approximately 2 minutes and turn the fish over. Transfer to oven and cook to desired doneness.

To assemble this dish, make a mound with the barley in the center of the plate, using circle molds if available. Spoon the vinaigrette around the perimeter. Place the hazelnut salmon on top. ✳

 TRADE SECRET: *It is very important to start with lightly toasted hazelnuts, beige in color. The crust takes on more color after it has been oven-roasted and the nuts have a tendency to get bitter.*

HERB CRUSTED PRAWNS WITH A WARM MUSHROOM POTATO SALAD AND TRUFFLE ESSENCE

Serves 4

Preparation Time: 45 Minutes

Stock Ingredients:

¼ cup onion, diced
1 carrot, diced
½ stalk celery, diced
2 Tbsps. olive oil
Shells from 12 prawns (see following prawn recipe)

¼ cup white wine
1 Tbsp. tomato paste
2½ cups fish stock
1 bay leaf
2 sprigs thyme
5 peppercorns, crushed

Mushroom Potato Salad Ingredients:

6 to 8 fingerling potatoes, cut in half and sliced
4 Tbsps. olive oil
4 cups assorted mushrooms, sliced (oyster, cepes, portabello, shiitake, chanterelle)

¼ cup shallots, chopped
Salt and pepper to taste

Truffle Butter Ingredients:

¼ lb. butter, room temperature

1 Tbsp. truffle oil

Prawn Ingredients:

12 prawns, shelled, deveined
1 egg white, lightly frothed
¼ cup mixed fresh herbs, chopped
2 Tbsps. olive oil
¼ cup sherry vinegar

1 cup shrimp stock
3 Tbsps. truffle butter
Salt and pepper to taste
½ lemon, juiced

WINE PAIRING: The earthiness of the truffles naturally calls for the classic accompaniment of White Burgundy. Domaine Leflaive makes an exceptional Batard-Montrachet from their vineyards in Puligny Montrachet. This wine combines intense flavors with Old World earthiness that does justice to this dish. Another fine choice would be a Meursault from Domaine Comte Lafon.

FOR THE STOCK: In a stock pot over medium heat, sauté the onion, carrot and celery in oil until lightly caramelized. Add the prawn shells and stir until the shells turn pink. Deglaze with white wine and reduce until dry. Stir in the tomato paste. Add the fish stock, herbs and peppercorns. Bring to a boil, then reduce heat and simmer for 15 to 20 minutes. Strain the liquid, making sure to press down on the solids to extract all the flavor. Return the liquid to a saucepan, and over medium-low heat, let reduce until liquid yields 1½ cups. While the stock is simmering, prepare the mushroom potato salad.

FOR THE MUSHROOM POTATO SALAD: In a sauté pan over medium heat, cook the potatoes in 2 Tbsps. olive oil until golden brown and tender. Keep warm.

In a sauté pan over medium-high heat, cook the mushrooms in small batches in 2 Tbsps. olive oil until golden brown. Toss in some shallots at the end of each batch and season with salt and pepper.

Mix potatoes and mushrooms together, season with salt and pepper and keep warm.

FOR THE PRAWNS AND TRUFFLE BUTTER: In a food processor, add the butter, and with the machine running, slowly drizzle in the truffle oil. Transfer to a storage container and refrigerate. Lightly coat the prawns in the egg white and dredge them in the herb mix. In a sauté pan over medium heat, cook the shrimp for approximately 1 minute on each side in olive oil. Remove the shrimp and deglaze the pan with sherry vinegar. Reduce by half, add the shrimp stock, and bring to a boil. Reduce the heat and swirl in the truffle butter. Season with salt, pepper and lemon juice. Set aside.

To serve, place a generous spoonful of the warm potato mushroom salad in the middle of a shallow bowl. Drizzle sauce over the salad and place four prawns on top. ✱

Lidia Bastianich

FELIDIA RISTORANTE • NEW YORK, NEW YORK

Lidia and Felice Bastianich opened Felidia in 1981 after a decade of success in running two Italian restaurants in the Borough of Queens. Together, they converted an old brownstone into a polished elegant ristorante, then graced the new east side establishment with their combined given names.

Lidia has become involved in a number of new and related ventures including the opening of two Manhattan restaurants, Becco and Frico Bar, with her son Joseph. She also runs a specialty food line and travel company and continues to write books and articles and appear on television.

Although she has gained celebrity status, guests will still find Lidia in the dining room greeting them on arrival or preparing a fresh seasonal sauce to go with their pasta — giving this elegant establishment an added Italian country home touch.

A teacher in food anthropology and physiology, this knowledgeable chef cares deeply about her profession. The food at Felidia predominantly derives from Northern Italy and from the region of Istria, a peninsula that has belonged to the Republic of Venice, the Austro-Hungarian Empire, Italy and Croatia. Exciting examples of her dishes include Vegetable Soup with Fennel and a delicate Risotto with Squab.

VEGETABLE SOUP WITH FENNEL

Serves 12

Preparation Time: 1¹/₂ Hours (note soaking time)
© La Cucina Di Lidia

2 cups white beans

2 fresh pork hocks,
   optional

2 large Idaho potatoes,
   peeled

2 large carrots

5 fresh bay leaves

4 garlic cloves,
   chopped fine

4 Tbsps. olive oil

1 cup tomatoes,
   peeled, chopped

1 lb. spinach, shredded

1 lb. Swiss chard,
   shredded

10 oz. corn kernels,
   fresh or frozen

10 oz. peas, fresh
   or frozen

1 lb. fennel, diced fine

Salt and freshly
   ground pepper
   to taste

TRADE SECRET: *One fresh and one smoked pork hock may be used to infuse the soup with a somewhat more intriguing flavor. If frozen corn kernels and peas are used, they should not be parboiled and their final cooking time should be reduced by half.*

Pick over and rinse the beans, and soak them overnight in plenty of water. In a large pot, bring 5 qts. of water to a boil. Add the drained beans, pork hocks, potatoes, carrots and bay leaves.

In a skillet, lightly sauté the garlic in the olive oil until golden, add the tomatoes and sauté 10 minutes longer. Add the garlic tomato mixture to the boiling pot, lower the heat, and simmer gently, covered, for 1 hour.

Meanwhile, in a large saucepan, bring 3 qts. of water to a boil. Add the spinach, Swiss chard, corn, peas and fennel, and parboil for 10 minutes. Drain and set aside.

At the end of the first hour, remove the carrots and potatoes from the pot, mash them together with a fork, and return them to the soup. Add the reserved vegetables, season to taste and simmer about 30 minutes, uncovered, skimming and stirring occasionally. Remove the pork hocks (which may be eaten separately) and the bay leaves. Adjust the seasoning and serve with crusty Italian bread or focaccia. ✳

RISOTTO WITH SQUAB

Serves 4

Preparation Time: 1¹/₂ Hours
© La Cucina Di Lidia

Squab Ingredients:

4 medium squab	1 tsp. fresh rosemary
¹/₂ cup olive oil	4 whole cloves
1 large onion, chopped	Salt and freshly ground pepper
2 slices lean bacon, diced	1 cup dry white wine
	1¹/₂ Tbsps. tomato paste
3 bay leaves	2 cups chicken stock

Risotto Ingredients:

3 Tbsps. olive oil	Salt and freshly ground pepper to taste
1 cup onion, minced	
2 Tbsps. shallots, minced	2 Tbsps. butter, cut into slices
2 cups Arborio rice	
¹/₂ cup dry white wine	¹/₂ cup Parmesan cheese, freshly grated
6 cups chicken stock, hot	

FOR THE SQUAB: Remove the backbones from the squab and quarter each bird. Wash each squab, removing any traces of viscera and pat dry with paper towels.

In a large skillet, heat the oil over moderate heat, adding the onion, bacon, bay leaves, rosemary and cloves. Sauté until the onion is wilted, 3 minutes.

Add the squab and brown on both sides, turning in about 5 minutes and reducing the heat as necessary to prevent burning the onion. Add salt and pepper to taste.

Add the wine and let evaporate. Then add the tomato paste and cook over medium heat for 10 minutes. Add ¹/₂ cup of the stock. Stir, adding the remaining stock ¹/₂ cup at time.

Cook at a gentle simmer until the squab is tender when pierced with a fork or skewer, about 30 to 45 minutes, depending on the quality of the birds.

Remove the squab to a heated platter and cover with foil. When cool, remove the meat from the bones and break into small pieces. Strain the sauce through a fine sieve into a saucepan and skim off as much fat as possible. Add the squab meat and simmer to reduce the sauce, about 15 minutes, skimming frequently. Season to taste. Keep warm.

FOR THE RISOTTO: In a heavy skillet, heat the olive oil and sauté the onion and shallots until golden. Add the rice and stir, to coat with oil. Add the wine, stir well and add ¹/₂ cup hot stock and ¹/₂ tsp. salt. Cook, stirring constantly, until all liquid has been absorbed.

Add squab sauce and then continue to add hot stock in small batches (just enough to completely moisten rice) and cook until each successive batch has been absorbed, stirring constantly until rice mixture is creamy but al dente.

Remove from heat. Stir in the butter and half the grated cheese. Season with salt and freshly ground pepper.

Serve on individual plates and top each serving with additional grated cheese to taste. ✳

Gerard Bechler

PATISSERIE BECHLER • PACIFIC GROVE, CALIFORNIA

KUGELHOPF

Serves 8

Preparation Time: 1¹/₂ Hours (note bread rising time)
Pre-heat oven to 400°

3 cups all-purpose flour	2 eggs, lightly mixed
5 Tbsps. sugar	³/₄ cup warm milk
Pinch of salt	²/₃ cup raisins
2 tsps. dry yeast	2 Tbsps. Kirsch (brandy)
(rapid rise) or ¹/₂ oz.	8 to 10 almonds
fresh yeast	2 Tbsps. soft butter
10 Tbsps. soft butter	Confectioner's sugar

Gerard Bechler began his career at the age of 14 under the tutelage of his father's boulangerie in France. His rising reputation for making great pastry with love and care moved him into international culinary circles, where he landed a job as head pastry chef at the world-famous Auberge de L'Ill restaurant in the Alsace-Lorraine region of France.

In the 1980's Gerard opened his own bakery, Pastisserie Bechler, to the delight of locals in Pacific Grove, California. "Through the years, we have built a clientele that appreciates the work and love that goes into our pastry," says Gerard, who usually has 19 cakes on display on any given day.

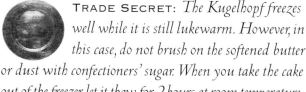

TRADE SECRET: *The Kugelhopf freezes well while it is still lukewarm. However, in this case, do not brush on the softened butter or dust with confectioners' sugar. When you take the cake out of the freezer, let it thaw for 2 hours at room temperature and then bake at 325° for 10 minutes to warm the cake. It may then be finished as indicated above.*

In an electric mixer bowl, combine the flour, sugar, salt and yeast. Work in the butter as if making pastry.

In a separate bowl, mix the eggs and milk and add to the flour mixture. Beat hard for at least 5 minutes until the dough starts to come away from the sides of the bowl. Add an additional pinch of flour if necessary to achieve this state. Allow the dough to rise in the bowl for as long as it takes to double in bulk, about 2 hours.

Soak the raisins in the kirsch. When the dough has risen, punch it down and knead in the raisins.

Butter a Kugelhopf mold and place an almond in each tunnel. Press in the dough. Cover with a cloth and let rise until doubled.

Bake the loaf for about 45 minutes or until it is golden brown on top. Turn it out immediately. It should be evenly browned all over. If it is too pale, return unmolded to oven for 5 to 10 minutes. Let cool on rack, brush with softened butter and sprinkle with confectioner's sugar. ✳

Jan Birnbaum

CATAHOULA RESTAURANT & SALOON • CALISTOGA, CALIFORNIA

Jan Birnbaum has received critical acclaim from major international and national wine, food and lifestyle magazines. Born and raised in Baton Rouge, Louisiana, he began his culinary apprenticeship in Chef Paul Prudhomme's internationally acclaimed K-Paul's Kitchen.

On his mentors, Birnbaum remarks: "Prudhomme is a master of taste. He taught me about flavor, tradition and innovation. From Jimmy Schmidt at the Rattlesnake Club in Denver I learned about organization and combining ingredients and from Bradley Ogden of the Lark Creek Inn, I learned about the importance of an enthusiastic staff."

A firm believer in the virtues of bold and exciting cuisine, Birnbaum uses cooking techniques that combine tradition, creativity, the freshest ingredients and solid professional kitchen procedures. "Food doesn't have to be hot, but it has to be exciting in your mouth," he says. "It has to make you want to take the next bite." Several examples of his cooking style are Shrimp and Corn Soup and Corn Hominy Cakes with the Season's Best Vegetables and Smoky Onion Vinaigrette.

SHRIMP AND CORN SOUP

Yields 1½ gallons

Preparation Time: 1 Hour

Shrimp Stock Ingredients:

3 lbs. shrimp heads
  and shells
  (see below)

4 Tbsps. olive oil

8 garlic cloves, smashed

1 celery stalk, roughly
  chopped

1 onion, roughly
  chopped

2 leeks, roughly
  chopped

3 carrots, roughly
  chopped

8 corncobs (corn
  reserved for soup)

1 tsp. peppercorns

Soup Base Ingredients:

2 leeks, white part
  only, chopped

2 onions, sliced

3 garlic cloves, sliced

1½ Tbsps. butter

2½ cups corn

2 cups white wine
  Sachet of
  bouquet garni

8 cups shrimp stock
  White pepper
  to taste

1½ tsps. Tabasco
  Salt to taste

4 cups cream

1 large sweet potato,
  peeled, ½-inch
  cubes, blanched

1 lb. shrimp, heads
  removed, peeled,
  deveined,

½ cup scallions,
  sliced thin

1 large poblano
  pepper, roasted,
  peeled, diced

FOR THE SHRIMP STOCK: Try to buy shrimp with the heads on; they make great stock. In a medium-size stockpot, sauté shrimp shells and heads in olive oil. Add the remaining ingredients and cover with water to 1½ inches over the top of the vegetables. Bring to a boil, then reduce heat and simmer for 25 minutes. Remove, strain and cool. Set aside.

FOR THE SOUP BASE: Sauté the leeks, onions and garlic in butter over medium heat. Cook until soft. Add 2 cups corn and sauté. Add the wine and sachet of bouquet garni. Reduce the liquid by half.

Add the shrimp stock and bring to a boil. Reduce heat and simmer. Season soup with white pepper, Tabasco and salt.

Purée soup in a blender. Add the cream and return to heat, bringing the mixture to a boil. Pass through a chinois (fine strainer). Adjust seasonings to taste.

Before serving, add the sweet potato, peeled shrimp, scallions, remaining ½ cup corn kernels and peppers. Heat through and ladle into soup bowls. ✳

CORN HOMINY CAKES WITH THE SEASON'S BEST VEGETABLES AND SMOKY ONION VINAIGRETTE

Serves 6

Preparation Time: 45 Minutes (note marinating time)

Smoky Onion Ingredients:

2 cups water	½ bay leaf
2 Tbsps. white vinegar	1 Tbsp. whole black peppercorns, crushed
¾ cup kosher salt	
¾ cup brown sugar	1 onion, cut in half
8 garlic cloves	

Corn Hominy Cakes Ingredients:

1½ cups whole milk	3 medium parsnips
½ cup unsalted butter	2 heads fennel
Salt and pepper to taste	1 large yam
1 cup grits	3 heads Belgian endive, cut in half
1 tsp. garlic, chopped	
⅓ cup chives, sliced	4 Tbsps. balsamic vinegar
Clarified butter for sautéing	½ cup virgin olive oil
2 large red onions, peeled, quartered	1 Tbsp. champagne vinegar
4 medium carrots with tops	1 Tbsp. fresh thyme, chopped
	Parmesan cheese to taste

Smoky Onion Vinaigrette Ingredients:

2 Tbsps. lemon juice	1 cup olive oil
1 Tbsp. red wine vinegar	1 smoked onion, julienned
2 Tbsps. balsamic vinegar	

FOR THE SMOKY ONION: Combine all the ingredients, adding the onion last. Marinate the onion in the smoking cure for 2 to 4 hours. Grill the onion halves over hot coals along with the vegetables until it is tender all the way through. When it is cool enough to handle, thinly slice and add to the Smoky Onion Vinaigrette.

FOR THE CORN HOMINY CAKES: Bring the milk, butter, salt and pepper to a boil. Slowly whisk in the grits. Cook 5 minutes, stirring regularly. Fold in the garlic and chives. Pour onto parchment-lined 8-inch x 8-inch x ½-inch deep baking pan. Refrigerate. When the hominy cakes are set, use a cookie cutter to cut out round discs about 1 to 1½ inches in diameter.

Prepare a barbecue grill. Clean and peel the vegetables. Marinate the endive in balsamic vinegar and 4 Tbsps. of the olive oil. Toss the remaining vegetables in the rest of the olive oil, champagne vinegar and thyme. Over hot coals, grill the vegetables to your liking.

In a large sauté pan or on a griddle, using a small amount of clarified butter, brown both sides of the hominy cakes over medium heat. Hold warm.

FOR THE VINAIGRETTE: In a small mixing bowl, whisk together the lemon juice and both vinegars. Add the smoked onion. Drizzle in the olive oil in a fine stream, whisking constantly. Adjust the acidity if necessary. Set aside.

To serve, ladle the smoky onion vinaigrette onto a serving platter and top with the hominy cakes. Arrange the vegetables attractively over the hominy cakes. Shave Parmesan cheese over the top. ✳

Wendy Brodie

Wendy Brodie, a fourth generation native Californian, has created her own, very personal California Ranch Cuisine. During her seven year tenure as Executive Chef at the celebrated Rancho San Carlos on the Pacific Central Coast and her four years as the Executive Chef at Stonepine, the Relais et Chateau estate resort in Carmel Valley, the Chef explored the extraordinary bounty of both venues. Brodie's signature is her gift of deliciously combining the natural foods and wildlife of the area with spectacular table settings reflecting her artistic as well as culinary background.

She is a popular teacher, lecturer and regular contributor to "Adventures in Dining" and the Carmel Pine Cone.

A graduate of the prestigious California Culinary Academy in San Francisco, she is an active member of the American Culinary Federation, Les Toques Blanches, Confrerie de la Chaine des Rotisseurs, Knights of the Vine and the American Institute of Wine & Food. She is a past president of the Monterey Peninsula's Chef's Association, who honored her as the Chef of the Year in 1982.

We are pleased to feature her recipes for Chile Cured Beef and Chocolate Pine Nut Torte with Caramel Citrus Sauce.

CHILE CURED BEEF

Serves 8

Preparation Time: 1¹/₂ Hours

6 lbs. whole tenderloin of beef	1 Tbsp. garlic, chopped
1 Tbsp. salt	2 Tbsps. brown sugar
4 Tbsps. chile powder	¹/₂ cup peanut or salad oil
2 Tbsps. cumin powder	2 tsps. dried oregano or tarragon
1 tsp. cinnamon	

Trim and clean the tenderloin. Set aside.

In a mixing bowl, make a paste of the salt, chile and cumin powder, cinnamon, garlic and brown sugar. Slowly stir in the oil. Add the oregano or tarragon.

Coat the beef generously with the mixture and marinate in the refrigerator overnight. Grill to desired doneness.

Alternatively, the beef may be seared on all sides in a large, heavy skillet with a little oil in the bottom. A little bacon fat gives good flavor. The tenderloin should then be placed on sheet pan and roasted with meat thermometer if needed. Approximate cooking time will be about 7 to 10 minutes per pound. Let meat rest about 10 to 15 minutes before slicing. ✳

CHOCOLATE PINE NUT TORTE WITH CARAMEL CITRUS SAUCE

Serves 8

Preparation Time: 30 Minutes (note refrigeration time)
Fills one 10-inch Spring Form Pan

2¹/₂ cups dark bitter-sweet chocolate, coarsely chopped	¹/₂ cup lime juice
2 cups heavy cream	¹/₄ cup orange juice
¹/₂ cup pine nuts	¹/₄ cup lemon juice
2 cups sugar	Zest from fruit, optional
2 Tbsps. water	Cocoa powder garnish, optional

Line the bottom of a 10-inch spring form pan with parchment paper.

Melt the chocolate and ¹/₂ cup cream in a double boiler. When the mixture is well combined, add the pine nuts.

Pour the chocolate mixture into the pan and chill for several hours or until chocolate has set.

Prepare the Caramel Citrus Sauce in a saucepan by combining the sugar and water over low heat, cooking until it turns a caramel color, about 15 minutes. Add 1¹/₂ cups cream and mix thoroughly. Remove from heat. Add the citrus juices and zest. Cool to room temperature.

Serve the torte in a pool of citrus sauce. Garnish with cocoa powder. ✳

Giuliano Bugialli

This popular Italian cooking teacher consistently draws record-breaking audiences for his classes and lectures. Deep knowledge, remarkable technique and theatrical charisma cause him to be booked more than a year in advance, with his classes having long waiting lists. His popular weekly television show, in Italian, was carried for more than 5 years on cable in many American cities and abroad.

Born in Florence, Bugialli grew up in a villa outside the city where his father was a director of one of Italy's large wineries. His native city has consistently honored him with, among other things, the Caterina de Medici award for outstanding contribution to Italian cooking, as well as the Ponte Vecchio award for his contribution to the city of Florence and the region of Tuscany.

CARTA DA MUSICA

Serves 8

Preparation Time: 30 Minutes (note resting time)

The Bread:

4 large disks Carta da Musica bread
  (sweet Italian bread) or 8 individual small ones

Cream Ingredients:

12 oz. ricotta cheese,
  well drained

½ cup heavy cream

3 Tbsps. sugar
  Grated peel of ½
  lemon or orange,
  optional

1 pt. strawberries or
  raspberries

1 Tbsp. Vernaccia
  wine (sweet wine)

2 Tbsps. sugar

8 Tbsps. honey,
  warmed

8 sprigs fresh mint

FOR THE BREAD: If you are using the large pieces of Carta da Musica bread, divide them into roughly broken individual pieces, about 5 x 5-inches. Place 1 piece on each plate.

FOR THE CREAM: Place the ricotta, heavy cream and 1 Tbsp. sugar in a blender or food processor and lightly blend for 20 seconds, or until the mixture almost has the texture of whipped cream. Add the lemon or orange peel.

Transfer this "cream" to a crockery or glass bowl and let rest, covered, in the refrigerator for at least 2 hours before serving.

In a mixing bowl, combine the berries with the wine and 2 Tbsps. sugar.

Before serving, spoon the cream onto the prepared bread pieces and top with the berries. At the very last moment before serving, drip some of the warmed honey over everything and add sprigs of mint.

The classic way to eat this dessert is to break off a piece of the bread and use it as a spoon. ✳

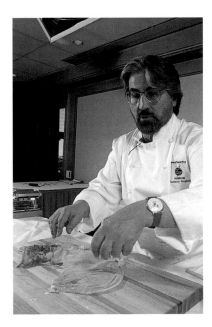

Laura Chenel

CHENEL'S CHÈVRE, INC. • SONOMA, CALIFORNIA

Laura Chenel, founder and owner of Laura Chenel's Chèvre, Inc., originated American chèvre in 1979. Her cheese quickly became a signature ingredient in the newly emerging American cuisine, inspiring producers to develop new varieties and providing chefs with a new range of ingredients.

Born in 1949 in Sonoma County, California, Chenel has long championed flavorful food. Her innate curiosity took her to Holland and the rest of Europe as an exchange student at 17. Later she became an organic gardener and was general manager of her parents' Sebastopol restaurant. Her interest in gardening expanded to small animal husbandry, including dairy goats. Intrigued by the rich flavor and abundance of goats' milk, she began her experiments with cheese making.

With the recognition of her unique influence on the development of American cuisine, she was among the first 50 inductees in *Who's Who of Cooking in America.* Success and growth have not modified her original inspiration: an unyielding desire to make exceptional goat cheeses. Her creative cooking style is reflected in the recipe for Broccoli, Shiitake and Goat Cheese.

BROCCOLI, SHIITAKE AND GOAT CHEESE

Serves 4

Preparation Time: 40 Minutes
Pre-heat oven to 350°

½ lb. broccoli florets	3 Tbsps. white wine
2 medium garlic cloves, chopped	2 Tbsps. lemon juice
3 Tbsps. olive oil	2 oz. fresh chèvre,
¼ tsp. each salt and pepper	crumbled into large chunks
3 large shiitake mushrooms, stemmed, julienned	

Toss together the broccoli and garlic with olive oil, salt and pepper in an oven-proof casserole. Bake 10 minutes, stirring once.

Add the shiitakes and wine and bake 20 minutes more. Remove from the oven. Stir in the lemon juice and chèvre and serve. ✳

Michael Chiarello

TRA VIGNE RESTAURANT • ST. HELENA, CALIFORNIA

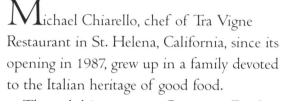

Michael Chiarello, chef of Tra Vigne Restaurant in St. Helena, California, since its opening in 1987, grew up in a family devoted to the Italian heritage of good food.

Through his company, Consorzio Foods, Chiarello fueled the flavored-olive-oil cooking trend with his intensely flavored olive oils, including basil, roasted garlic and rosemary. In 1993 the specialty foods production and marketing company, Napa Valley Kitchens, was formed to develop and market specialty mustards and savory vinegars.

However, producing food products has not distracted Chiarello from his main love: cooking. In 1994 he opened two restaurants in Aspen, Colorado — Bump's and Ajax Tavern. He has also opened Caffé Museo, in the new San Francisco Museum of Modern Art and Tomatina, a casual pizza and pasta restaurant adjacent to Tra Vigne. In addition, he has written two cookbooks, *Flavored Oils: 50 Recipes for Cooking with Infused Oils* and *Flavored Vinegars*, published by Chronicle Books.

Chiarello's passion for perfection in basic raw ingredients shaped his development as a cook and chef. His food is simple, straightforward, Italian in inspiration and expressive of its location. The results are the dishes such as those here — Harvest Focaccia, Fettuccine with Grilled Artichokes and a delicious Brodetto.

HARVEST FOCACCIA

Serves 4

Preparation Time: 45 Minutes (note rising time)

1 small cake fresh	1 cup fresh grapes
yeast or 2½ tsps.	1 cup golden raisins
dry	2 Tbsps. fresh
½ cup warm milk	rosemary
2 Tbsps. sugar	1⅛ cups virgin olive oil
8 cups all-purpose	2 cups warm water
flour	1 Tbsp. coarse salt

Mix the yeast, milk, 1 Tbsp. sugar and ½ cup flour in mixing bowl. Let stand to foam for 15 minutes.

Prepare the filling by warming 1 cup olive oil over medium heat. Add the grapes, raisins and rosemary. When warm, remove from heat and set aside until room temperature.

Mix half of the filling into the yeast mixture. Add 4 cups flour and the warm water and mix, using dough attachment on mixer. Mix until smooth, adding salt and remaining flour one cup at a time. Knead in machine for 3 minutes. Dough should be velvety and elastic. Set in an oiled bowl with damp cloth on top to rise, approximately 1 hour.

Coat a sheet pan with olive oil. Roll out dough to fit inside the pan. Cover with a damp cloth and rise a second time, until doubled in volume. Make finger indents into dough, making sure not to press all the way through. Spread the remaining topping over dough. Sprinkle with 1 Tbsp. each sugar and salt and bake in 350° oven until golden brown. ✷

FETTUCCINE WITH GRILLED ARTICHOKES

Serves 4

Preparation Time: 30 Minutes

4 fresh artichokes	2 Tbsps. chervil,
1 lemon, juiced	chopped
4 Tbsps. olive oil	2 tsps. marjoram,
1 garlic head, peeled,	chopped
cloves crushed	3 Tbsps. butter
4 cups chicken stock	Salt & pepper to taste
½ cup corn	1 lb. fresh fettuccine

Prepare the artichoke hearts by rubbing with lemon juice and 2 Tbsps. olive oil. Grill until tender. Slice thin.

In a large sauté pan, heat 2 Tbsps. olive oil to the smoking point, then reduce heat to medium. Add the garlic and sauté until golden brown. Add the sliced artichokes and toss well. Add the chicken stock and reduce until the sauce begins to take on body. Add the corn, chervil, marjoram and butter. Simmer until the butter has been incorporated, then adjust the seasonings with salt and pepper as needed.

Cook fresh pasta in rapidly boiling salted water until firm to the tooth, or al dente. Drain and toss with the sauce.

Serve immediately. ✷

WINE PAIRING: Artichokes can be a difficult pairing. Matanzas Creek Winery Sauvignon Blanc often bridges the gap with its distinctive, grassy flavors, perfume and balance of oak.

BRODETTO

Serves 4

Preparation Time: 45 Minutes

1 live Dungeness crab, 2 to 3 lbs.	4 Tbsps. Pernod
3 cups white wine	4 cups tomatoes, peeled, seeded, diced
2 lemons, juiced	Pinch of saffron
4 bay leaves	4 cups fish stock
2 Tbsps. pickling spice	2 lbs. fresh clams
¼ cup salt	2 lbs. fresh mussels
1 lb. prawns, peeled, deveined, reserve shells	½ tsp. chile flakes
5 Tbsps. olive oil	1 Tbsp. butter
1 Tbsp. plus 1 tsp. garlic, chopped	1 sprig each basil, Italian parsley and tarragon, chopped

Prepare the crab by blanching in a solution of 1½ gallons water and 2 cups white wine, lemon juice, bay leaves, pickling spice and salt. Bring liquid to a rapid boil. Add the crab, return to a boil and simmer for 6 to 8 minutes. Remove and cool. Clean and crack legs and body to remove crab meat.

Prepare the stock by toasting shrimp shells in 1 Tbsp. hot olive oil until golden brown. Add 1 Tbsp. garlic and caramelize. Deglaze with 2 Tbsps. Pernod. Add 2 cups chopped tomatoes and 1 cup white wine. Add saffron and simmer for 5 minutes. Add the fish stock and cook until reduced by half. Strain and reserve.

To assemble the brodetto, heat 4 Tbsps. olive oil in a large sauté pan. Add clams and mussels. When shells open, add shrimp and sauté to a golden brown. Remove the seafood and set aside with prepared crab.

To the same pan, add 1 tsp. garlic and chile flakes. When the garlic is golden brown, deglaze the pan with the remaining Pernod. Add remaining tomatoes and the brodetto stock. Simmer until the sauce begins to thicken slightly. Add the reserved seafood, butter and fresh herbs. ✳

Julia Child

BEST-SELLING COOKBOOK AUTHOR • CAMBRIDGE, MASSACHUSETTS

Julia Child was born in Pasadena, California and went on to graduate from Smith College. Later, the opportunity to travel arose when she took a position with the O.S.S. (Office of Strategic Services) during World War II. Her first overseas assignment was in Ceylon, where she met Paul Child, also with the O.S.S.

Marriage and a move to France followed, where Julia fell in love with French cooking, literally after the first bite. As soon as she and Paul were settled, she enrolled in the Cordon Bleu, where she attended classes and studied privately. Through mutual friends, Julia met Simone Beck, who invited her to join the French women's gastronomical society, "Le Cercle des Gourmettes." Madame Beck introduced her to Louisette Bertholle, and the three women eventually opened their own cooking school in Paris, "L' Ecole des Trois Gourmandes" or, the "School of the Three Hearty Eaters."

Mastering the Art of French Cooking by Child, Beck and Bertholle was published by Alfred A. Knopf in 1961. Child was asked to do three pilot television shows which were well received — there was no TV cooking at that time. She and "The French Chef" went on the air February 11, 1963 and her cooking shows have been aired and repeated without interruption ever since.

Julia Child is very much committed not only to the furthering of gastronomy as a recognized discipline but also to the encouragement of young people to enter the profession.

Her principal interest, however, is the American Institute of Wine and Food, of which she and Robert Mondavi are among the founders and honorary chairpersons. The Institute's objective is to provide a focus for the study, development, and appreciation of gastronomy in all its manifestations, from growing and farming through preparation, presentation, and consumption. She generously shares with us some of the secrets of her lasting popularity with the following two recipes, Monterey Bay Sole Food Stew and Stove-Top Duck.

MONTEREY BAY SOLE FOOD STEW

Serves 6

Preparation Time: 45 Minutes
© The Way To Cook

---

2 medium-sized
  carrots
2 leeks, white part
  only
2 celery stalks,
  medium-size, young
  and tender
1 yellow onion,
  2½-inch diameter
3 Tbsps. unsalted
  butter
Salt and white
  pepper
2 medium branches
  fresh tarragon or
  ¼ tsp. fragrant
  dried tarragon

2 firm ripe red
  tomatoes
2½ cups dry white
  Monterey wine
  such as a young
  Chardonnay
2½ cups fish stock or
  chicken broth
1 Tbsp. cornstarch
  blended with
  2 Tbsps. white wine
1½ lbs. Monterey
  sole filets
2 egg yolks blended
  with 1 cup sour
  cream
  Chopped fresh
  parsley

For the soup base, peel and trim the vegetables and cut into very thin (less than ⅛-inch) julienne slices 1½-inches long. Sauté them slowly over moderately low heat with the butter, salting lightly and covering the pan. Watch carefully that they do not brown. When tender, in 10 minutes or so, add the tarragon, the wine and the fish stock or chicken broth. Bring to the simmer for 5 minutes and remove from heat.

When the soup base is ready, blend dribbles of hot soup into the cornstarch and after about a cup has gone in, blend the mixture back into the rest of the hot soup. Simmer 2 minutes, then fold in the diced tomatoes and the fish. Bring just to the simmer. Carefully taste and correct seasoning. Blend a cup of hot soup by dribbles into the egg yolks and sour cream; fold this back into the hot soup. Remove from heat.

Before serving, reheat to below the simmer, folding gently with several Tbsps. of chopped parsley. Taste again and correct seasoning.
Turn into a warmed tureen or hot soup bowls. ✳

STOVE TOP DUCK

Serves 4

Preparation Time: 2½ Hours
© The Way To Cook

This dish contains a formidable number of steps, all of which, except for the final assembly, may be accomplished even a day in advance. So take your time; it will be worth your while. Note that once the stock is made, many of the steps may be done at the same time, such as braising the onions while sautéing the mushrooms and cooking the duck legs, etc.

Cover-cooked with spices, onions and mushrooms, this is a great way to cook a duck. You have complete control over its meat and can produce rosy breasts and tender legs with remarkably good flavor, while the bones and scraps are simmered into a rich sauce.

Rich Brown Duck Stock Ingredients:
Yields 2 cups

1 roaster duckling weighing 5 to 5½ lbs., with giblets	2 Italian plum tomatoes, cored, peeled, chopped
1 Tbsp. spice marinade (recipe follows) Rendered duck fat or vegetable oil	2 cups veal or chicken stock plus water as needed
1 celery stalk, peeled, chopped	1 medium herb bouquet (2 branches fresh thyme or ¼ tsp. dried thyme,
2 onions, peeled, chopped	4 sprigs fresh parsley and 4 allspice berries
1 carrot, peeled, chopped	all tied together in washed cheesecloth)

FOR THE DUCK STOCK: Disjoint a fine roaster duckling to give you 2 boneless breasts and 2 legs with thighs, reserving the bones for the stock. Season with 1 Tbsp. of the spice marinade (recipe follows) and reserve, refrigerated, until ready to sear.

Place the scraps of fat in a sauté pan over medium-low heat and render the fat. Chop the duck carcass into 1-inch pieces, the smaller the better.

Transfer a Tbsp. or so of the rendered duck fat or vegetable oil into a heavy 2½ qt. saucepan. Stir in the celery, onions and carrot; sauté over low heat for 10 minutes or so, until tender and just beginning to brown. Stir in the tomatoes. While the vegetables are cooking, brown the carcass pieces and reserved bones in a roomy frying pan, using another Tbsp. of duck fat or oil.

Transfer the carcass pieces from the frying pan to the saucepan with the vegetables. Reserve the fat for searing the breasts, legs and thighs. Pour the stock in the frying pan, scraping with a wooden spoon to deglaze it. Pour the stock into the saucepan and add the herb bouquet with enough water to cover the ingredients by ½-inch.

Bring to the simmer, skimming off scum as necessary. Cover loosely and let simmer quietly for an hour, adding a little water if needed. Strain into a smaller pan, pressing juices out of the ingredients before you discard them. Degrease thoroughly (a fat separator pitcher is very useful here) and boil the stock down rather slowly until you have about 2 cups of rich brown duck essence. You may concentrate it further, if you wish.

May be prepared in advance to this point. When cool, cover and refrigerate where it will keep for several days, or it may be frozen for a month or more.

Spice Marinade Ingredients:
Yields 1¼ cups   OR:
  1 part ground allspice
  2 parts paprika
  5 parts freshly ground
    white peppercorns

  1 Tbsp. each: allspice, cinnamon, savory
  2 Tbsps. each: clove, mace, nutmeg, paprika and imported bay
  5 Tbsps. white peppercorns

FOR THE SPICE MARINADE: A few hours' sojourn in a spice mixture gives pork chops and roasts, goose and duck, as well as sausage meat and pates an exceptionally fine flavor and is particularly recommended when these meats are to be served cold. You can make a simple mix you can use on the spot, but it is convenient to have a ready-made jar on hand.

I pulverize my spices and dried herbs in a cheap little electric coffee grinder that I keep just for this purpose. The amount to use is up to ½ tsp. per lb. of boneless meat, plus 1 tsp. salt.

Stove Top Duck Ingredients:

The reserved duck breasts and legs with thighs	12 small white onions, 1¼-inch diameter, peeled, with ½-inch crosses cut in root ends
The reserved rendered duck fat	
1 to 2 cups strong duck stock	8 rounds of cooked yellow polenta, 3 by ½-inch
2 cups fresh mushrooms, wild and/or cultivated, trimmed, cleaned and ready to cook	Sprigs of fresh parsley

TO FINISH THE STOVE TOP DUCK: Set a sauté pan over moderate heat and when hot, film it with a spoonful or so of the rendered duck fat. Brown the skin sides of the duck pieces slowly, turning the legs about in the pan with tongs to obtain an even, dark walnut brown. Then brown the flesh sides of the breast pieces briefly and remove to a side dish. This should take 10 to 12 minutes and the breasts should still be rare and slightly squishy to the touch; they will finish cooking later.

Film a smaller frying pan with duck fat and arrange the leg-thighs in it. Cover and cook over moderately low heat, moving and checking on them every several minutes. They are done in 20 minutes or so, when the flesh of the legs is beginning to soften.

Heat a sauté pan to moderately hot with a filming of duck fat, then sauté the mushrooms briefly to brown very lightly. Turn them into the pan with the duck breasts.

Adding a little more duck fat if needed, and with the sauté pan over moderately high heat, brown the peeled onions briefly, tossing them around gently in the pan. Pour in 2-inches of duck stock bring to the simmer, cover the pan and let simmer for about 20 minutes, checking on it now and then and adding a little water if needed, until the onions are tender when pierced.

Brown the polenta rounds lightly in a little duck fat and keep warm on a baking sheet in a 200° oven.

Wipe out a sauté pan. Place the duck breast and leg pieces in it, along with the mushrooms and the onions with their juices. Pour in 1 cup or so of the duck stock and cover the pan loosely. Plan to serve in 20 to 30 minutes. Warm the dinner plates.

Cover the sauté pan and bring to the simmer for several minutes, frequently spooning the sauce over the duck and mushrooms. When warmed through, rapidly remove the duck pieces to a cutting board and cut the breast and thigh meat into slanting crosswise slices. Arrange 2 rounds of the warm sautéed polenta down the center of each plate and set slices of duck meat off center upon them. Bring the sauce in the pan to the boil as you swiftly spoon mushrooms and onions about each serving, finishing with a good dollop of the hot sauce. Decorate with 2 or 3 sprigs of parsley. ✳

WINE PAIRING: A Pinot Noir here would be classic, however, a Merlot, especially from the great Duckhorn Vineyards, would be a fine choice. This Merlot, in particular, has enough tannin to stand up to the richness of the finished sauce.

Patrick Clark

TAVERN ON THE GREEN • NEW YORK, NEW YORK

Born in Brooklyn, New York, Chef Patrick Clark embarked on his culinary course at age 9, when "I started puttering in the kitchen. You see, my father was a chef, and I had gotten to see the back of the house of restaurants where he worked — places like the Four Seasons and La Fonda del Sol. I wanted to recreate what I had seen there." So intent was he on emulating his father's profession that, while other boys were squandering their allowances on baseball cards, Clark saved his to buy cream cheese. "I loved to make cheesecake. By the time I was 17, I had perfected my recipe. It's one I still use today."

However, not all of Clark's gastronomical expertise was self-taught. He enrolled in the hotel and restaurant curriculum at New York City Technical College before refining his skills at Great Britain's Bournemouth Technical College.

His trademark fusion of progressive American food with flourishes of French cuisine continues to shine with signature dishes such as his Corn and Mushroom Ravioli with Mushroom Coulis. Indeed, one guest was so overwhelmed by his meal that he dashed out to purchase a bottle of champagne for Chef Clark. He had it gift wrapped and returned to present it, with great fanfare in the kitchen, to the man he considers "the best chef in America".

CORN AND MUSHROOM RAVIOLI WITH MUSHROOM COULIS

Serves 4

Preparation Time: 45 Minutes

Ravioli Ingredients:

1 Tbsp. unsalted butter

1 small sweet onion, minced

½ tsp. Madras curry powder

2 ears sweet yellow corn, shucked (reserve cobs)

2 Tbsps. olive oil

½ lb. mixed wild mushrooms

1 garlic clove, minced

1 sprig fresh thyme, chopped

2 Tbsps. parsley, chopped

Salt and freshly ground pepper to taste

1 package wonton skins

1 egg, beaten with 1 Tbsp. milk

Coulis Ingredients:

4 ears of corn, shucked (reserve cobs)

1 spice bag: parsley stem, black pepper, thyme and bay leaf

1½ qts. water

1 sweet onion, minced

1 Tbsp. butter

Salt and pepper to taste

FOR THE RAVIOLI: Melt the butter and sweat the onion until translucent. Add the curry powder and cook until fragrant. Add the corn and season to taste. Cook 3 to 4 minutes, then set aside.

Heat the olive oil in a sauté pan and add the mushrooms. Cook until all liquid is evaporated, then add the garlic and thyme. Cook 1 minute, then drain.

Chop mushrooms coarsely and mix with the corn-onion mixture. Stir in parsley and the salt and pepper to taste. Set aside to cool. Fashion ravioli by stuffing mixture into wonton skins, using the egg wash to seal. Cook in boiling salted water until they float. Drain and set aside.

FOR THE COULIS: In a medium-size stockpot, make the corn stock by boiling shucked cobs and spice bag in the water for about 30 minutes. Remove cobs and spice bag.

Add the onions and corn to stock and simmer for 15 minutes. Pour mixture into blender and blend until smooth. Return coulis to saucepan and bring to boil. Remove from heat and whisk in butter. Season with salt and pepper to taste.

Serve the ravioli with the corn coulis. ✳

WINE PAIRING: A spicy, full flavored, white wine would play off of the hint of curry very well here. A Gewürztraminer or Tokay Pinot Gris from Domaine Zind-Humbrecht in Alsace, France would complement the hint of curry very well here.

Lisa and Anthony Damiano

DAMIANO'S • DELRAY BEACH, FLORIDA

SHRIMP PAMPUSKY WITH ORANGE VODKA SAUCE

Serves 4

Preparation Time: 30 Minutes

4 Idaho potatoes	1¾ cups orange
⅔ cup all-purpose	marmalade
flour	6 oz. vodka
2 tsps. baking soda	¼ cup brown sugar
⅛ tsp. salt	2 Tbsps. Marsala
⅛ tsp. pepper	1 Tbsp. cilantro,
Pinch of	finely chopped
cayenne pepper	Oil for deep-frying
3 eggs	12 medium-size
1 to 1½ cups beer	shrimp, peeled,
	deveined

Lisa and Anthony Damiano have made loyal fans throughout the Sunshine State with their trademark "Florasian" cuisine, uniting the bounty of Florida with the clean, elegant tastes of Asia. Critics are at no loss for words to describe the spectacular fare at this four-star restaurant housed in an exquisite landmark home in the heart of Delray Beach's Pineapple District. The menu offers a cross-cultural marriage of flavors encompassing dishes that bridge the European continent.

The Damianos have been delighting diners since their New York days, when Tony was executive chef and Lisa took over the dessert kitchen at the famous Russian Tea Room. Together, they have established an extensive "fat free" menu using techniques for deepening flavors while drastically cutting fat and calories.

They favor us with appetizers that are simple in essence but stunningly original in presentation: Shrimp Pampusky with Orange Vodka Sauce, Smoked Salmon and Caviar Tart, and Mushrooms à la Russe.

Peel and shred potatoes and set aside in cold water.

In a large mixing bowl combine the flour, baking soda, salt and peppers. Blend in the eggs and beer. Batter should be fairly thick to adhere to shrimp. Drain the potatoes well, squeezing dry and add to batter.

Prepare the orange vodka sauce in a large mixing bowl by whisking together the marmalade, vodka, brown sugar and Marsala. Add the cilantro and set aside.

In a heavy, medium-size sauce pot, heat oil for deep-frying. Dry the shrimp on paper towels so that the batter will adhere. Dip the shrimp into the potato batter and deep-fry in hot oil. Serve immediately with the orange vodka sauce. ✳

SMOKED SALMON AND CAVIAR TART

Serves 8

Preparation Time: 30 Minutes
Pre-heat oven to 400°

---

1 sheet frozen puff
  pastry, thawed, cut
  into a 12-inch
  round rectangles
3 hard-boiled eggs,
  peeled, finely
  chopped
½ medium red onion,
  finely diced
1 green onion, finely
  chopped

½ cup sour cream
  Salt to taste
1 Tbsp. vodka
1 tsp. lemon juice
8 oz. smoked salmon,
  thinly sliced
  Caviar for garnish
3 Tbsps. fresh dill,
  finely chopped

For the crust, prick the puff pastry with a fork
and bake at 400° for 10 to 15 minutes, until
golden. Allow to cool.

In a medium bowl, mix together the eggs, red
onion and green onion. Add the sour cream and
dill and season with salt. Slowly drizzle in the
vodka and lemon juice.

Carefully spread the mixture onto the pastry.
Arrange the smoked salmon over the filling, dot
with caviar, and garnish with chopped dill. ✳

MUSHROOMS À LA RUSSE

Serves 4

Preparation Time: 20 Minutes

½ lb. mushrooms
⅓ cup onions,
  chopped fine
2 Tbsps. vegetable oil
1 Tbsp. fresh dill,
  chopped fine
2 tsps. white wine
  vinegar

1 tsp. Dijon mustard
  Salt and pepper
  to taste
1 loaf French or
  dark rye bread, cut
  into ½-inch slices,
  brushed with butter
  and toasted

Boil mushrooms in salted water for 5 to 10 minutes.
Drain and chop fine. Mix with the remaining
ingredients. Season to taste.

Serve on the bread croutons. ✳

Traci Des Jardins

JARDINIÈRE • SAN FRANCISCO, CALIFORNIA

A California native, Traci was inspired by her Cajun and Mexican grandparents' love for their native foods. She knew at an early age that her life's passion was cooking. Four apprenticeships in France and ten more years spent cooking in French restaurants in the United States provided her with a solid foundation for developing her own style.

San Francisco Chronicle Food Critic Michael Bauer wrote, "Although she is only 30 and was named as the rising-star chef last year at the James Beard Awards, Des Jardins' cooking has a maturity and sophistication beyond her years."

Her exquisite skill is well represented in the recipe she prepared for us, Seared Foie Gras with Sautéed Turnips and Tamarind Glaze.

SEARED FOIE GRAS WITH SAUTÉED TURNIPS AND TAMARIND GLAZE

Serves 4

Preparation time: 25 Minutes

3 shallots, peeled, sliced

½ cup butter

2 Tbsps. champagne vinegar

2 Tbsps. sugar

3 Tbsps. tamarind paste

1½ cups duck demi-glace

1 lb. turnips, peeled

8 slices or scallops of foie gras, 2-oz. portions, sliced thin and flattened

Sweat the shallots in 2 Tbsps. of the butter. Do not allow to brown. Deglaze with the champagne vinegar and reduce completely. Add the tamarind paste and the duck stock, and reduce to a fairly thick consistency. Set aside.

Cube the turnips and sauté in remaining butter until cooked through and slightly caramelized.

Sear the foie gras over very high heat. Place on a bed of turnips and spoon the tamarind sauce over it. ✷

Roberto Donna

GALILEO • WASHINGTON, D.C.

Born in the Piedmont region of Italy, Chef Roberto Donna has been working in restaurants since he was a child. He would visit the restaurant near his parent's grocery store in Torino, keeping a sharp eye on the chefs. The kitchen became his playground and by the age of nine he was cooking. He enrolled in a professional cooking school when he was 13 and finished school with the highest grade. By 1977, he was the executive chef at one of Torino's finest restaurants. Ready to expand his culinary horizons, Roberto then worked in kitchens across England, France and Switzerland.

By 1984, he opened his first restaurant, Galileo, and created a very strong following that looked to him for innovative Italian specialties — cuisine that changed the character of Italian restaurants and fine dining in Washington. His success with Galileo led him to open six other establishments.

With continued applause from patrons and peers, Roberto has achieved world-wide praise. In 1990 Roberto was named "One of the Ten Best Chefs in America" by *Food & Wine* Magazine and the accolades have flourished. Recent recognition includes the James Beard Award for 1996 Best Chef/Mid-Atlantic, the induction of Galileo into *Nation's Restaurant News* Fine Dining Hall of Fame, and the 1996 reader-selected Traveler's Choice Award from *Washington Flyer Magazine.*

Ravioli Filled with Beans and Leeks served in a Tomato Purée flavored with Shallots, and Roasted Halibut with Potato Purée and Mushroom Ragu are exciting examples of how he has updated the traditional cuisine with dishes using modern preparation without compromising the intensity of flavors.

RAVIOLI FILLED WITH BEANS AND LEEKS SERVED IN A TOMATO PURÉE FLAVORED WITH SHALLOTS

Serves 4

Preparation Time: 45 Minutes (note refrigeration time)

Dough Ingredients:

⅓ cup all-purpose flour

⅓ cup durum wheat flour

2 eggs, beaten

Filling and Sauce Ingredients

1 cup cranberry beans or shell beans, cooked in salted water

½ cup leeks, chopped very fine

6 sage leaves

½ garlic clove

2 Tbsps. olive oil

2 Tbsps. shallots, chopped very fine

½ cup fresh tomato, peeled, cut in small cubes

Salt and freshly ground black pepper

Parmesan cheese, optional

FOR THE DOUGH: Prepare the dough in a large mixing bowl by combining the flours and eggs to form a firm dough. Let rest for 2 hours, refrigerated. Roll out in thin layers.

FOR THE FILLING: Drain the beans and sauté with the leeks, 4 sage leaves and garlic in 1 Tbsp. olive oil until they are soft and dry. Purée them in a blender and place the purée in a bowl to cool.

FOR THE SAUCE: Sauté the shallots in 1 Tbsp. olive oil with 2 sage leaves for 2 minutes. Add the tomato and cook for 5 minutes. Season with salt and pepper.

To assemble, cut the layers of pasta into 2-inch squares. Place a tsp. of bean filling in the middle and then close the ravioli.

Boil the pasta in salted water until al dente. Serve with the tomato sauce and, if desired, sprinkle with a touch of grated Parmesan cheese. ✳

WINE PAIRING: A light-to-medium-bodied red wine from the Tuscany or Piedmont region of Italy would go well with the chef's cooking style. A Sangiovese from a lighter vintage would be a good choice to complement the tomato-based sauce.

ROASTED HALIBUT WITH POTATO PURÉE AND MUSHROOM RAGU

Serves 4

Preparation Time: 45 Minutes (note marinating time)

1½ lbs. halibut filet
4 Tbsps. fresh
  rosemary, chopped
4 sage stalks, chopped
2 garlic cloves,
  chopped
4 Tbsps. olive oil
  Salt and pepper
  to taste

4 potatoes, cooked
  and puréed
⅓ cup fat-free
  sour cream
½ onion, chopped fine
¾ lb. wild mushrooms,
  chopped

Marinate the halibut with 2 Tbsps. each rosemary, sage, garlic and olive oil for 2 hours. Salt and pepper to taste. Refrigerate.

To the cooked and puréed potatoes, add the sour cream and keep warm.

In a heavy braising skillet with just enough water to cover, cook the onion along with 2 Tbsps. each chopped rosemary and sage until the onion is tender. Add the chopped mushrooms and cook until tender, approximately 15 minutes. Season with salt and pepper.

Drain the fish and dry well. In a large sauté pan, heat the remaining olive oil and sauté the fish until it is cooked through and golden in color. Serve with the potato purée and mushroom ragu. ✱

WINE PAIRING: The mushrooms add a woodsiness to the delicacy of the halibut, making it possible to select either a white or a light red wine. If white wine is desired, Chappellet Vineyards Chardonnay, Eisile Vineyard Sauvignon Blanc from Araujo Wine Estates, or Long Vineyards Pinot Gris all work equally well. ✱ Pinot Noirs from Etude Wines or Saintsbury Winery, with their light, crushed fruit flavors, are styled nicely to go with this dish.

Todd English

OLIVES • CHARLESTOWN, MASSACHUSETTS

Todd English began his cooking career at the age of 15 when he first entered the doors of a professional kitchen. At 20, he attended the Culinary Institute of America, graduating with honors. He went on to hone his craft at New York's La Cote Basque and then to Italy, at Dal Pescatore and Paraccuchi. It was in Italy where Todd developed his unique style and approach to food and cooking. He returned to the United States at age 25 to open, as executive chef, the award-winning Northern Italian restaurant, Michela's.

Today you will find Todd in his kitchens as chef/owner of Olives and Figs, located in Massachusetts. His skill with interpretive European cuisine continues to draw national and international attention.

We are pleased to feature his special recipes for Roasted Oysters, Risotto with Wild Mushrooms and Asparagus, Marinated Lamb Sandwich with Spicy Aïoli, and Soup of Potato with Porcini Mascarpone en Brodo with Shaved Truffles and Parmigiano.

ROASTED OYSTERS

Serves 4

Preparation Time: 30 Minutes

24 oysters

1 lemon, juiced, zested

1 Tbsp. balsamic vinegar

1 cup mascarpone cheese

2 Tbsps. sour cream

1 head radicchio, shredded

5 scallions, cut lengthwise

1 Tbsp. fresh thyme, roughly chopped

Salt and pepper to taste

Rock salt

Shuck oysters. Set aside.

In a medium-size bowl, combine the lemon juice, zest, vinegar, mascarpone and sour cream until blended.

Fold in the radicchio and scallions. Season with thyme, salt and pepper.

Pre-heat oven broiler, fitting rack about 3 inches under the heating element. Place a heaping Tbsp. of the mascarpone mixture onto each oyster. Set oysters snugly in the rock salt.

Broil until done, about 3 to 4 minutes. ✳

RISOTTO WITH WILD MUSHROOMS AND ASPARAGUS

Serves 6

Preparation Time: 30 Minutes

1 bunch asparagus, peeled

6 to 8 cups beef or veal stock

$\frac{1}{4}$ cup ($\frac{1}{2}$ stick) butter

2 cups button mushrooms, thinly sliced

2 cups wild mushrooms, thinly sliced

1 large onion, finely chopped

2$\frac{1}{2}$ cups short-grain Arborio rice

1 cup dry white wine

$\frac{1}{2}$ cup Parmesan cheese, grated

Salt and pepper to taste

$\frac{1}{2}$ bunch Italian parsley, chopped

Boil 4 cups water and blanch the asparagus until bright green.

Cut off the top 2-inches of each asparagus spear and set aside. In a food processor, purée the asparagus stems with 1 cup of stock.

In a large saucepan, melt half the butter over medium heat. Sauté the mushrooms and onion. Add the rice and stir to coat. Deglaze with wine, then bring to a boil.

Add one cup of stock at a time, stirring until the rice absorbs the liquid. Continue adding all the stock until the rice is cooked.

Stir in the remaining butter and Parmesan. Season to taste with salt and pepper. Garnish with reserved asparagus and parsley. ✳

MARINATED LAMB SANDWICH WITH SPICY AÏOLI

Serves 6

Preparation Time: 45 Minutes (note marinating time)

Lamb Ingredients:

1 leg of lamb, 6 lbs., butterflied	1 recipe lamb marinade (recipe follows)
	6 slices of bread, ¾-inch thick

Marinade Ingredients:

½ cup paprika	2 Tbsps. turmeric
4 Tbsps. cumin	½ tsp. cinnamon
4 Tbsps. fresh rosemary	¼ tsp. nutmeg
1 tsp. cayenne pepper	8 garlic cloves
	1 cup olive oil

Spicy Aïoli Ingredients:

3 red bell peppers	2 egg yolks
1 large garlic clove, peeled	1 cup olive oil
4 Tbsps. lamb marinade	5 Tbsps. water
4 tsps. lemon juice	Salt and pepper to taste

FOR THE MARINATED LAMB: Combine all the marinade ingredients except the olive oil in a food processor. Pulse a few times to roughly chop the herbs. Add the olive oil and purée.

Trim any excess fat from the leg of lamb. Cover the entire leg with the marinade, reserving ¼ cup for aïoli. Place the lamb in a shallow dish, cover, and refrigerate at least 3 hours or up to 48 hours.

Grill the lamb 12 to 15 minutes on each side. Remove from heat and let stand 5 to 10 minutes.

Toast bread on the grill until brown, 2 to 3 minutes each side.

Slice lamb thinly and drizzle with 2 Tbsps. marinade. Pile slices on top of each piece of toast and serve with spicy aïoli.

FOR THE AÏOLI: Place the red peppers on a grill or under a broiler until skins are blackened. Remove from grill and place them in a paper bag to steam. When cool, remove the skins and seeds.

Place the garlic, lamb marinade, lemon juice and egg yolks in a food processor and purée. While the machine is running, add the olive oil in a thin stream. Process until the mixture is thick and creamy. Add water to thin if necessary. Salt and pepper to taste. ✳

WINE PAIRING: In a word, Zinfandel. Doug Nalle of Nalle Vineyard makes a lovely, soft, fruit-rich wine from the Dry Creek Region, known for this American varietal. Ridge Vineyards, Geyserville, Pagani Ranch and Ravenswood Dickerson Vineyard all make exceptional selections.

SOUP OF POTATO WITH PORCINI MASCARPONE EN BRODO WITH SHAVED TRUFFLES AND PARMIGIANO

Serves 6

Preparation Time: 1 Hour

1 onion, (Spanish preferred), minced

2 garlic cloves, minced

1 leek, white part only, cleaned, minced

6 Tbsps. olive oil

2 cups porcini mushrooms, stems removed, roughly chopped

5 cups chicken stock

1 lb. new potatoes, peeled, quartered

3 oz. fresh or frozen black truffles

1 cup heavy cream

½ cup mascarpone cheese

¼ fresh Parmesan cheese, grated

Truffle oil, optional

Salt and pepper to taste

Over medium heat, sauté the onion, garlic and leek in 3 Tbsps. olive oil until the onion becomes clear. Be careful not to brown. Set aside.

Sauté the porcini mushrooms over medium heat until soft. Combine with the onion and garlic, cover with chicken stock, bring to a slow boil, then lower heat.

Boil potatoes until soft. Drain, cool, set aside.

Finely slice the truffles, reserving some shavings for garnish. Over low heat, steam the truffle slices in ½ cup heavy cream for 10 minutes. Remove from heat and set aside.

Combine the remaining ½ cup cream with the mascarpone cheese.

In a large mixing bowl, pass potatoes through a ricer. Using a whisk, add the truffles and cream, mascarpone mixture and Parmesan cheese.

To serve, divide the potato mixture into six soup bowls, ladling the porcini stock over the mixture until it covers the potatoes. Dot each serving with a few truffle slices and a few shavings of Parmesan. Finish with truffle oil, if desired. Salt and pepper to taste. ✴

Dean Fearing

THE MANSION ON TURTLE CREEK • DALLAS, TEXAS

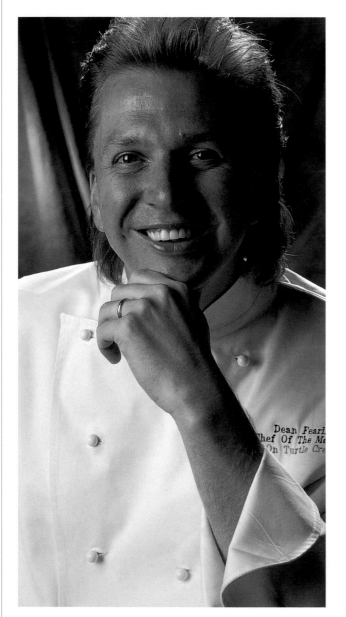

Such notable personages as the Queen of England and presidents George Bush and Bill Clinton have expressed delight upon tasting the Southwest cuisine prepared at The Mansion on Turtle Creek in Dallas. The hotel restaurant's creator, Chef Dean Fearing, was at the forefront of developing the new Southwest cuisine genre when he became The Mansion's executive chef in 1985.

Unrelentingly creative, the exuberant Chef Fearing creates new dishes each week. Most begin with seasonal native ingredients which he then complements with an intriguing array of flavors from around the world. The result is both exotic and harmonious.

A decade after opening the restaurant and countless culinary awards later, Chef Fearing buzzes around both kitchen and dining room in chef's whites and brightly hued Lucchese cowboy boots, clearly in his element. When he is not stirring pots, you will find him playing progressive Texas country on his guitar with his group of musical chefs called The Barbwires.

He has given us his frequently requested recipe for Grilled Chicken Breast with Drunken Black Beans, Smoked Tomato Ranchero and Tart Tomatillo Relish.

GRILLED CHICKEN BREAST WITH DRUNKEN BLACK BEANS, SMOKED TOMATO RANCHERO AND TART TOMATILLO RELISH

Serves 4

*Preparation Time: Approximately 4 Hours
(note marinating time)*

Chicken Ingredients:

- 4 whole chicken breasts, boneless, skinless
- 1 large onion, peeled, sliced
- 2 garlic cloves, peeled, minced
- 3 jalapeño chiles, stems removed, finely chopped
- 1 small bunch fresh cilantro, washed, picked, chopped
- 1½ tsps. crushed cracked black pepper
- Salt to taste
- ½ cup corn or olive oil
- Drunken Black Beans (recipe follows)
- Smoked Tomato Ranchero (recipe follows)
- Cotija queso and fresh cilantro for final garnish

Drunken Black Beans Ingredients:

- 1 lb. black turtle beans
- ¼ lb. smoked bacon, cut into medium dice
- ¼ lb. Mexican chorizo sausage, skin removed
- 2 onions, peeled, cut into small dice
- 1 carrot, peeled, cut into small dice
- 3 garlic cloves, peeled and minced
- 3 jalapeños, skins removed, minced
- 1 smoked ham hock
- ½ Tbsp. epazote, (herb) chopped fine
- 1 bottle dark Mexican beer
- 2 qts. rich chicken stock
- ¼ cup cornstarch
- ¼ cup tequila
- 1 small bunch of fresh cilantro, chopped
- Lime juice to taste
- Salt to taste

FOR THE CHICKEN: Prepare the smoker for cold smoke.

Place chicken breasts on rack and cold smoke with as little heat as possible for 15 to 20 minutes. Remove breasts from smoker and place in a large bowl along with the onion, garlic, chiles, cilantro, pepper, salt and oil. Mix to combine and let marinate overnight or at least 8 hours.

FOR THE BLACK BEANS: Place beans onto a large tray and pick through them. Wash beans and set aside.

Render fat from bacon in a large stockpot over medium heat. Add the chorizo and cook until the sausage breaks apart, about 4 to 5 minutes. Add the onions and carrot and sauté for 3 minutes. Add garlic, jalapeños, ham hock and epazote, and sauté for 1 minute. Add the beer and reduce for 3 minutes. Add beans and chicken stock and bring to a boil.

Dissolve the cornstarch in the tequila and stir into the boiling chicken stock little by little until mixture thickens slightly. Reduce heat to a simmer, season with salt, and cook, stirring occasionally for 1 hour or until beans are soft.

The beans at this stage should be thick. Remove ham hock. Add cilantro and lime juice. Adjust seasoning, if necessary.

Tart Tomatillo Relish Ingredients:

8 large tomatillos,
husked, cut into
⅛-inch dice

½ red bell pepper,
seeded, membranes
removed, cut into
⅛-inch dice

½ yellow bell pepper,
seeded, membranes
removed, cut into
⅛-inch dice

2 jalapeños, seeded,
cut into ⅛-inch dice

2 shallots, peeled, cut
into ⅛-inch dice

1 garlic clove, peeled,
minced

4 large limes, juiced

Maple syrup to taste

Salt to taste

Ancho Chile Paste Ingredients:

4 ancho chiles,
chopped

1 small onion, peeled,
chopped

1 garlic clove, peeled,
chopped

1 jalapeño, chopped

1 serrano chile,
chopped

1 chipotle chile,
chopped

1 small bunch fresh
cilantro

1 cup rich chicken
stock

Smoked Tomato Ranchero Ingredients:

Pre-heat oven to 350°

3 tomatoes, peeled,
seeded, cut into
small dice

1½ Tbsps. olive oil

8 garlic cloves, peeled

2 onions, peeled,
cut into small dice

1 carrot, peeled,
cut into small dice

½ tsp. fresh thyme,
chopped fine

½ tsp. fresh oregano,
chopped fine

½ tsp. ground cumin

½ tsp. ground coriander

½ tsp. cracked black
peppercorns

1 bay leaf

1 cup veal demi-glace

2 cups rich chicken
stock

½ cup ancho chile paste

1 small roasted red bell
pepper, skinned,
seeded, cut into
small dice

1 small roasted yellow
bell pepper, skinned,
seeded, cut into
small dice

1 small poblano chile,
skinned, seeded,
cut into small dice

1 small bunch of
cilantro, picked,
chopped

Lime juice to taste

Salt to taste

FOR THE TOMATILLO RELISH: Mix all ingredients together and adjust seasonings to taste.

FOR THE ANCHO CHILE PASTE: Place all ingredients in a medium-size saucepan over medium heat. Bring to a boil, then simmer for 10 minutes. Pour into a blender and purée until smooth. Set aside until ready to use.

FOR THE SMOKED TOMATO RANCHERO: Prepare the smoker for cold smoke. Place the tomatoes on a tray and cold smoke with as little heat as possible for 12 to 15 minutes. Remove from smoker and set aside.

Heat ½ Tbsp. oil in a small ovenproof sauté pan over medium heat. When hot, add the garlic cloves and sauté for 3 minutes or until golden brown. Place in a 350° oven and roast for 6 to 8 minutes or until each clove is soft, stirring occasionally to prevent burning. Remove from oven. Remove garlic from pan and allow to cool. Set aside until ready to use.

Place remaining 1 Tbsp. oil in a large saucepan over medium heat. When hot, add the onions and carrot and sauté for 5 minutes, or until the onions are golden brown. Add the thyme, oregano, cumin, coriander, black peppercorn and bay leaf, and sauté for 1 minute. Add the demi-glace, chicken stock and ancho chile paste, and bring to boil. Lower heat and simmer for 30 minutes. Skim any fat that may have settled on top. Add smoked tomatoes, roasted garlic, roasted red and yellow bell peppers and roasted poblano chiles. Simmer for 10 minutes to combine flavors. Remove from heat and add cilantro, lime juice and salt. Hold warm.

FOR THE FINAL ASSEMBLY: Mix all ingredients together and adjust seasonings to taste.

Prepare the grill. Make sure grates are clean and lightly rubbed or brushed with oil. Remove chicken from marinade and place skin side down on hot grill. Cook for 4 minutes. Turn and grill other side for 3 minutes, or until chicken is cooked through. Remove from grill and keep warm.

To serve, spoon a portion of the Drunken Black Beans in the middle of each warm plate. Surround the beans with a ladle of the Smoked Tomato Ranchero. Place a chicken breast slightly off center in the middle of each plate, showing a small portion of beans. Top each chicken breast with a small spoonful of Tart Tomatillo Relish. Sprinkle the middle of each plate with Cotija queso and garnish with a large sprig of cilantro. ✳

 TRADE SECRET: *Cotija queso is a Mexican hard cheese that is crumbly like feta, but not as salty. It is usually available in supermarkets in the Southwest or Latin American markets around the country.*

Bruno Feldeisen

FIFTY SEVEN FIFTY SEVEN RESTAURANT AND BAR
FOUR SEASONS HOTEL• NEW YORK, NEW YORK

French-born pastry chef Bruno Feldeisen has a natural fascination and affection for traditional American sweets. With classical training from his native land, he enjoys bringing them to them to new heights. The result is a repertoire of desserts that deliciously translate classic French style into American favorites.

As the executive pastry chef for the Four Seasons Hotel and its signature restaurant Fifty Seven Fifty Seven, Feldeisen is responsible for the creative development of all desserts served in both the restaurant and the hotel. Developing innovative delights on a daily basis is no new challenge for Feldeisen, who made his mark at such world-famous eateries as Patina, L'Hotel de Paris and Pinot Bistro.

He has been honored with awards such as First Place in the Quady Dessert Pairing Competition and the Seagrams/Godiva Pastry Cup in 1993. Recently, *Chocolatier* magazine named Feldeisen one of the Ten Best Pastry Chefs in the country.

Inside his customized chocolate kitchen at the Four Seasons Hotel, Feldeisen toils over his work much like "a scientist in a laboratory," he says with chuckle. The results, such as delicately flavored truffles, are a sensation to both the eye and the palate. He illustrates his point well and deliciously with two dessert recipes: Chocolate Croissant Pudding and Chocolate Crème Brûlée.

CHOCOLATE CROISSANT PUDDING

Serves 6

Preparation Time: 1 Hour
Pre-heat oven to 350°

9 croissants	1 vanilla bean, split
10 oz. bittersweet	lengthwise
chocolate, chopped	9 egg yolks
in small pieces	1 cup sugar
1 qt. heavy cream	

Begin by dicing croissants into small ½-inch cubes. Place cubed croissants on a baking sheet and bake in a 350° oven for approximately 20 minutes or until golden brown.

Fill 6 ramekins, 5-inches in diameter with the chopped chocolate, about ¾-inch deep. Top with toasted croissant cubes.

Meanwhile, in a 4-quart saucepan, bring the cream and vanilla bean to a boil. Remove from heat.

In a large mixing bowl, combine egg yolks and sugar, whisking until pale yellow in color. Slowly whisk the hot cream into the egg mixture. Remove the vanilla bean.

Place ramekins into a large baking dish. Pour hot water into the baking dish to come ½-inch up the sides of the ramekins. Pour custard mixture into the ramekins. Cover the baking dish with aluminum foil and bake for 30 minutes. Serve warm. ✳

CHOCOLATE CRÈME BRÛLÉE

Serves 10

Preparation Time: 30 Minutes (note refrigeration time)
Pre-heat oven to 290°

10 oz. extra bitter	8 egg yolks
chocolate, chopped	1 cup granulated
in small pieces	sugar
1 qt. heavy cream	1¼ cups raw sugar
1 cup milk	(to caramelize)
¼ vanilla bean,	
split in half	

Place chocolate in a small stainless steel bowl fit over a larger bowl of very hot water.

In a medium-size saucepan over high heat, bring the cream, milk and vanilla bean to a boil.

In a medium-size mixing bowl, whisk the egg yolks with the sugar until the mixture becomes a pale yellow. Pour over the cream mixture and stir well. Add the melted chocolate. Allow to sit for a few minutes. Mix well and strain the whole mixture.

Pour creme brûlée mixture into individual ramekins, about 4-inches in diameter and ½-inch deep, and place in a water bath. Bake for 30 minutes. Chill in refrigerator for 3 hours.

Sprinkle the tops with raw sugar and caramelize under the oven broiler or with a propane torch. ✳

Larry Forgione

AN AMERICAN PLACE • MANHATTAN, NEW YORK

For more than 17 years, Larry Forgione has been regarded as one of America's leading chefs and is considered by many to be the catalyst behind the "New" American cuisine. Larry is a recipient of numerous culinary distinctions.

Born on Long Island in 1952, Larry began his career as a graduate of the Culinary Institute of America. In 1976 he was a silver medalist in the British Culinary Olympics before becoming the first American chef to be awarded a Mention of Honor in the Prix Pierre Taittinger competitions in Paris. He returned to the United States in 1977 to hold executive chef positions at New York's El Morocco, Regine's and The River Café in Brooklyn, where he earned a reputation as one of the first American "star" chefs.

In 1983, Larry opened An American Place on Manhattan's Upper East Side, a restaurant with a formal 50-seat dining room and a fixed price menu featuring only American grown and produced products. We are pleased to feature his recipes for Country Ham, Cheese and Scallion Biscuits and Sautéed Breast of Chicken with Bacon, Mushrooms and Wilted Spinach.

COUNTRY HAM, CHEESE AND SCALLION BISCUITS

12 2-inch biscuits

Preparation Time: 45 Minutes
Pre-heat oven to 375°
© An American Place cookbook

2 cups unbleached all-purpose flour	3 Tbsps. country ham, finely chopped
1 Tbsp. baking powder	2 Tbsps. scallions, minced
2 tsps. sugar	
1 tsp. salt	¾ cup heavy cream
3 Tbsps. sharp Cheddar cheese, finely grated	3 Tbsps. unsalted butter, softened

In a large bowl, whisk together the flour, baking powder, sugar and salt. Add the cheese, ham, scallions and cream, and mix gently with a wooden spoon and then your fingertips to make a soft, moist dough.

Turn the dough out onto a lightly floured surface and knead for 1 to 2 minutes just until cohesive. Do not overknead. Pat the dough out to a thickness of about 1-inch. Using a 2-inch biscuit cutter, cut out 12 biscuits. Brush each biscuit with the butter and lay the biscuits 1-inch apart on ungreased baking sheets.

Bake for 18 to 20 minutes, or until golden brown. Serve hot. ✳

TRADE SECRET: *These simple country biscuits are made in the classic style of American baking powder biscuits and they're what you find in every basket at An American Place. They are delicious — make a lot!*

SAUTÉED BREAST OF CHICKEN WITH BACON, MUSHROOMS AND WILTED SPINACH

Serves 4

Preparation Time: 45 Minutes
© An American Place cookbook

4 large chicken breasts, boneless, skinless	½ tsp. garlic, minced
Salt and freshly ground black pepper	¼ cup dry white wine
	½ cup chicken stock
3 Tbsps. olive oil	1 Tbsp. cornstarch
2 cups white mushrooms, sliced	¾ cup heavy cream
	4 cups lightly packed spinach leaves, washed and dried
4 strips smoked bacon, coarsely chopped, cooked crisp	¼ cup flat-leaf parsley, chopped

Season the chicken breasts with salt and pepper.

In a large sauté pan, heat 2 Tbsps. of oil over medium-high heat. Add the chicken, lower the heat to medium, and cook until lightly browned. Transfer to a plate and set aside.

Add the mushrooms, bacon and garlic to the pan, and cook, stirring for 2 to 3 minutes. Add the wine and stock, bring to a boil over high heat, and cook until reduced by half.

Stir the cornstarch into the cream until smooth and add to the pan. Bring to a simmer, stirring, and add the chicken breasts. Simmer until the sauce thickens. Remove from heat and cover.

In a large skillet, heat the remaining oil over medium-high heat; add the spinach, salt and pepper, and increase the heat to high. Cook until the spinach is wilted and drain on paper towels. Divide the spinach among four plates and place the chicken breasts on top. Bring the sauce to a boil and season to taste. Spoon the sauce over the chicken and sprinkle with parsley.

Gale Gand

BRASSERIE T • NORTHFIELD, ILLINOIS

Gale Gand has always been an artist, having spent her college years studying silver and goldsmithing. When she took a year off and went to work in a restaurant, she discovered that the skills she had learned in art translated well to cuisine. She started her own catering company and also worked three years at the Strathallen Hotel in Rochester, N.Y. There she met Chef Greg Broman, who mentored her and Rick Tramonto, whom she later married.

In 1994, Gand received the Robert Mondavi Award for Culinary Excellence. That same year, she and her husband, Rick, were named among the Top Ten Best New Chefs by Food & Wine. Together, they have opened 13 restaurants, including Bice and Bella Luna in Chicago.

They were hired to transform the kitchen and cuisine of the Stapleford Park Hotel outside London, an opportunity which opened other doors to live and work in France and Spain, as well. It was while living in England that Gand discovered that most English wheat simply won't make good bread. Undaunted, she found a miller who would grind the type of flour she needed to bake her singular pastries and breads.

Since its opening in July 1995, the Brasserie T quickly became a hit and is considered one of the hottest kitchens on the North Shore. Gand and Tramonto are known for their rustic French, Italian and American food — "Familiar dishes turned inside out," as they describe it, "with a lot of slow cooking and roasting to bring out the fullest flavor."

Gand's desserts have consistently received stellar reviews, with descriptions such as "sensational, sinful and oh-so satisfying." Her recipes for Chocolate Sour Cream Marble Cake and Plum Crostata demonstrate her flare and creativity.

CHOCOLATE SOUR CREAM MARBLE CAKE

6 mini-bundt cakes

Preparation Time: 1 Hour
Pre-heat oven to 350°

½ cup butter	½ cup sour cream
1¼ cups sugar	2 Tbsps. half & half
2 eggs, separated	¼ cup cocoa powder
1¼ cups all-purpose flour	¼ cup coffee
2 tsps. baking powder	Pinch of baking soda

In the bowl of an electric mixer, cream the butter and 1 cup of the sugar until fluffy. Add the yolks, incorporating well. Sift together the flour and baking powder. With the mixer on low speed, add the flour mixture to the butter mixture, alternately adding the sour cream and half & half.

In a clean mixing bowl, whip the whites until stiff. Gradually add the remaining sugar and whip until glossy. Fold into the batter. Remove half of the batter to another bowl.

In a small bowl, stir together the cocoa, coffee and baking soda. Blend the cocoa mixture into one of the bowls of batter.

Alternately drop spoonfuls of each batter into 6 non-stick mini-Bundt cake pans. Bake for 35 to 40 minutes or until firm to the touch. Let cool in pan, then turn out. ✳

TRADE SECRET: *Serve with warm chocolate sauce and banana-walnut ice cream.*

PLUM CROSTATA

Serves 8

Preparation Time: 1 Hour
Pre-heat oven to 375°

2 cups flour	6 plums, cut into wedges
½ cup sugar	½ pt. raspberries
1 lemon, zested	1 Tbsp. honey
½ cup unsalted butter, sliced	2 Tbsps. cream or milk
1 medium egg	2 Tbsps. coarse sugar
1 egg yolk	
2 Tbsps. raspberry jam	

In a mixing bowl with a paddle, blend the flour, sugar and lemon zest. Add the butter and continue mixing on low until the mixture is sandy looking.

Meanwhile, in a small bowl, whisk together the egg and the yolk. Add to the flour mixture and blend on low, just until it comes together. Form into a ball and chill.

Roll dough out to a 14-inch circle and place on a sheet pan lined with parchment paper. Fold over ½-inch of the crust to form a rustic edge.

Spread jam on center of tart, then fan around wedges of plums and dot with raspberries. Drizzle honey over plums, brush edge with cream, and sprinkle with coarse sugar.

Bake until the fruit is tender and crust is cooked on the under side, about 25 to 30 minutes. ✳

Michael Ginor

HUDSON VALLEY FOIE GRAS • FERNDALE, NEW YORK

Michael is the co-founder, co-owner, and president of Hudson Valley Foie Gras and New York State Foie Gras, the largest and most comprehensive foie gras producer in the world.

Born in Seattle, Washington, he is a graduate of Brandeis University and studied for his MBA at New York University. After four years on Wall Street as a senior vice president with David Lerner Associates (at 23, the youngest in the history of the firm), he decided to take a revolutionary step: Michael joined the Israeli Defense Forces, where he served as a Defense Forces spokesman. It was in Israel that Michael discovered the potential of modern age foie gras processing and the possibilities of total and comprehensive production.

While Hudson Valley Foie Gras is the bedrock of Michael's pursuits, he also is a consultant to the gourmet food industry, organizer of an inter-cultural culinary exchange program and a guest writer for *Food Arts Magazine, James Beard Magazine, Art Culinaire,* and *Great Britain's Great Hospitality.* He is working on his first cookbook, which will be, naturally, dedicated to the ancient and classic delicacy of foie gras. He shares with us his recipes for Sautéed Foie Gras with Balsamic Sauce and Charcoal Grilled Foie Gras with Fig Chutney on Pita Bread.

SAUTÉED FOIE GRAS WITH BALSAMIC SAUCE

Serves 6

Preparation Time: 20 Minutes

1 cup balsamic vinegar	6 whole cepes,
1 cup veal stock	trimmed or similar
Salt and freshly	amount of other
ground white pepper	wild mushroom
to taste	1 shallot, peeled,
1½ lbs. duck foie gras,	chopped
sliced into 12 ½-inch	3 sprigs parsley
thick medallions	3 sprigs thyme
1½ Tbsps. peanut oil	6 long chives

For the sauce, reduce the balsamic vinegar by about ⁴/₅. Add the veal stock and reduce by an additional ²/₃ to a light sauce. Adjust the seasoning. Hold warm in a bain marie water bath.

For the foie gras, score the medallions in a criss-cross pattern, sprinkle generously with salt and pepper, and set aside. Heat a heavy skillet over high heat until very hot. Sear the foie gras medallions for approximately 30 seconds and turn over for an additional 15 seconds. Remove to a warmed plate and drain on paper towels.

For the mushroom garnish, heat the oil in a skillet and sauté the mushrooms for 2 to 3 minutes until they are crisp on the outside. Add the chopped shallot, parsley and thyme. Continue to sauté until the chopped shallot becomes translucent. Season to taste with salt and pepper.

To serve, cover the center of each plate with sauce. Center the foie gras medallions over the sauce and garnish with mushrooms and chive. ✳

CHARCOAL GRILLED FOIE GRAS WITH FIG CHUTNEY ON PITA BREAD

Serves 6

Preparation Time: 20 Minutes

1 lb. figs, fresh or dry,	Salt and pepper
diced	6 pita bread
½ cup balsamic	Olive oil
vinegar	Sea salt
1 cup port	Fresh chives for
1 duck foie gras,	garnish
about 1½ lbs.	

For the fig chutney, combine the diced figs with the vinegar and the port. Cook over low heat until the liquid has almost completely evaporated.

Allow the foie gras to come to room temperature and separate into two lobes. Using a knife warmed in hot water, cube the foie gras into 18 cubes, about 1 oz. each. Season with salt and pepper and arrange on 6 skewers.

Grill the foie gras rare over charcoal while controlling any flare-ups.

Slice the pita into wedges, brush with olive oil, sprinkle with sea salt, and grill over charcoal.

To serve, arrange 3 grilled pita wedges topped with a dollop of fig chutney. Place a skewer of grilled foie gras on top of the chutney. Garnish with a chive spear, using the chutney as a base. ✳

 TRADE SECRET: *Foie gras should be seared on both sides while the middle remains rare. One critical mistake is overcooking foie gras — this robs it of its rich and silky texture.*

Joyce Goldstein
CONSULTANT • SAN FRANCISCO, CALIFORNIA

Along with her work as a consultant to the restaurant and food industries, Joyce Goldstein is an author of consistently best-selling cookbooks. Her extensive list of award-winning titles includes *The Mediterranean Kitchen, Mediterranean the Beautiful* and *Back to Square One: Old World Food in a New World Kitchen.* She also has written three books for the Williams Sonoma Kitchen library: *Beef and Fish, Festive Occasions* and *Casual Occasions.* In September, *Taverna* will be published by Sunset Books, and *Kitchen Conversations* will be published by William Morrow. Joyce is also at work on a book on Italian Jewish cooking.

For 12 years she was the chef/owner of the ground-breaking pan-Mediterranean restaurant, Square One, in San Francisco, where she won numerous awards for food, wine and service. Joyce featured classic dishes from around the world, although Mediterranean food is her primary passion. She describes her food as "tasty, big flavors, as authentic to the spirit of the country as possible, using good ingredients and some finesse." Her inspiration for these dishes came from her library of 3,000 cookbooks, from travel, and from tasting.

Joyce's menu presents the foods of Italy, Spain, France, Greece, Turkey, the Middle East and North Africa. We are fortunate here to have her imaginative recipes for Bastilla—Moroccan Chicken and Filo Pie, Grilled Lamb Brochettes with Moroccan Spices and Vegetable Tagine with Sweet Preserved Lemon.

BASTILLA-MOROCCAN CHICKEN AND FILO PIE

Serves 8

Preparation Time: Two Hours
Pre-heat oven to 400°
©The Mediterranean Kitchen

2 chickens,
    about 1½ lbs., or
2 chicken breasts,
    about 2 lbs., to yield
3 to 4 cups of
    shredded, cooked
    chicken
20 Tbsps. unsalted
    butter
2 cups yellow onions,
    chopped
2 tsps. ground ginger
1 tsp. ground cumin
½ tsp. cayenne
½ tsp. turmeric
1 Tbsp. plus 2 tsps.
    cinnamon

¼ tsp. saffron,
    crumbled fine
2 Tbsps. cilantro,
    chopped
1 Tbsp. parsley,
    chopped
1 cup water
1½ cups blanched
    almonds, slivered
    or sliced
2 Tbsps. sugar
7 eggs
1 lb. filo dough
3 Tbsps. confectioners
    sugar

Cut the chicken or chicken breasts in half. There is no need to remove the bones. However, if you have boned chicken breasts, you may use them; simply reduce your cooking time.

Melt 8 Tbsps. of butter in a heavy sauté pan. Add the chicken and brown evenly, turning often. Set aside. You may omit this step, if you like, but if you want to use the skin then you'll want to sauté the chicken for color. Add the onions and cook until tender and translucent. Add the ginger, cumin, cayenne, turmeric, 2 tsps. of the cinnamon and the saffron, and cook for 5 minutes. Then add the herbs and water, bring to a boil and stir to blend. Add the chicken and its juices to the pan. Cover the pan and reduce heat to low. Simmer until the chicken is tender, about 30 minutes for half chickens and 15 minutes for boneless breasts.

Place the almonds on a sheet pan and toast until golden, about 7 minutes at 400°. Chop the almonds coarsely in a food processor, pulsing on and off. Place them in a bowl and toss them with 1 tsp. of cinnamon mixed with the granulated sugar. Set aside. Reduce oven heat to 350°.

When the chicken is cooked, remove from the pan, and place on a platter. Cook the onion mixture for about 20 minutes, reducing the excess liquids. Beat the eggs. Stir the beaten eggs gradually into the hot spiced onions, stirring constantly over low heat until soft curds form. The mixture will look like softly scrambled eggs. Season the mixture with salt and pepper to taste. Pour egg mixture into a bowl and cool.

When the chicken is cool enough to handle, remove the skin and meat from the bones, if any and tear into strips that are about 1-inch wide and 2-inches long. Slice the skin into strips if you want to add it to the pie.

Melt the remaining butter. Butter a 15-inch pizza pan. Brush melted butter on filo sheets, one at a time, and place them in an overlapping circular pattern in the pan, allowing the edges to hang over the edge of the pan, and brushing them with butter. After you have built up about 10 layers, add a few sheets in the center, and brush them with butter. Sprinkle with half the almonds and add half the egg mixture. Distribute the chicken strips on top. Cover with the rest of the egg mixture and then the last of the almonds. Fold the overlapping filo over the top and brush with butter.

Now, again working with 1 filo sheet at a time and brushing each sheet with butter, arrange 12 sheets over the filling in the same pinwheel fashion. Tuck the overhanging ends under the pie. At this point, you may cover the pie loosely with foil and refrigerate overnight. Do not press the foil on the buttered filo, or the filo will tear when you remove the foil.

Bake the pie at 350° until pale golden in color, about 20 minutes. Carefully tilt the pan to drain the excess butter. Place a second 15-inch pizza pan over the pie and invert, turning the pie onto the second pan. Return to the oven and bake until golden brown, about 25 minutes. Invert the pie again onto the original pan so that the smoother side of the filo is on top.

Mix the remaining cinnamon and the confectioners sugar. Sprinkle over the top of the pie while still warm. You may lay a grid of paper strips over the pie to form a pattern, or just sprinkle freely.

Let the pie cool just a bit, then cut into wedges. Eat the pie Moroccan style, with your fingers, or with a fork. A salad of sliced oranges sprinkled with cinnamon-sugar is a tasty accompaniment. ✳

WINE PAIRING: The complexity of the spices in this dish creates a pairing challenge. A Vouvray (Chenin Blanc) from the Loire Valley of France in the demi-sec style or a well-made Viognier, with its exotic flavors of peach, would do well, providing it's not too high in alcohol. ✳ Another wine that might work well here is made by Caymus Vineyards, aptly called Conundrum. It is off-dry and comprises five separate varietals. It resembles, in many regards, the exotic nature of a Viognier.

GRILLED LAMB BROCHETTES WITH MOROCCAN SPICES

Serves 4

Preparation Time: 25 Minutes (note marinating time)

Marinated Lamb Ingredients:

2 lbs. leg of lamb, well-trimmed, cut into 1½-inch cubes

1 small onion, diced

4 garlic cloves, minced

1 Tbsp. ground cumin

1 Tbsp. paprika

½ tsp. ground ginger

½ tsp. cayenne pepper

1 tsp. black pepper, freshly ground

3 Tbsps. lemon juice

⅔ cup olive oil

2 Tbsps. cilantro, chopped

Harissa Ingredients:

1 Tbsp. cayenne pepper

2 tsps. ground cumin

2 Tbsps. lemon juice

Salt to taste

4 to 6 Tbsps. olive oil

FOR THE MARINATED LAMB: For the marinade, purée the onion, garlic and spices in the bowl of a food processor. Add the lemon juice and pulse a few times. Stir in the olive oil and cilantro by hand.

Place the cubed lamb in a shallow glass, stainless steel, or ceramic dish, and pour the marinade over the meat. Toss the meat in the mixture. Refrigerate overnight, or leave at room temperature before grilling or broiling.

Pre-heat the broiler or light a charcoal fire. Thread the meat onto skewers and sprinkle with salt. Broil about 3 to 4 minutes per side. It should be medium-rare (the timing is dependent on the heat of your fire or broiler).

FOR THE HARISSA: Combine the cayenne and cumin in a small bowl, and grind to a paste with the lemon juice. A mortar and pestle are ideal for this task. Then add salt to taste and enough olive oil to make a somewhat thick but spoonable sauce. ✷

TRADE SECRET: *Serve the brochettes with steamed couscous and broiled eggplant and peppers that have been brushed with the marinade. You may accompany this with harissa, a hot sauce of cayenne and cumin.*

WINE PAIRING: Chinon from Domaine Charles Joguet or Babcock Vineyard are light and fruity red wines that are low in alcohol — all sought-after qualities that work nicely with this dish. Fathom Cabernet Franc, Chinon-like in its fruitiness and structure, would also do well here.

VEGETABLE TAGINE WITH SWEET PRESERVED LEMON

Serves 6

Preparation Time: 1 Hour (note soaking time)
Pre-heat oven to 400°

12 little potatoes, preferably Finnish yellow

2 Tbsps. olive oil

Salt and pepper to taste

1½ cups fennel bulbs, sliced or quartered

6 carrots, peeled, cut into chunks

3 Tbsps. olive oil

2 cups yellow onions, diced

4 garlic cloves, minced fine

1 Tbsp. ground coriander

2 tsps. black pepper

2 tsps. ground cumin

¼ to ½ tsp. cayenne pepper

3 Tbsps. cilantro, chopped

2 Tbsps. mint, chopped

1 cup plum tomatoes, diced, some of their liquid, optional

½ cup chicken stock or water as needed

3 cups spinach or Swiss chard, finely sliced

Finely julienned zest of 2 lemons (not the traditional salted preserved lemons of Morocco)

Sugar and water

For the tagine, rub the potatoes with the olive oil, and sprinkle with salt and pepper. Roast in a 400° oven for about 20 to 30 minutes, until cooked but firm. Set aside to cool and then cut into chunks.

Blanch the fennel and carrots and refresh in cold water.

Heat the olive oil in a large sauté pan. Add the chopped onions and cook for about 5 minutes. When the onions are tender and translucent, add the garlic and spices, and cook for 2 minutes. Add 1 Tbsp. of the chopped cilantro, 1 Tbsp. mint, the optional tomatoes and chicken stock or water, and simmer for 2 minutes. Add the cheffonnade of greens and the cooked vegetables to the sauce, simmer for 2 to 3 minutes. Season with salt and pepper to taste.

For the sweet preserved lemon, boil the zest in water for about 3 minutes, then drain and soak in cold water for an hour.

Make a light syrup of 2 parts sugar to 1 part water and simmer the zest in the syrup for about 5 minutes. Drain the zest and reserve the syrup for another use.

Add the preserved lemon zest to the tagine. Garnish with the remaining chopped cilantro and mint just before serving. ✳

Fred Halpert

BRAVA TERRACE • ST. HELENA, CALIFORNIA

GRATIN OF FENNEL

Serves 4

Preparation Time: 45 Minutes
Pre-heat oven to 350°

4 large fennel bulbs	Salt and white
1½ qts. chicken stock	pepper to taste
1 Tbsp. softened	2 Tbsps. grated
butter	Emmenthal cheese
1½ cups heavy cream	

Wash and trim fennel, set leaves aside. Halve fennel bulbs lengthwise and simmer gently in stock. When tender, transfer to a shallow, lightly buttered dish.

In mixing bowl, season cream with salt and pepper. Pour over the fennel bulbs. Chop fennel leaves coarsely and place on top of bulbs, then add the grated cheese on top.

Bake in a 350° oven until cream thickens and the cheese is lightly browned. ✳

"Cuisines of the Sun" is how Chef Fred Halpert describes the food at his wine country bistro, Brava Terrace in California's Napa Valley. "The wines, the grapes, the fresh herbs and produce, and the terrain of Napa all remind me of southern France," he says. This abundance of fresh ingredients plays an integral role in Halpert's cooking style and menu selections.

According to Halpert, "Provencal cooking doesn't try to mask the flavors of food but brings it out. These techniques really open up the possibilities for matching food with the wonderful flavors of Napa Valley wines."

He brings us his recipes for a delicious Gratin of Fennel, Cassoulet of Lentils with Lamb, Sausage, and Pork, and Roasted Breast of Chicken with Fava Beans, Grilled Portobella Mushrooms and Tarragon.

CASSOULET OF LENTILS WITH LAMB, SAUSAGE AND PORK

Serves 8

Preparation Time: 45 Minutes

1 carrot, diced	1 lb. boneless leg of
1 medium onion,	lamb, trimmed
diced	Clarified butter
2 celery stalks, diced	or olive oil
¼ cup olive oil	1 lb. link sausages
2 cups lentils	2 Tbsps. unsalted
1 bay leaf	butter
2 thyme sprigs	1 lb. mushrooms,
1¼ cups chicken stock	quartered
Salt and white	1 bunch chives,
pepper to taste	chopped, for garnish
1 lb. pork loin	

Sauté the carrot, onion and celery in olive oil over medium heat. Add the lentils, bay leaf and thyme, and sauté 1 minute. Add the chicken stock and bring to a boil. Cover and cook for 15 minutes on medium heat or until lentils are al dente, stirring occasionally. Remove from heat.

Cut the pork loin and lamb in half. Season with salt and pepper. In a large sauté pan, heat a small amount of clarified butter or oil. Sear the pork and lamb over high heat just until rare. Remove from pan and quarter lamb and pork pieces.

Cut sausages in half and sear the sausages in the same manner. Remove from heat and set aside.

In another large sauté pan over medium-high heat, sauté mushrooms in butter.

Return lentils to heat. Add all ingredients to lentils and cook until meats reach desired doneness (2 minutes rare, 4 minutes medium, 6 minutes well-done). Season to taste.

Divide among 8 individual serving bowls and garnish with chives. ✳

 TRADE SECRET: *Try duck, venison, or specialty game sausages for variation.*

WINE PAIRING: Cabernet-based wines are often paired with lamb. However, with this preparation, a Pinot Noir or red Burgundy works very well and is especially nice with the earthy flavors of the lentils. A young Volnay from Domaine Comte Lafon would work beautifully with its bright flavors, the firm acidity acting as a tannin to cut the richness of the lamb.

ROASTED BREAST OF CHICKEN WITH FAVA BEANS, GRILLED PORTOBELLA MUSHROOMS, AND TARRAGON

Serves 4

Preparation Time: 1½ Hours
Pre-heat oven to 450°

3 Tbsps. olive oil

1 lb. chicken bones

4 carrots, medium dice

4 celery stalks, medium dice

2 yellow onions, medium dice

4 whole garlic cloves

4 sprigs fresh thyme

½ lb. Yukon Gold potatoes

8 Tbsps. butter

4 Tbsps. shallots, finely chopped

Salt and white pepper

4 chicken breasts, boneless

1 cup fava beans, shelled

5 Tbsps. olive oil

½ lb. portobella mushrooms

½ bunch tarragon, chopped

In a large roasting pan, heat the olive oil over medium heat and add the chicken bones, turning occasionally, until lightly browned. Add the carrots, celery, onions, garlic and thyme, and roast in the oven for 1 hour, stirring occasionally. Remove from oven, place in stock pot, and cover bones with water. Bring to a boil, turn down to simmer, and reduce by ⅔. Strain and set aside.

Prepare the barbecue grill for the mushrooms.

Slice potatoes crosswise ¼-inch thick. In a large sauté pan over medium-high heat, sauté the potatoes in 4 Tbsps. butter with 2 Tbsps. shallots. Season with salt and white pepper.

In separate pan, sauté favas in 2 Tbsps. olive oil with the remaining shallots; do not overcook. Season with salt and white pepper. Hold warm.

Heat a sauté pan with 2 Tbsps. olive oil. Season chicken breasts, sear skin side down and finish cooking to medium temperature in oven.

Season portobellas with salt, white pepper and 1 Tbsp. olive oil. Grill to medium rare.

To assemble, slice the mushrooms in half and mix with the potatoes and favas. Add the tarragon. Place the vegetables in the middle of the plate. Reheat the stock reduction and adjust the seasonings. Place chicken on the vegetables and ladle the reduction over the top. ✳

WINE PAIRING: When asked which food is paired best with Chateau Lafite Rothschild, Baron Eric de Rothschild's reply was simply, "Grilled chicken." A dish like this allows the complexity of the wine to shine completely through, while the portobella will underscore the earthiness of the wine. Other Cabernet-based wines may suffice in the event that no Lafite is on hand.

Giuliano Hazan

BEST-SELLING COOKBOOK AUTHOR • SARASOTA, FLORIDA

Giuliano Hazan is the author of the best-selling cookbook, *The Classic Pasta Cookbook,* which has been translated into 12 languages and is sold in 16 countries.

Giuliano had the best of all possible teachers of Italian cooking: his mother, Marcella Hazan, celebrated for her classic Italian cooking and best-selling author of four cookbooks, including the new *Essentials of Classic Italian Cooking.*

He began his education as a chef before he could reach the counter, and by the age of 17, he was a hard-working assistant at Marcella Hazan's renowned School of Classic Italian Cooking in Bologna.

Giuliano has been a guest lecturer at the Smithsonian Institution and the National Geographic Society in Washington, D.C. He now works as a consultant for Italian restaurants and teaches classes in Italian cooking at more than 30 cooking schools throughout North America and at the Cipriani Hotel in Venice, Italy. He is currently living in Sarasota, Florida, where he is working on his second book, on quick and easy Italian cooking, scheduled to be published by Scribner's.

We are pleased to offer his recipe for Spaghetti with Shrimp and Porcini.

SPAGHETTI WITH SHRIMP AND PORCINI

Serves 4

Preparation Time: 25 Minutes (note soaking time)

1 oz. dried porcini mushrooms

⅓ cup extra virgin olive oil

¾ cup yellow onion, thinly sliced lengthwise

¾ lb. cremini mushrooms, sliced thin

Salt and freshly ground black pepper to taste

½ cup fresh Roma tomatoes, peeled, seeded, diced into ½-inch pieces

¾ lb. medium shrimp, peeled, cut into thirds

½ cup heavy cream

1 lb. spaghetti

Soak the dried mushrooms in a bowl with 1 cup lukewarm water for at least 20 minutes. Lift them out, squeezing the excess water back into the bowl. Rinse them under cold running water and coarsely chop them. Filter the soaking water through a paper towel or coffee filter and set aside.

Place the olive oil and onion in a sauté pan over medium heat, and cook until the onion turns a rich golden color. Add the reconstituted porcini and their water. Raise the heat to medium-high and cook until most of the water has evaporated.

In a large stock pot bring 4 quarts of water to a boil.

Add the sliced mushrooms to the sauté pan, season with salt and pepper, cook until they are tender and all the liquid has evaporated, about 10 minutes.

Add the tomatoes, cook for another 2 minutes, then stir in the shrimp. Add the cream and cook until it has reduced by half. Adjust seasonings to taste, then remove from the heat and set aside.

Add salt to the boiling water, drop in the pasta, and stir well. When the pasta is al dente, drain and toss with the sauce.

Serve at once. ✳

WINE PAIRING: Despite the fact that shrimp are used in this dish, a red wine is called for to balance the influence of the tomatoes. The earthy, dried mushrooms make appropriate the Old World character of a super Tuscan, such as Antinori's Tignanello or perhaps a Vino Nobile di Montepulciano by Avignonesi.

Marcella Hazan

BEST-SELLING COOKBOOK AUTHOR • VENICE, ITALY

To *Time Magazine* Marcella Hazan is "the most authoritative exponent of Italian cooking in America." Craig Claiborne, who helped introduce her to American audiences in the early seventies, considers her a "national treasure." And for Julia Child, she is "my mentor in all things Italian." Marcella truly is the first name in Italian cooking and as *People Magazine* states, ". . .what makes her books indispensable is as simple and rare as this: Her recipes always work."

Pointing out that the best cooking in Italy takes place not in restaurants but in the home, Marcella's recipes are often beguilingly simple, yet brimming with flavor. No one's influence on Italian gastronomy in this country goes back as far, as deeply, or continues to be as pervasive as Marcella Hazan's. Her recipes introduced Americans to Italian cooking, and many of the Italian ingredients and preparations that have penetrated even the far reaches of America — pesto, good olive oil, risotto — were championed first in this country by Marcella. "The first time that I brought out squid, " she says, "everybody screamed. Now they call it calamari."

There is no doubt that in kitchens across the country, Marcella has indeed become not only the first name but also the last word in Italian cooking. The following recipe for Risotto with Artichokes is simple in essence but stunningly original in presentation.

RISOTTO WITH ARTICHOKES

Serves 4

Preparation Time: 1¼ Hours
© Marcella's Italian Kitchen

Risotto and Artichoke Ingredients:

2 Tbsps. extra virgin olive oil

¼ cup onion, chopped

2 tsps. garlic, chopped very fine

½ cup parsley, chopped

4 large artichokes, cleaned, cut into 1-inch wedges, sliced thin

½ cup water
Salt and pepper to taste

1½ cups Italian Arborio rice

5 cups meat broth (recipe follows) or 1 bouillon cube dissolved in 5 cups water or ¾ cup canned meat broth diluted with 4¼ cups water

4 Tbsps. butter

⅓ cup Parmesan, freshly grated

Homemade Meat Broth Ingredients:

1 tsp. salt

1 carrot, peeled

1 small to medium yellow onion, peeled

1 or 2 stalks celery

½ green or red pepper, stripped of its seeds

1 small potato, peeled

1 tomato, preferably canned Italian plum tomato, drained

5 lbs. assorted pieces of meat and bones, of which at least 1½ lbs. are all meat

FOR THE RISOTTO AND ARTICHOKES:

Select a heavy-bottomed pot large enough to accommodate the risotto later. Pour in the oil, add the onion, and turn on the heat to medium-high.

When the onion becomes translucent, add the garlic. Cook until the garlic becomes a pale gold in color, then add half the chopped parsley. Stir, then add the sliced artichokes.

Cook the artichokes for about 3 minutes, turning them frequently. Then add the water and a pinch of salt. Turn the artichokes once, cover the pot, turn down the heat to low, and cook for 20 to 30 minutes, depending on the freshness and youth of the artichokes, until they are very soft. Check the pot occasionally to make sure there is enough liquid for the artichokes to cook in without sticking and, if necessary, add a little water from time to time. Bring the broth to a gentle simmer in a saucepan over medium-low heat.

Test the artichokes for tenderness by pricking them with a fork. When they are soft and all the water has evaporated, add the rice, turn up to heat to medium high and keep the pan uncovered. Stir the rice thoroughly several times to coat the grains well with the contents of the pot.

Add a ladleful of broth and stir the rice constantly to wipe it away from the bottom and sides of the pot. When all the broth in the pot has been absorbed, add another ladleful. Stir steadily to keep the rice from sticking, adding more broth, a ladleful at a time, as required. Repeat the procedure until the rice is done. It should be firm but tender, without a chalky center. If you should run out of broth, add warm water.

Remove the pot from the heat, add salt and liberal grindings of pepper, the butter, grated cheese, the remaining half of the chopped parsley, and stir quickly and thoroughly. Serve at once.

FOR THE MEAT BROTH: Place all the ingredients in a stock pot and add enough cold water to cover by 2 inches. Set the cover askew, turn on the heat to medium and bring to a boil. As soon as the liquid starts to boil, turn it down so that it bubbles at a gentle simmer.

Skim off the scum that floats to the surface, fairly frequently at first, then only from time to time. Cook for 3 hours, never any more rapidly than at a simmer.

Strain the broth through a large wire strainer lined with paper towels, pouring it into a non-metallic bowl. Allow to cool completely, uncovered.

When cool, place in the refrigerator long enough for any fat to come to the surface and solidify. Remove the fat and pour the clear broth into ice-cube trays. Freeze, then divide up the cubes into four or five small plastic bags. Seal the bags tightly and return to the freezer compartment until needed. ✻

Jean Joho

EVEREST • BRASSERIE JO • CHICAGO, ILLINOIS

Jean Joho, a native of Alsace, France, began cooking at a young age while helping his family in Auberge de L'Ill. Working his way from the bottom, Joho began his career at age 13 as a chef's apprentice, washing vegetables and peeling potatoes in the kitchen of Paul Haeberlin. He continued his training in kitchens throughout France and Switzerland and by age 23, Joho had become the chef of a two-star Michelin restaurant in Switzerland. His schooling included the Hotel School in Strasbourg, where he learned the hotel and restaurant business as well as specializing in pastry, cheesemaking and wine.

In 1984, Jean Joho came to Chicago to open Maxim's. Shortly thereafter he met Richard Melman of Lettuce Entertain You Enterprises, Inc. One year later, Everest was born with a four-star rating that continues to shine. In 1995, Joho introduced Brasserie Jo, his latest creation and the first authentic brasserie to open in Chicago, featuring his culinary expertise in a classic French brasserie setting.

Chef Joho's light cooking style is an art form. He uses the finest seasonal American ingredients and creative presentation to personalize each dish with simplicity and style. He illustrates his points well and deliciously in two recipes, Everest Tarte Flambé and Roasted Lobster with Ginger and Alsace Gewürztraminer.

EVEREST TARTE FLAMBÉ

Yields 24 pieces

Preparation Time: 45 Minutes
Pre-heat oven to 450°

½ lb. bread dough	2 oz. smoked bacon, cut in strips
⅔ cup double (Devonshire) cream	6 oz. smoked salmon
⅓ cup sour cream	6 oz. Osetra caviar
2 egg yolks	1 bunch chervil
Salt and pepper	
2 shallots, sliced	

Allow the bread to rise once, punch down, then roll out very thin. Cut into circles 2-inches in diameter. Place on a heavy sheet pan, lightly greased.

In a mixing bowl, combine the double cream, sour cream, egg yolks, salt and pepper. Spread on each circle a little bit of the cream mixture. Place shallots and bacon on top. Bake for 8 minutes. The underside will be golden in color.

Remove from the sheet pan. Garnish with thinly sliced smoked salmon and caviar. Top with chervil before serving. ✳

ROASTED LOBSTER WITH GINGER AND ALSACE GEWÜRZTRAMINER

Serves 4

Preparation Time: Two Hours
Pre-heat oven to 425°

2 live lobsters or buy fresh-cooked lobster, 1½ lbs. each	1½ cups Gewürztraminer
	2 Tbsps. olive oil
3½ cups water	15 Tbsps. butter
2 Tbsps. sugar	1 lb. fresh spinach
1 piece fresh ginger, 2½ inches x ¼ inch, peeled, cut into match-stick-size strips	Salt and pepper to taste
	1 Tbsp. fresh lime juice
	1½ Tbsps. lime peel, green part only

Bring a large pot of water to boil over high heat. Plunge live lobsters into water and cover. Boil 5 minutes. Transfer lobsters to bowl of cold water.

Bring 3½ cups of water, 1 Tbsp. sugar and ginger to a boil in heavy saucepan over medium-high heat. Boil until ginger is tender and liquid is almost evaporated, about 45 minutes. Add wine and boil until liquid is reduced to 2 Tbsps., about 15 minutes. Remove from heat. Drain lobsters. This can be prepared 1 day ahead. Cover ginger reduction and lobsters separately and refrigerate.

Remove lobster tail and claw meat from shells. Brush lobster meat with olive oil. Place in heavy, large oven-proof skillet in 425° oven and roast for 10 minutes.

Meanwhile, melt 3 Tbsps. butter in heavy large skillet over medium heat. Add the spinach and sprinkle with remaining 1 Tbsp. sugar. Sauté until wilted, about 4 minutes. Season to taste with salt and pepper. Divide spinach among plates.

Heat the ginger reduction in a heavy, small saucepan over medium heat. Gradually whisk in the remaining 12 Tbsps. butter. Whisk in the lime juice and peel. Season to taste with salt and pepper.

Cut the lobster tails diagonally into slices. Fan tails atop spinach and garnish with claw meat. Drizzle sauce over lobster and serve. ✳

WINE PAIRING: Trimbach is an exceptional producer of Gewürztraminer. On the same plane, Hugel's Cuvée Tradition, Léon Beyer Cuvée des Comtes de Eguisheim and Domaine Zind-Hubrecht's Clos Windsbuhl Gewürztraminer would all be lovely here.

Madeleine Kamman

BERINGER VINEYARDS' SCHOOL FOR AMERICAN CHEFS • ST. HELENA, CALIFORNIA

Along with being one of America's outstanding chefs, Madeleine Kamman is also the Director of Beringer Vineyards' School for American Chefs. Situated in the heart of the Napa Valley wine country, it is the only graduate-level scholarship seminar program for working chefs at a winery. She has more than 30 years of experience in the food profession and is a renowned teacher of chefs, the author of several prestigious cookbooks and an indefatigable culinary scholar.

Since 1973, she has been teaching students of the culinary professions, both in the United States and in France. No stranger to the public eye, she has been a frequent contributor to food magazines and is currently featured in the PBS television series, *"Madeleine Cooks".*

Madeleine's dedication to the world of food and wine was recognized by a Doctorate Honoris Causa from Johnson and Wales University and nomination by the French Minister of Culture to the title of "Chevalier" in the French Order of Arts and Letters. The following recipe, Salmon in Winter, is a beautiful dish that will delight your senses.

SALMON IN WINTER

Serves 6

Preparation Time: 1¹/₂ Hours

6 large salmon steaks
and backbone trim
12 Manila clams
6 Green lip mussels
2 medium onions,
chopped
8 shallots, chopped
Sprig of thyme
1 small bay leaf
1 bottle of Riesling
or other dry
white wine
6 large (not jumbo)
shrimp in shells,
uncooked
1 Tbsp. olive oil
1¹/₂ lbs. Maine or other
fresh live lobster
12 Kumamoto oysters
or other small
Pacific or Eastern
oysters

Cooking juice of
all shellfish
Shrimp shells all
shrimp, chopped
Abdomen (meaty
part) and small legs
of lobster, chopped
Oyster juices and
adductor muscle
scraps
3 cups fish fumet
or home-made
chicken stock
1 cup bottled
clam juice
1 bouquet garni
1 large bouquet of
chervil, some leaves
reserved for garnish,
the rest chopped
1 large bouquet of
parsley, chopped
1 cup heavy cream
Butter to taste
Creme fraîche
to taste
6 scallions, green part
only, blanched,
chopped

Remove the salmon skin and all pin (pectoral) bones. Lift meat off the backbone and dice into even cubes. Reserve backbone. Skewer on half bamboo skewers. Keep refrigerated under plastic cover. To cook, season and cook over steam at 450° for 3 to 4 minutes.

Place Manila clams and mussels in a large pot; add 1 chopped onion, 2 chopped shallots, 1 sprig of thyme, bay leaf and 1²/₃ cup Riesling or other dry white wine of your choice. Steam open 3 to 4 minutes, taking care not to overcook. Store shellfish in shells in large dish covered with plastic. Strain the cooking liquid and reserve.

Pull the shrimp vein out in the raw state; if no black vein comes, the vein is empty. Heat 1 Tbsp. olive oil in a large skillet and sear shrimp on both sides until bright red. Remove the shells, reserving them for the sauce. Store the shrimp in a dish covered with plastic.

Parboil the lobster 3 to 4 minutes in boiling salted water, then shock on ice until firm. Shell lobster, reserving abdomen and small legs for sauce but discarding tomalley.

Shuck the oysters, carefully depositing each on a flat strainer, allowing all the juices to drip into the container of reserved cooking liquid from the clams and mussels. Scrape each oyster's adductor muscles from shell lid and add to juices. Keep oysters refrigerated until ready to use.

Prepare the sauce in a flat sauté pan by placing the salmon backbones, the reserved cooking juices of all shellfish, shrimp shells, well-chopped abdomen and small legs of the lobsters, oyster juices and scraps of adductor muscle, fish fumet or chicken stock, clam juice, wine, bouquet garni, chervil and parsley.

Reduce by ²/₃. Do not strain. In a clean sauté pan, add alternately the heavy cream and the reduction on high heat, stirring constantly and reducing further. When the sauce coats a spatula lightly, strain it into a saucepan and add the butter and creme fraîche to taste.

Place the scallions in a blender, add ²/₃ of the sauce, and liquefy until sauce has turned green. Correct seasonings as you taste with the wine and a small piece of salmon. The remaining third of the sauce will remain white and be used to grill the oysters.

Put ½ tsp. hot white sauce into each oyster shell, add one oyster, and top with another half tsp. of white sauce. Grill or broil until sauce is golden. Reheat clams and mussels over steaming salted water. Reheat lobster and shrimp by gently sautéing them in very little butter until hot.

Pan steam salmon in oven at 450°. Arrange the plate as follows: A pool of green sauce in the center, a piece of lobster at 9 o'clock, a green lip in her shell at 3 o'clock, a shrimp — and in the crook of the shrimp — one clam at 6 o'clock, another clam at 12 o'clock, at the very center of the plate a salmon skewer posed between all other elements at a 45° angle, an oyster at 10 o'clock, a second oyster at 8 o'clock. Drizzle the remainder of both sauces in drops around the shellfish. Dot the plate all around with tiny leaves of chervil. ✳

TRADE SECRET: *The salmon in winter is out at sea, so all this shellfish helps it look more opulent on the plate. The white wine may be Alsatian Riesling or California Sauvignon Blanc or Chardonnay.*

Diana Kennedy

BEST-SELLING COOKBOOK AUTHOR • MICHOACAN, MEXICO

PEPPERED OYSTERS

Serves 6

Preparation Time: 25 Minutes
© Mexican Regional Cooking

4 dozen oysters, removed from shells, liquid reserved	6 garlic cloves
2 tsps. whole peppercorns	1 Tbsp. lime juice, more if desired
½ tsp. salt, or to taste	2 Tbsps. olive oil
	2 bay leaves

Heat the liquid from the oysters to the simmering point, then add the oysters and poach for 2 to 3 minutes, or until the edges start to curl up. Drain the oysters, reserving the broth.

Pound the peppercorns in a mortar with the salt until finely ground. Pound in the garlic and gradually add the lime juice. Last of all, add about 3 Tbsps. of the reserved oyster broth. Mix well.

Heat the olive oil in a saucepan. Add the bay leaves and the peppercorn mixture, and cook over high heat for about 2 minutes, stirring constantly. Remove the pan from the flame and add the oysters. Adjust the seasoning, then add a squeeze of lime juice and a little more of the oyster liquid if desired.

Set aside to cool and serve as suggested above, or leave to season overnight. ✳

People who know Diana Kennedy say that she cooks like a Mexican grandmother, even though she was born in England. Considered the doyenne of Mexican cookery, Kennedy not only pursues off-the-beaten-track recipes but also lives an off-the-beaten-track life. Her Quinta Diana, an 8-acre ranch in the tiny village of San Francisco Coatepec de Morelos in the state of Michoacan, is 100 miles west of Mexico City, outside the city of Zitacuaro.

Back in her "laboratory," as she calls her kitchen in the British manner, she usually tests recipes according to the season and the contents of her garden. The precision she brings to her tasks mirrors and shapes the purity of the ingredients she selects.

The following recipes for Peppered Oysters and Shrimps in Pumpkin-Seed Sauce are simple in essence but stunningly original in presentation.

SHRIMPS IN PUMPKIN-SEED SAUCE

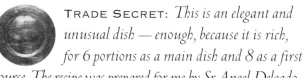

Serves 6

Preparation Time: 45 Minutes
© Mexican Regional Cooking

1½ lbs. medium-sized shrimps, shelled, deveined (shells reserved)	8 sprigs fresh coriander
2½ cups cold water	3 fresh chiles serranos or any fresh, hot green chiles, wiped clean
1 tsp. salt, or to taste Freshly ground pepper	½ small white onion
1 cup pumpkin seeds hulled, unroasted, unsalted	1 Tbsp. unsalted butter
	½ cup sour cream or creme fraîche, preferably homemade

TRADE SECRET: *This is an elegant and unusual dish — enough, because it is rich, for 6 portions as a main dish and 8 as a first course. The recipe was prepared for me by Sr. Angel Delgado, the owner of Las Diligencias in Tampico, which has had the reputation of being one of the serious eating places outside Mexico City — perhaps the best thing one can say of any restaurant. I have altered Señor Delgado's recipe by reducing the amount of butter considerably — the sour cream is quite rich enough — and by using shrimp broth rather than milk to blend the sauce. The shrimps of Tampico also deserve mention. I would go out of my way any day to have a plateful of camarones al natural in Tampico — served unskinned with head and tail still on. But you should specify whether you want those from the lagoons along the coastal area or from the sea. I'd take those from the sea every time.*

Put the shrimp shells, tails and heads, if any, into a saucepan, add the water and salt, and cook over medium heat for about 20 minutes, to extract the flavor and make a light broth. Strain and discard the shells, reserving the cooking liquid. Add the shrimps and cook over gentle heat for about 3 minutes, or until they are just turning opaque. Drain the shrimps, reserving the broth.

In a heavy, ungreased frying pan, toast the pumpkin seeds lightly, stirring them often, until they begin to swell up and start to pop about — do not let them brown. Set them aside to cool and then grind them finely in a coffee-spice grinder. Alternatively, they can just be added to the blender with the broth in the next step, but the sauce will not be as smooth.

Place the shrimp broth, pumpkin seeds, coriander, chiles and onion in a blender or food processor, and blend until smooth.

Melt the butter in a heavy saucepan. Add the blended pumpkin-seed sauce and cook over very low heat, stirring and scraping the bottom of the pan constantly, for about 10 minutes. Stir in the cream, adjust seasoning and just heat through — about 5 minutes. Then add the shrimps and heat through for another 5 minutes. The sauce should be of a medium consistency.

Serve with fresh, hot tortillas or crusty French bread — no butter. And never serve it on top of rice or all that lovely sauce will be absorbed and lost. ✳

Mark Kiffin

COYOTE CAFÉ • COCINAS OF THE SOUTHWEST • SANTA FE, NEW MEXICO

Mark Kiffin is the corporate executive chef at Coyote Café in Santa Fe, New Mexico and corporate executive chef and partner at the Coyote Café in the MGM Grand Hotel, Las Vegas, Nevada and the Coyote Café in Austin, Texas.

Chosen as one of the Rising Star chefs of 1995 by *Restaurant Hospitality* magazine, Kiffin is a graduate of the Culinary Institute of America. His expertise and experience in Southwestern cuisine were recognized by Mark Miller, who recruited him.

In 1992, Kiffin assisted with the opening of Miller's award-winning Red Sage restaurant in Washington D.C. More recently he opened the new Coyote Cafés in Las Vegas and Austin. In addition, Kiffin has been active in the product design, development and testing for the Coyote Cocina line of premier Southwestern food products. He jointly authored with Miller *Coyote's Pantry*, *The Great Salsa Book*, and the *Indian Market Week Cookbook.*

We are fortunate to include recipe for his Red Chile Crusted Sea Bass with Roasted Clams, Mussels and Calamari Risotto with Fire-Roasted Tomato Chipotle Salsa.

RED CHILE CRUSTED SEA BASS WITH ROASTED CLAMS, MUSSELS AND CALAMARI RISOTTO AND FIRE-ROASTED TOMATO CHIPOTLE SALSA

Serves 4

Preparation Time: 1¹/₂ Hours

Sea Bass Ingredients:

2 lbs. sea bass filets	1 recipe Picante Dried Red Chile Rub (recipe follows)

Chile Rub Ingredients:

2 Tbsps. chile caribe	1 Tbsp. sugar
1 Tbsp. dried oregano	1 tsp. salt
³/₄ cup red chile powder	

Clams and Mussels Ingredients:

3 Tbsps. olive oil	1 bunch fresh thyme
¹/₂ white onion, chopped	1 lb. manila clams
2 garlic cloves, sliced	1 lb. black mussels, debearded
2 bay leaves	¹/₂ cup white wine
	2 cups fish stock or clam juice

Risotto Ingredients:

2 Tbsps. olive oil	2 cups fish stock (clam juice can be substituted)
1 shallot, minced	
¹/₂ cup Arborio rice	
¹/₂ cup cooking liquid from clams and mussels, strained	¹/₂ cup Parmesan cheese, freshly grated

FOR THE SEA BASS: Rub bass with chile rub and refrigerate.

FOR THE CHILE RUB: Place the chile caribe and oregano in a dry skillet, and toast over medium heat for 2 minutes until fragrant. Transfer to a spice grinder and pulse until smooth. Place in a bowl and combine thoroughly with the chile powder, sugar and salt.

FOR THE CLAMS AND MUSSELS: Heat the olive oil in a large, shallow saucepan over medium-high heat. Sweat the onion, garlic and herbs in the olive oil. Add the clams and cook for 1 minute. Add the mussels and cook for another minute. Deglaze with the wine, then add the fish stock and cook until the shellfish just pops open. Remove from heat and cool in the liquid. Remove shellfish from the shells, discard shells, and strain the cooking liquid (be careful to avoid sand). Should yield ¹/₂ cup.

FOR THE RISOTTO: Heat the olive oil and add the shallots. Cook for 1 minute over medium-low heat without browning. Add the rice and stir in the strained cooking liquid. While stirring constantly, add the fish stock in parts, allowing the rice to absorb the liquid. Cook to al dente stage, creamy but firm. Fold in the cheese. Keep hot.

Yields: 2 cups

Fire-Roasted Tomato Chipotle Salsa Ingredients:

2½ Tbsps. virgin olive oil

¼ onion, small diced

1 lb. Roma tomatoes, blackened

2 tsps. roasted garlic, minced

¼ cup fresh cilantro, minced

2 chipotle chiles, chopped

2 Tbsps. red wine vinegar

1½ tsps. salt

½ tsp. sugar

2 cups good red wine, Rhone or burgundy style

Assembly Ingredients:

4 Tbsps. olive oil

1 lb. calamari, cleaned, sliced into rounds

2 lbs. chile-rubbed sea bass

1 Tbsp. fresh chives, minced

1 Tbsp. fresh marjoram, minced

TRADE SECRET: *You may also substitute 1 pound of tomatillos for the tomatoes. Husk and rinse the tomatillos, and blacken them before using.*

FOR THE SALSA: Heat ½ Tbsp. olive oil in a sauté pan over medium heat until lightly smoking. Add the onion and sauté until caramelized, about 10 minutes. Transfer the onion, half the blackened tomatoes and garlic to a food processor or blender, and pulse until finely chopped but not puréed. Add the cilantro and chipotle chiles, and pulse again to mix.

Peel, seed and chop the remaining tomatoes and fold together with the remaining 2 Tbsps. olive oil, vinegar, salt and sugar. Add to preceding mixture.

Reduce the red wine to ½ cup and add to the cooled salsa. Heat for service.

FOR THE ASSEMBLY: Heat 2 Tbsps. olive oil and sauté the calamari just until tender. Fold into the risotto along with the clams, mussels and fresh herbs.

Heat remaining 2 Tbsps. olive oil and sauté the fish to desired doneness. Keep hot.

To serve, spoon the risotto onto plates and ladle the salsa around. Center sea bass on rice. ✳

Susur Lee

LOTUS • TORONTO, CANADA

Reviewers seem almost speechless when trying to describe a visit to Susur Lee's celebrated Lotus. They use words like "magic," "astonishing," and "the stuff of food-related daydreams." All these however, merely hint at the mystery, the mastery that is Lee's cuisine.

You can't place it — Lee trained in French techniques at Hong Kong's Peninsula Hotel and practiced his craft at Toronto's Westbury Hotel, Le Trou and Peter Pan. But he's also highly knowledgeable about Chinese cooking and Asian ingredients, and this is only the beginning of his multicultural culinary repertoire.

You can't predict it — Lee's menu changes nightly, reflecting his morning forays into local street markets. You certainly can't rush through it — his dinners are a ritual that Lee describes as "a performance, just like a play." His fame has spread far beyond Canadian borders with feature stories in *Art Culinaire*, *Food Arts*, *Gourmet*, *Esquire*, and *Travel Holiday*.

So what is Lee up to? Oriental Lobster Ravioli with Sun-dried Tomato and Smoky Chile Sauce.

ORIENTAL LOBSTER RAVIOLI WITH SUN-DRIED TOMATO AND SMOKY CHILE SAUCE

Serves 6

Preparation Time: 45 Minutes

Dough Ingredients:

1³/₄ cups all-purpose
  flour
¼ tsp. salt

1½ Tbsps. extra virgin
  olive oil
½ cup cold water
5 egg yolks

Stuffing Ingredients:

¼ cup fresh leeks,
  diced
1 cup fresh (not
  frozen) sea scallops
½ egg white
  Salt and pinch
  of freshly ground
  white pepper
3 drops sesame oil
  (Japanese dark
  roasted)

1 ice cube
1 tsp. ginger,
  finely diced
½ tsp. coriander,
  chopped
1 fresh lobster, about
  ²/₃ lb., cooked half
  way, shelled, diced

Sun-dried Tomato Sauce Ingredients:

3 pieces sun-dried
  tomato in olive oil
3 garlic cloves,
  chopped

1½ Tbsps. Kikkoman
  soy sauce
1 Tbsp. shallots,
  chopped
3 Tbsps. extra-virgin
  olive oil

FOR THE DOUGH: Mix all ingredients in a bowl until a ball is formed. Wrap in Saran wrap and refrigerate.

FOR THE STUFFING: Blanch the leeks and place in a large mixing bowl. Set aside.

In a food processor, add the sea scallops, egg white, salt, pepper, sesame oil and 1 ice cube. Process until a mousse consistency is achieved. Set aside.

Add to the leeks the ginger, coriander and diced lobster. Fold in the mousse.

Roll out the dough with a pasta machine or by hand to about ³/₁₆-inch thick and cut out circle shapes about 3-inches in diameter. Place some mousse on one side of the dough and fold over the dough to cover. Pinch sides to close.

Bring salted water to a boil. Drop in ravioli and cook for 18 minutes. Remove from water and drain.

Place on individual serving dishes and drizzle with warm Sun-dried Tomato Sauce.

FOR THE SUN-DRIED TOMATO SAUCE: In a small bowl, combine the tomato, garlic, soy sauce and shallots.

In a thick cast-iron pan with a lid, heat the olive oil until smoking. Turn off heat and place mixture in the oil. Cover quickly, as mixture will spit. Let stand for 30 seconds and spoon over ravioli. ✳

Nobuyuki Matsuhisa

MATSUHISA • BEVERLY HILLS, CALIFORNIA
NOBU • TRIBECA, NEW YORK

CUCUMBER AND WAKAME SUNOMONO

Serves 4

Preparation Time: 10 Minutes (note soaking time)

8 oz dried wakame*	½ cup soy sauce
(edible seaweed)	½ cup sugar
1 cucumber	1 lemon, juice only
1 cup rice vinegar	1 Tbsp. sesame seeds

Soak wakame in water for 30 minutes before using.

Slice the cucumber paper thin, and squeeze out excess water with your hands.

Combine the vinegar, soy sauce, sugar, lemon juice in a bowl. Mix well until sugar is dissolved.

Add the cucumber and wakame to the dressing, and garnish with sesame seeds. ✳

Wakame, a dark green edible seaweed, is available both in fresh and dried form in Asian markets.

Sashimi Salad with Matsuhisa Soy Sauce Dressing, Hamachi Sashimi with Jalapeños, Squid Pasta with Light Garlic Sauce, and Baked Cod in Miso represent the multitude of imaginative dishes that led *Food & Wine* to name Nobuyuki Matsuhisa one of America's "10 Best New Chefs".

Born and raised in Japan, Matsuhisa apprenticed in the sushi bars in Tokyo before he ventured overseas to Lima, Peru. Classically trained, Matsuhisa was challenged by the culture and regional ingredients that inspired his inventive style.

Next, he went to Buenos Aires, Argentina, then back to Japan, to Alaska, and finally to Los Angeles, where he opened his restaurant, Matsuhisa, in Beverly Hills, in 1987. He opened Nobu in New York City with actor Robert De Niro in 1994, whereby the James Beard Foundation awarded him the honor of "Best New Restaurant."

We are fortunate to have his imaginative recipes for Cucumber and Wakame Sunomono, Santa Barbara Shrimp with Spicy Lemon Garlic Sauce, and Sautéed Japanese Mushroom with Yuzu Dressing.

SANTA BARBARA SHRIMP WITH SPICY LEMON GARLIC SAUCE

Serves 4

Preparation Time: 20 Minutes

8 large shrimp, peeled	2 Tbsps. lemon juice
2 Tbsps. + 1 tsp. extra-virgin olive oil	1 tsp. yuzu* juice
	Pinch of cayenne
3 Tbsps. sake	pepper
2 Tbsps. soy sauce	½ red beet, julienne
½ tsp. minced garlic	

Butterfly the shrimp lengthwise on the back side and devein. Rinse thoroughly and pat dry. Place shrimp on a grill and cook until just opaque in the thickest part, about 2 minutes.

In a small saucepan heat the olive oil, sake, soy sauce and garlic until boiling. Remove pan from heat and add lemon juice, yuzu juice and cayenne.

Arrange 2 shrimp on each plate and drizzle with sauce. Top with beet as garnish and serve. ✳

Yuzu is a sour citrus fruit available in Japanese markets.

SAUTÉED JAPANESE MUSHROOM WITH YUZU DRESSING

Serves 4

Preparation Time: 30 Minutes

½ cup extra-virgin olive oil	½ cup trumpet mushrooms, chopped
3 Tbsps. soy sauce	1 cup shiitake mushrooms, chopped
3 Tbsps. yuzu* juice	
1½ tsps. water	
1½ tsps. minced garlic	½ cup enoki mushrooms
4 Tbsps. sake	
½ tsp. black pepper	½ bunch chives, chopped
4 Tbsps. butter (½ stick)	1 whole yuzu fruit, juiced, rind zested

In a small bowl, mix the olive oil, soy sauce, yuzu juice, water, minced garlic, sake, and black pepper and whisk thoroughly.

In a large sauté pan, melt butter over medium-high heat. Add all the mushrooms, reserving enokis, and sauté. Mix sautéed mushrooms and raw enoki together, and toss with the dressing. Garnish with chives and yuzu. ✳

Yuzu is a sour citrus fruit available in Japanese markets.

Mark Militello

MARK'S PLACE • NORTH MIAMI, FLORIDA
MARK'S LAS OLAS • FT. LAUDERDALE, FLORIDA
MARK'S IN THE GROVE • COCONUT GROVE, FLORIDA

Born in El Paso, Texas, and raised in upstate New York, Mark was a pre-med student before discovering his true love was cooking. He switched schools and careers, obtaining culinary degrees in Florida and New York.

Over the years, Mark has received numerous awards and accolades for his cooking. This 40-year-old chef weaves Caribbean ingredients, Californian and Mediterranean cooking techniques, and an international array of recipes into a cuisine that's uniquely his own. The results are exhibited here in the two dishes he gives us: Stone Crab Salad with Pickled Japanese Relish and Ginger and Creole Spiny Lobster with Fresh Conch.

STONE CRAB SALAD WITH PICKLED JAPANESE RELISH AND GINGER

Serves 4

Preparation Time: 30 Minutes

Stone Crab Salad Ingredients:

- 1 oz. dried wakame* seaweed, softened with warm water
- ½ European cucumber, thinly sliced
- 1 Tbsp. pickled daikon, julienne
- 1 tsp. ginger, julienne
- ¼ cup ginger soy vinaigrette (recipe follows)
- ¼ lb. fresh stone crab meat
- 1 tsp. scallion, chopped
- 1 tsp. white sesame seeds, toasted

Ginger Soy Vinaigrette Ingredients:

- ½ cup fish stock
- ½ cup rice vinegar
- ½ cup light soy sauce
- 1 Tbsp. sugar
- 1½ Tbsps. fresh ginger juice
- 1½ Tbsps. orange juice

FOR THE STONE CRAB SALAD:
Soften wakame seaweed in warm water until fully reconstituted. Cool in ice bath.

Cut the wakame into 1 x 1-inch slices, and place in a large mixing bowl along with the cucumber, pickled daikon, ginger soy vinaigrette and crab meat. Toss lightly without breaking up the crab meat.

Place the salad ingredients in the form of a mound in the center of a serving plate. Garnish with scallion and sesame seeds.

FOR THE GINGER SOY VINAIGRETTE:
In a small bowl, whisk all ingredients to blend. ✳

Wakame, a dark green edible seaweed, is available both in fresh and dried form in Asian markets.

CREOLE SPINY LOBSTER WITH FRESH CONCH

Serves 6

Preparation Time: 45 Minutes (note marinating time)

Lobster Ingredients:

6 spiny lobsters,
  1½ pounds each

½ cup extra-virgin
  olive oil

½ cup dry white wine

4 limes, juiced

Sauce Ingredients:

2 Tbsps. extra-virgin
  olive oil

2 Tbsps. garlic, minced

½ cup onion, diced

½ cup red bell pepper,
  diced

1 scotch bonnet chile,
  seeded, minced

1½ Tbsps. curry powder

½ cup dry
  Spanish sherry

½ cup tomatoes,
  peeled, seeded,
  finely chopped

2 cups lobster or
  fish stock

½ cup fresh corn
  kernels, cut off
  the cob

½ cup chayote*, diced

½ cup yellow yam,
  diced

½ cup butternut squash
  or calabaza, diced

¾ cup ground
  fresh conch

2 Tbsps. fresh
  thyme leaves

2 Tbsps. parsley,
  chopped

Salt and freshly
  ground black pepper

FOR THE LOBSTER: Cut the lobsters in half lengthwise. Remove the entrails.

In a shallow pan, combine the olive oil, wine and lime juice. Add the lobsters and marinate for 30 minutes.

FOR THE SAUCE: Heat the oil in a large sauté pan. Add the garlic, onion, bell pepper and chile. Cook over medium heat for 3 minutes, or until translucent.

Stir in the curry powder and cook for 2 minutes. Stir in the sherry and boil until the mixture is reduced by half.

Add the tomatoes and lobster or fish stock and bring to a boil. Reduce heat and gently simmer the mixture for 15 minutes.

Pass the sauce through a food mill fitted with a fine grate into a clean saucepan. Return the pan to the heat.

Add the corn, chayote, yam, squash and conch, and simmer for 15 minutes. Stir in the thyme and parsley. Correct the seasonings to taste, adding salt and pepper .

Preheat the grill. Grill the lobsters for 8 to 10 minutes, preferably over a hardwood or charcoal fire. Place two lobster halves on each plate and spoon the sauce over and around them. ✱

*Chayote, a pear-shaped member of the gourd family and known in France as Christophene, is widely available in grocery stores and Latin American stores throughout the year.

 TRADE SECRET: *The flavorful spicy sauce is sweetened by the addition of fresh conch. The best way to grind the conch is in a meat grinder, but you can also use a food processor. Here, the lobster is grilled with the heads on, but you can also remove the heads, split the tails, brown them in olive oil, then simmer them briefly in the sauce.*

Nancy Oakes

BOULEVARD • SAN FRANCISCO, CALIFORNIA

From the beginning, the principles that define Nancy Oakes' cooking have been clear and unshakable. She has always believed that her diners need to be comforted by her food as well as the surroundings and service and that the room and food presentation should flatter them in a way that makes each person feel personally cared for.

In the kitchen, Nancy and her crew continue to cook for each diner personally. "When you order a chicken, we actually cook it to order for you over an open fire in our wood-burning oven and do a modern confit on the leg. There are no shortcuts," she says. "Even our pastries and cookies are made in small batches so they have a home-baked quality. We choose diver scallops rather than dredged; fish caught with hook and line rather than netted;

fruits and vegetables straight from the farm or the farmer's market and natural chickens and duck."

Her team derives great satisfaction in delivering consistently inspired and sumptuous plates to their dining room. Her cuisine has been honored by the capacity crowds that have gathered each day and evening since Boulevard's opening two years ago. And through it all, the accolades accumulate from *Zagat, San Francisco Focus, Food & Wine, Gourmet,* Robert Mondavi Rising Star Chefs and the James Beard Foundation.

We are fortunate here to have her imaginative Crab Cakes with Tartar Sauce, an Asian Dipping Sauce, White Chocolate Banana Cream Pie and Maple-Cured Pork Loin with White Corn.

CRAB CAKES WITH TARTAR SAUCE

Serves 6

Preparation Time: 45 Minutes
Pre-heat oven to 350°

Crab Cake Ingredients:

2 cups fresh
  bread crumbs
  (size of a pea)
2 Tbsps. olive oil
1 lb. fresh crab meat
2/3 cup celery, finely
  chopped
1/2 cup red onion,
  finely chopped
1 1/2 tsps. Worcestershire
  sauce

1/4 cup parsley,
  finely chopped
2 Tbsps. fresh thyme,
  chopped
1 Tbsp. Dijon
  mustard
1 tsp. Tabasco sauce
1/2 tsp. pepper flakes
3 eggs, separated
Salt & pepper

Tartar Sauce Ingredients:

1 1/2 cups Best Foods
  Mayonnaise
  (Hellman's east of
  the Rockies)
1/2 cup green onion,
  finely chopped

1/4 cup fresh parsley,
  finely chopped
1/2 cup dill pickle,
  finely chopped
1/2 cup capers,
  finely chopped
1 tsp. coarse
  black pepper

FOR THE CRAB CAKES: In a large mixing bowl, toss the bread crumbs in the olive oil. Add the crab, celery, onion, Worcestershire, herbs, mustard, Tabasco and pepper flakes. Mix in the egg yolks.

Whip the egg whites to stiff peaks, then fold gently into the crab mixture. Form into balls approximately 3-inches in diameter.

In a hot sauté pan filmed with oil, brown on one side, turn over and finish cooking in a 350° oven for 5 minutes, or until cooked through.

FOR THE TARTAR SAUCE: In a mixing bowl, combine all ingredients. Refrigerate until needed. ✳

ASIAN DIPPING SAUCE

Makes 3 1/2 to 4 cups

Preparation Time: 10 Minutes

2 cups sweet Thai
  chile sauce*
1 cup rice vinegar
1/2 cup fish sauce or
  soy sauce
Juice of 2 limes

3 Tbsps. fresh ginger,
  finely chopped
1/4 cup green onions
  or scallions, finely
  chopped
Hot chile oil to
  taste, optional

Combine all the ingredients in a bowl and serve. The sauce will keep covered in the refrigerator for 7 to 10 days. Can be served with potstickers. ✳

Sweet Thai chile sauce made from the thin-fleshed Thai chile, adds a fiery punch that doesn't dissipate with cooking. Available in Asian markets.

WHITE CHOCOLATE BANANA CREAM PIE

Serves 6 to 8

Preparation Time: 45 Minutes
Pre-heat oven to 350°

White Chocolate Pastry Cream Ingredients:

4 cups milk

1 vanilla bean

1⅓ cups sugar

½ cup cornstarch

12 egg yolks

¼ cup butter, chopped

1 cup white chocolate, chopped

3 bananas, sliced

Fresh whipping cream

Pie Dough Ingredients:

2 sticks butter

2 tsps. sugar

3 cups flour

⅔ cup cream

FOR THE PASTRY CREAM: Heat the milk and vanilla bean in a heavy-bottomed pan.

Mix the sugar, cornstarch and yolks, and add to the milk. Over medium heat, whisk until thickened and add butter and ¾ cup white chocolate. Strain and refrigerate.

FOR THE PIE DOUGH: In a mixer with a paddle, combine the first three ingredients and mix until it resembles coarse meal. Then add the cream until the dough comes together and forms a ball. Roll out pastry dough to a ¼-inch thickness and line a 9-inch pie pan.

Bake the pastry shell until the edges start to turn golden brown, about 15 to 20 minutes. Remove from the oven and sprinkle ¼ cup chunks of white chocolate into the shell base.

Allow pastry shell to cool and then fill with cream mix. Fold sliced bananas into the pastry cream and serve with freshly whipped cream. ✳

MAPLE-CURED PORK LOIN WITH CIDER SAUCE

Serves 8

Preparation Time: 1 Hour (note marinating time)
Pre-heat oven to 325°

Pork Loin Ingredients:

1 pork loin, 10-rib rack about 9 lbs.	2 Tbsps. chile flakes
1 gallon hot water	¼ cup Dijon mustard
1 gallon hot cider	Salt and pepper to taste
3 cups maple sugar	
2 cups kosher salt	

Cider Sauce Ingredients:

Pre-heat oven to 350°

4 apples, chopped	½ bunch thyme
4 cloves garlic, chopped	12 whole peppercorns
1 large white onion, chopped	3 cups regular cider, reduced to 1 cup
2 cups hard cider	2 cups rich chicken or pork stock
⅔ cup cider vinegar	Salt and pepper to taste

FOR THE PORK LOIN: Mix all ingredients but salt and pepper and cool. Submerge pork loin in the curing mixture and refrigerate for 48 hours. Season with salt and pepper. Sear all sides in a hot sauté pan.

Roast in a 325° oven for approximately 1 hour, or until done.

FOR THE CIDER SAUCE: Lightly brown the apples, garlic and onion in saucepan. Place saucepan in 350° oven until vegetables are soft. Deglaze pan with hard cider and vinegar; add thyme and peppercorns, reduce by half. Add regular cider and reduce by half. Add stock, reduce by half, strain and season to taste. ✷

WINE PAIRING: A Spätlese from Weingut Franz Kunstler, Hochheimer Reichstal would be very special here. The strong, ripe apple flavors of this wine complement the concentrated flavors of the stock and cider nicely.

Bradley Ogden

THE LARK CREEK INN • LARKSPUR, CALIFORNIA
THE LARK CREEK CAFÉ • WALNUT CREEK, CALIFORNIA
ONE MARKET RESTAURANT • SAN FRANCISCO, CALIFORNIA

Bradley Ogden, the 42 year-old native of Traverse City, Michigan, has been inducted into the "Who's Who of American Cooking" by *Cooks* magazine. He has also been chosen as one of the Great American Chefs by the International Wine and Food Society, awarded the Golden Plate Award by the American Academy of Achievement and has been named Best California Chef by the prestigious James Beard Foundation.

Ogden believes perhaps the greatest influence on his cooking came from his early exposure to fresh, native American foods. "Coming from the Midwest, I grew up with freshly caught trout, free-range chickens, and hand-picked fruits and vegetables. As my culinary training exposed me to new techniques and ingredients, I never lost my appreciation for those basic tastes." His philosophy remains: "Keep it simple; use the freshest ingredients available and put them together in such a way that the flavors, colors and textures combine to bring out the best in each other."

He offers us his recipes for Creamy Wild Mushroom Polenta and Fire Roasted Ahi Tuna with Chopped Vegetable Salad and Ginger Glaze.

CREAMY WILD MUSHROOM POLENTA

Serves 6

Preparation Time: 1 Hour
Pre-heat oven to 350°

2 cups water
2 cups chicken stock
1 sprig of rosemary, 3-inches long
4 tsps. garlic, minced
1 cup polenta (cornmeal)
8 Tbsps. butter (1 stick), unsalted

½ lb. wild mushrooms, cleaned, trimmed, sliced ¼-inch thick
1 Tbsp. Kosher salt
1 tsp. ground white pepper
3 Tbsps. each parsley, sage and marjoram, chopped
1 cup sour cream or mascarpone

Bring the water and stock to a rolling boil in an oven-proof pot. Add the rosemary sprig, 2 tsps. garlic and polenta, stirring with a wooden spoon continuously, to ensure there are no lumps, for 5 to 10 minutes. Cover pot and place in oven for 45 minutes, stirring occasionally. Remove from oven and add half the butter. Keep warm in a double boiler.

Melt the remaining butter in a sauté pan. Add the mushrooms and sauté in the butter for 2 minutes. Add the remaining 2 tsps. garlic and season with salt and pepper to taste. Sauté for another 2 to 3 minutes, or until mushrooms are soft.

Add the mushrooms to the polenta with the herbs and sour cream. Season to taste if necessary and serve immediately. ✳

FIRE ROASTED AHI TUNA TENDERLOIN WITH CHOPPED VEGETABLE SALAD AND GINGER GLAZE

Serves 4

Preparation Time: 45 Minutes

1 lb. tuna filet, trimmed, 2¹/₂-inches thick, 8-inches long
2 Tbsps. extra-virgin olive oil
Kosher salt
Fresh black pepper
1 cup asparagus, blanched, cut into ¹/₂-inch dice
12 baby artichokes, cooked, cut in half
1 red bell pepper, roasted, diced
¹/₂ cup fava beans, blanched
1 cup Blue Lake beans, snapped, blanched
1 bunch golden beets, blanched
1 bunch Chioggia beets, blanched
2 fennel bulbs, peeled, chopped
¹/₂ bunch watercress, broken into small stems
¹/₂ cup tomato, chopped
3 Tbsps. Italian parsley
3 Tbsps. tarragon, chopped
2 Tbsps. lemon juice
Ginger glaze (recipe follows)

Brush the tuna with some olive oil and season with salt and pepper. Set aside.

Combine the remaining salad ingredients in a large mixing bowl and season with salt and pepper. Set aside.

Grill the tuna over very hot coals until rare. While grilling, baste the tuna with the ginger glaze.

Arrange the salad on serving plates and top with 2 slices of tuna. Finish by brushing a little glaze on the tuna and serve. ✳

GINGER GLAZE

Serves 4

Preparation Time: 20 Minutes

1 tsp. mustard seed
¹/₂ ancho chile, seeded
2 Tbsps. molasses
1 tsp. soy sauce
1 Tbsp. minced lemon grass
1 tsp. garlic, minced
3 Tbsps. white ginger, grated
1 cup sweet rice wine vinegar
4 Tbsps. lemon juice
4 Tbsps. cilantro, chopped
¹/₂ tsp. red pepper flakes
1 cup water

Combine all ingredients in a saucepan over medium heat and reduce to ¹/₃ cup. Strain. ✳

Charles Palmer

AUREOLE • ALVA • LENOX ROOM • NEW YORK, NEW YORK

When the Lenox Room opened in April 1995, it became Charles Palmer's third restaurant in New York City — joining the internationally celebrated Aureole and downtown's Alva.

Having worked hard to develop his own special culinary vision and style, Palmer has come into his own as a chef and restaurateur. Over the years he has succeeded in putting together a seasoned team with a keenly developed sense of what makes restaurants work — from ambiance, service and food to wine lists, cost controls and public relations. He has authored his first cookbook and is a partner in the Egg Farm Dairy, an upstate New York creamery that produces butter and wild ripened cheeses.

In 1995, Palmer released the first vintage of Aureole Cuvee, a sparkling wine blended and labeled exclusively for Aureole restaurant by Iron Horse Vineyard.

From restaurant management to product development to cookbook authorship, Palmer strives for a future filled with further food successes. He demonstrates his knowledge and expertise for us with Herb-Spiced Venison with Red Onion and New Potato Salad.

HERB-SPICED VENISON WITH RED ONION AND NEW POTATO SALAD

Serves 4

Preparation Time: 45 Minutes

½ tsp. cracked black pepper
½ tsp. ground cumin
½ tsp. ground allspice
1 tsp. salt
4 medium red potatoes
1 Tbsp. vegetable oil

2 small red onions, peeled, quartered
4 blocks of venison, cut from loin or leg, 3 oz. each, 1½-inch thick
20 arugula leaves

In a small bowl, combine pepper, cumin, allspice and salt. Set aside.

In a pot of salted water, bring potatoes to a boil and simmer for 15 to 18 minutes. Drain and cool.

Heat ½ Tbsp. oil in a sauté pan, and sauté the onions on all sides until browned and slightly soft, about 15 minutes. Set aside and keep warm.

Rub the spice mixture onto the venison. In the same sauté pan, heat the remaining ½ Tbsp. oil and sear the venison on all sides until brown, about 1 minute for each side. Cook to medium rare, 6 to 7 minutes total. Let the meat rest.

To serve, arrange the arugula on plates in a circle. Slice potatoes ½-inch thick and fan over the arugula. Place 2 onion quarters in center of each plate. Slice the venison against the grain and fan slices over the onions. Spoon the vinaigrette over top.

Vinaigrette Ingredients:

6 Tbsps. extra-virgin olive oil
2 Tbsps. red wine vinegar
1 Tbsp. Worcestershire sauce

½ Tbsp. Kosher salt
½ tsp. black pepper, milled
1 Tbsp. chives, finely minced

In a small bowl, mix all ingredients except chives. Add the chives just before serving. ✳

Anne Parker Johnson

HIGHLANDS INN • CARMEL, CALIFORNIA

After attending the Culinary Institute of America in Hyde Park, Anne completed a one-year internship at Tavern on the Green in New York City. In 1989, she led the three-person U.S. team to Paris to compete in the international World Pastry Cup competition. While in France, she accepted an offer to work for one year at a pastry shop in Belgium. On returning to New York, Anne worked for several restaurants before relocating to Carmel in 1993 as pâtissier at Highlands Inn.

EARL GREY TEA CHOCOLATE TRUFFLES

Yields 25 to 30

Preparation Time: 45 Minutes (note refrigeration time)

2½ cups heavy cream	½ lb. milk chocolate,
1¼ oz. bulk	chopped
Earl Grey tea	4 Tbsps. sweet butter,
1 lb. semisweet	softened
chocolate, such as	3 cups almonds,
Callebaut, chopped	toasted and
	chopped

Bring the cream to a boil and add the tea. Cover and infuse for 6 minutes. Meanwhile, place the semisweet chocolate and ½ lb. milk chocolate in a large bowl.

After the tea has infused for 6 minutes, bring the cream and tea back to a boil and pour through a strainer over the chocolate, separating out the tea leaves.

Using a whisk, stir to form a homogenous, smooth ganache. Mix in the soft butter and pour into a container. Cover with plastic wrap and refrigerate overnight.

Using a small-sized ice cream scoop, scoop the hardened truffle mix and roll into little balls. Refrigerate until firm.

Dip the balls into ½ lb. tempered melted milk chocolate and roll in toasted and chopped almonds.

Truffles may be stored in the refrigerator for up to 2 months and are best consumed at room temperature. ✳

François Payard

RESTAURANT DANIEL • NEW YORK, NEW YORK

François Payard, executive pastry chef of the famed Restaurant Daniel, came there by way of Le Bernardin in New York City and Lucas-Carton and Tour d'Argent in Paris. Winner of the James Beard Award as the 1995 Godiva Liqueur Pastry Chef of the Year, Payard features thirteen desserts on his menu, seven of which are chocolate, including a warm chocolate cake with an infusion of verbena.

A third-generation pastry chef, Payard left his family's pâtisserie in Nice at age 15 to strike out on his own. After three years of schooling at Ecole Lenôtre and five years of working in some of Paris' most renowned Michelin three-star restaurants, the chocolate brick road led him to America.

Most of Payard's days and nights are spent at Daniel, creating the head-turning desserts that have set new standards for pastry chefs throughout America. Even when he's not in the kitchen, he is always thinking of new things to do with pastry. Whether he is reading old country cookbooks late into the night or flipping through his ever-growing stack of French and American culinary magazines on his days off, this pastry artist never rests.

His dream dessert recipe for Upside Down Chocolate Soufflés with Chocolate Spaghetti and Bittersweet Chocolate Sorbet is airy, rich and smooth — everything a dessert should be.

Upside Down Chocolate Soufflés with Chocolate Spaghetti and Bittersweet Chocolate Sorbet

Yields 20

Preparation Time: 2 Hours
Pre-heat oven to 375°

Soufflés Ingredients:

7 eggs, separated	1¼ cups butter, melted
1 Tbsp. flour	½ lemon, juiced
6 Tbsps. sugar	1 Tbsp. butter,
12 oz. extra bitter	softened
chocolate, finely	¼ cup extra fine sugar
chopped	

Bittersweet Chocolate Sorbet Ingredients:

3 cups water	1 cup extra bitter
¼ cup creme fraîche	chocolate, finely
1 cup sugar	chopped

Chocolate Spaghetti Ingredients:

Pre-heat oven to 350°

½ cup butter, (1 stick)	2 Tbsps. cocoa
softened	powder, sifted
½ cup confectioner's	3 egg whites
sugar	
⅓ cup flour, sifted	

FOR THE SOUFFLÉS: In a mixing bowl, with a wire whisk, beat the egg yolks. Gradually incorporate the flour and 5 Tbsps. sugar. Continue to beat the mixture until it becomes light and fluffy and turns lemon color.

Place the chocolate in a small bowl and add the warm melted butter. Stir with a whisk until completely smooth. Add to the egg yolk mixture and blend well.

In a large mixing bowl, beat the egg whites and lemon juice until soft peaks are formed. Add remaining 1 Tbsp. sugar and continue to beat until stiff. Gently fold the egg whites into the chocolate and egg mixture until fully incorporated.

Butter 20 four oz. soufflé cups, 3-inches in diameter, and coat with sugar. Use a pastry bag to fill the soufflé cups ¾ full. Place filled cups in a bain marie and bake 5 to 6 minutes. Remove and unmold immediately onto serving plates.

FOR THE CHOCOLATE SORBET: In a saucepan over medium heat, bring the water, creme fraîche and sugar to a boil. Add the cocoa and stir until dissolved. Remove from the heat, add chocolate and stir until completely melted and smooth. Let cool, then churn in ice cream machine.

FOR THE CHOCOLATE SPAGHETTI: In a mixing bowl, cream the butter with a wooden spoon. Incorporate the confectioner's sugar, flour, cocoa and egg whites. Blend well. Refrigerate for 30 minutes.

Using a cake decorating comb and working in a lengthwise direction, spread the mixture on a non-stick baking mat (silpat or exopat) making a striated pattern. Bake 4 to 5 minutes.

While they are still warm, remove bands of 7 to 8 strips of the chocolate spaghetti and wrap around each individual soufflé. (The chocolate spaghetti can be prepared in advance and wrapped around molds the same size as the soufflé cups.)

Garnish each soufflé with a scoop of sorbet before serving. ✳

Michel Richard

CITRUS RESTAURANT ON MELROSE AVENUE • LOS ANGELES, CALIFORNIA
BROADWAY DELI • SANTA MONICA, CALIFORNIA
CITRONELLE • SANTA BARBARA, CALIFORNIA AND WASHINGTON, D.C.

Michel Richard grew up in Brittany, one of five children who had to go to work early to help support the family. When he was 9, Richard knew he wanted to become a chef. By the time Richard was 14, he was an apprentice to the pastry chef in a small hotel in northeastern France and had won an award as the best neophyte pâtissier in Champagne. At 21, Richard moved to Paris and was hired by one of the great mentors of his life, Chef Gaston Le Notre.

By 1987, Richard was ready for his own full-service restaurant. He opened Citrus Restaurant on Melrose Avenue, which allowed him the freedom to express his unending creativity. As Richard's restaurant empire continues to grow, he is still hailed for his simple, lightly sauced, innovative dishes with strong, fresh flavors.

These days, this restaurateur's schedule is kept busy with traveling from coast to coast, checking in at his restaurants, making promotional appearances for his cookbook and donating his time to work with charitable organizations. Richard and his wife of 11 years live in Los Angeles, California, with their six children.

We are fortunate to feature two of his mouth-watering creations: Chocolate Hazelnut Bar with Raspberry Sauce, and Saint Tropez Terrine with Shallot Vinaigrette.

CHOCOLATE HAZELNUT BAR WITH RASPBERRY SAUCE

Serves 12

Preparation Time: 45 Minutes (note refrigeration time)

1¾ cups milk chocolate
   or Gianduja
   chocolate, chopped
1½ cups praline
¼ cup peanut oil
¾ cup gaufrette*
   cookie, crumbled

1¼ cups bittersweet
   chocolate, chopped
2¾ cups heavy cream
   Cocoa powder
   for dusting
1 basket of raspberries
   Sugar to taste

Melt the chocolate in a double boiler to just above 99° temperature.

Meanwhile, soften the praline in a mixer with the peanut oil.

Stir together the melted chocolate, the praline and the gaufrette cookie. Pour the mixture into a shallow mold with a removable bottom. This recipe fills a 22 x 4 x 1¼-inch mold very nicely.

Melt the bittersweet chocolate in a large bowl in a double boiler to just above 99° temperature.

Meanwhile, whip the heavy cream to soft peaks. Quickly fold the whipped cream into the melted chocolate. Spread this mixture onto the base in the mold, and refrigerate until set.

Cut the chocolate cake away from the sides of the mold and lift out of the mold.

Dust with cocoa powder and cut the cake into thin bars. Serve 3 or 4 bars per person at room temperature.

FOR THE RASPBERRY SAUCE: Place 1 basket of raspberries with some sugar to taste in a blender and purée. Strain and serve with chocolate hazelnut bars. ✱

*Gaufrette cookies, available in most food stores, are thin, lightly sweet, fan-shaped wafers. When baked on a special gaufrette iron (similar to a waffle iron), the wafer's surface is waffled.

SAINT TROPEZ TERRINE WITH SHALLOT VINAIGRETTE

Serves 8

Preparation Time: 2¹/₂ Hours (note refrigeration time)

Terrine Ingredients:

2¹/₂ lbs. tomatoes (about 10 large), peeled

¹/₂ cup chopped onion

2 garlic cloves, peeled

¹/₃ cup beet juice

1¹/₂ cups tomato juice

Salt and freshly ground black pepper to taste

2 large eggplants, about 3 lbs. total

1 cup olive oil

1 Tbsp. unflavored gelatin

1 cup fresh basil, coarsely chopped

Shallot Vinaigrette Ingredients:

2 Tbsps. red wine vinegar

1 Tbsp. balsamic vinegar

¹/₄ cup olive oil

1 medium shallot, minced

Salt and freshly ground black pepper to taste

FOR THE TERRINE: Line a tray with parchment or waxed paper. Make a slit down the side of each tomato from stem to tip. Cut around the interior of each tomato to remove the pulp, gently opening and flattening it into a long strip as you cut. Reserve the strips on the prepared tray.

Place the tomato pulp in a small heavy saucepan. Cut any remaining interior ribs off the tomato strips and add them to the saucepan. Add the onion, garlic and beet juice. Bring the mixture to a boil, lower the heat and simmer 20 minutes, or until reduced and thickened to a sauce-like consistency, stirring occasionally.

Purée the mixture in a blender, pulsing on and off and stopping to scrape down the sides of the container. Strain the purée through a fine sieve into a 4-cups measuring cup, pressing on the ingredients. Add enough tomato juice to measure 3 cups. Clean the saucepan and return the tomato purée to the pan. Season the purée with salt and pepper. (This can be prepared ahead, covered and set aside at cool room temperature.)

Season the eggplant with salt and pepper. Line 2 large trays with several layers of paper towels. Heat ¹/₂-inch of olive oil in a heavy, large non-stick skillet until bubbling gently. Cook the eggplant, several slices at a time, until completely cooked, but not colored, turning halfway, for about 5 minutes total. Transfer to the prepared trays using a large slotted spatula. Add additional oil as necessary. This can be prepared ahead and set aside to cool to room temperature.

To assemble the terrine, sprinkle the gelatin over the tomato purée and stir gently over medium heat until dissolved. Stir the basil into the mixture. Cut a 15-inch wide piece of parchment paper 9-inches long, to fit a 9 x 5-inch loaf pan (or the length of whatever mold is used). Fold the parchment in half, short sides together. Place the parchment on a work surface with the fold running vertically. Blot any excess oil from the eggplant and season with salt and pepper. Arrange 4 large eggplant slices horizontally on each side of the fold with small ends overlapping slightly in the middle at the fold. Add more eggplant slices as necessary, until the paper is completely covered. Holding the short ends, gently insert the paper into the mold, eggplant side up, with the vertical fold down the center of the mold and the ends of the eggplant and paper overhanging the mold.

Spoon a ¼-inch layer of tomato purée into the bottom of the mold. Season the fresh tomato strips with salt and pepper, trim and arrange them in a single layer, covering the purée. Press the strips down firmly into the mold and brush generously with purée. Alternate layers of eggplant, tomato purée, tomato strips and tomato purée, ending with eggplant layer, until the mold is almost filled. Press down firmly after each layer. Fold the overhanging eggplant slices over the mold. Fold paper over all. Place loaf pan on tray. Top with a slightly smaller loaf pan and fill with weights. Refrigerate until the tomato purée is set, about 6 hours or overnight.

To serve, remove from the refrigerator and unmold 1 hour before serving, pouring off any accumulated liquid. Blot the terrine with paper towels. Use a serrated knife to cut the terrine into ½-inch wide slices. Using a wide spatula, place on a larger platter or 2 slices on each plate.

FOR THE VINAIGRETTE: Mix the red wine and balsamic vinegar in a small bowl. Whisk in the olive oil in a slow thin stream. Stir in the shallot and season with salt and pepper. (This can be prepared ahead, covered and set aside at cool room temperature.) Spoon several Tbsps. of the sauce alongside individual servings, or pass separately in a sauce boat. ✳

Guenter Seeger

THE RITZ-CARLTON, BUCKHEAD • ATLANTA, GEORGIA

Guenter Seeger realized a passion for cooking as a young boy, growing up in his parents' wholesale produce business in Baden Baden, Germany, where he learned early the importance of fresh ingredients. The resulting commitment has propelled him through a successful career and ultimately to international renown as executive chef of The Dining Room at The Ritz-Carlton, Buckhead.

To meet his demand for freshness and quality, he developed a unique network of local farmers and inspired them to grow produce not available in the regular markets especially for his Dining Room kitchen.

Chef Seeger and The Dining Room have received numerous honors, including AAA Five-Diamond (for seven consecutive years) and Zagat's "America's Top Restaurant" and "Triple Crown" awards. Featured in *"Who's Who in America,"* Chef Seeger appears frequently on local and international radio and television and is a sought-after guest for celebrity events such as Julia Child's "Merci Julia!" and dinner for the James Beard Foundation, which honored him with the 1996 award for Best Chef in the Southeast.

We are pleased to present his recipes for Fresh Tomato Soup with Tomato and Basil Salad and Rouget Filets in Herb Crust with Blood Orange Confit, Frisée Salad and Tangerine Oil.

FRESH TOMATO SOUP WITH TOMATO AND BASIL SALAD

Serves 4

Preparation Time: 25 Minutes

4 ripe Roma tomatoes, cored, quartered	Half of lemon, juiced
Salt and pepper	20 fried basil leaves
Olive oil	Basil oil
2 lbs. large ripe tomatoes, cored, quartered	

Slice tomatoes into circles and lay them on a sheet pan. Season with salt and pepper, sprinkle with olive oil and leave them to marinate.

Pass other tomatoes through a juicer. Season with lemon, salt and pepper. Ladle into shallow bowls.

Place basil leaves on the tomato slices, layering 5 high. Place the tomato salad in the center of the soup. Drizzle basil oil on top and serve. ✳

ROUGET FILETS IN HERB CRUST WITH BLOOD ORANGE CONFIT, FRISÉE SALAD AND TANGERINE OIL

Serves 6

Preparation Time: 45 Minutes

Orange Confit Ingredients:

1 cup white wine	3 Tbsps. powdered
1 Tbsp. arrowroot	sugar
1 Tbsp. lemon grass	6 blood oranges,
2 vanilla beans, split	sectioned
in half	

Filets in Herb Crust Ingredients:

5 slices of brioche,	6 rouget filets, about
crusts trimmed	6 oz. each, scaled,
1 bunch Italian	deboned
parsley	Salt and pepper
	Olive oil

Salad Ingredients:

1 bunch frisée	Balsamic vinegar
Olive oil to taste	to taste
1 lemon, juiced	Salt and pepper
	to taste
	Tangerine oil
	to taste

FOR THE ORANGE CONFIT: In a small bowl, pour 3 Tbsps. of the white wine over the arrowroot and whisk together.

In a saucepan, combine the remainder of the wine with the lemon grass, vanilla beans and powdered sugar and bring to a boil. Let simmer for 10 minutes. Pour in the arrowroot-wine mixture and thicken to a light syrup consistency. Strain over orange segments, cover with plastic wrap and let cool.

FOR THE FILETS AND HERB CRUST: Pre-heat oven broiler on high and arrange oven rack to within about 8-inches of heating element.

Using a food processor, pulse the brioche and parsley together to make very fine, green bread crumbs.

Season the fish with salt and pepper, brush with olive oil and sprinkle bread crumbs over the top of the filets. Arrange them in one layer in a heavy skillet and heat under the broiler until golden brown.

FOR THE SALAD: Mix frisée with the olive oil, lemon juice, balsamic vinegar, salt and pepper.

Spoon the orange confit on plates, and place the filets on the sauce. Arrange the frisée salad around the fish, drizzle with tangerine oil and serve immediately. ✱

Craig Shelton

THE RYLAND INN • WHITEHOUSE, NEW JERSEY

Despite his young age, Craig Shelton has a resumé that reads like a Who's Who of the world of haute cuisine. He has trained with many of the finest chefs of Europe such as Joël Robuchon, Paul Haeberlin and Gaston Le Notre, to name a few. In addition, Shelton has held important positions in many of America's top restaurants, including Ma Maison (Los Angeles), La Côte Basque, Le Bernardin, The Rainbow Room, Le Chantilly and Bouley.

Since taking over control of The Ryland Inn, Shelton has received extraordinary reviews and was recently rated "One of the Top 10 Country Restaurants in America" by *Gourmet Magazine*.

A dual citizen of France and America, chef Shelton received his degrees in Molecular Biophysics and Biochemistry from Yale University. When not cooking, he can be found tending his several-acre vegetable and herb garden on the 50-acre property of The Ryland Inn. His talent is demonstrated by the dish he gives us here, Charlotte of Asparagus and Maine Crabmeat with Leek Vinaigrette.

CHARLOTTE OF ASPARAGUS AND MAINE CRABMEAT WITH LEEK VINAIGRETTE

Serves 4

Asparagus Charlotte Ingredients:

Pencil-thin asparagus tips, cut to length of mold	½ lb. potatoes
	White truffle vinegar to taste
¼ tsp. sea salt and white pepper to taste	½ cup vegetable stock
	1 cup tomatoes, chopped
1½ Tbsps. extra-virgin olive oil	½ Lemon, juiced

Crab Ingredients:

1 lb. crab meat	3 lemons, juiced
2 Tbsps. tarragon chiffonade	

Leek Vinaigrette Ingredients:

1 bunch leeks, white part only, split lengthwise and cut into ⅛-inch rings	¼ cup extra-virgin olive oil
	White truffle vinegar to taste
¼ cup cold water	Fresh dill, chervil and tarragon
Salt and white pepper to taste	

FOR THE ASPARAGUS CHARLOTTE: Cook the asparagus tips in boiling salted water, uncovered, until only slight resistance is felt in the bite. Shock in ice water. Slice each asparagus tip lengthwise in half. Season with salt, white pepper and 1 Tbsp. of olive oil.

Boil the potatoes in salted water until fork tender. Peel and cut potatoes into ¼-inch dice. Season with white and black pepper, salt, white truffle vinegar and vegetable stock.

Season the chopped tomatoes with salt, white pepper, lemon juice and remaining ½ Tbsp. of olive oil. Set aside.

FOR THE CRAB: Remove any bones from crab meat. Combine all ingredients. Adjust seasoning as necessary. Reserve.

FOR THE VINAIGRETTE: Cook leeks in boiling salted water until tender. Shock in ice water. Process leeks in blender with enough cold water to ensure movement of purée. Season with salt and white pepper. At high speed, add enough olive oil and vinegar to create the beginning of an emulsion. Look for a change of tint to lighter green. Pass purée through chinois.

To assemble, place a small square of parchment paper on 4 small plates. Place the seasoned asparagus tips, flat side outward, along the inside of the 4 molds. Place 1 tsp. of potato in each mold.

Fill each mold to ¼-inch from top with the crab meat mixture. Place 1 Tbsp. of tomato concassé mixture on top, and level off so the surface is flat. ✳

Dawn Sieber

CHEECA LODGE • ISLAMORADA, FLORIDA

EXECUTIVE CHEF
DAWN SIEBER

Touted by *Esquire* magazine as "one of the chefs to watch in 1996," Chef Dawn Sieber has created menus that blend traditional Florida Keys recipes with her own style of "new American" cuisine. She is also setting the trend in environmental responsibility in her kitchens by encouraging recycling, removing endangered seafood species like conch from her menus, and featuring more farm-raised seafood.

Sieber's culinary creations have received accolades from such noted publications as *Esquire, Travel & Leisure, Food and Wine, Food Arts* and the *American Culinary Review.* Sieber participates in the prestigious Masters of Food and Wine presentations at Highlands Inn each year. She has appeared on the nationally televised "CBS This Morning Show," as well as Julia Child's 80th Birthday Celebration on PBS and "Great Chefs, Great Cities." Godiva Chocolatier hand-picked Sieber to prepare a luncheon for the nation's top food writers when the firm introduced its 1996 holiday line of products.

We are fortunate to feature her recipes for Onion Bass with Hearts of Palm and Boniato, Tower of the Islands White Chocolate Spice Ice Cream with Guava and Passion Fruit Ripple Sorbet on Ginger Tuiles.

ONION BASS WITH HEARTS OF PALM AND BONIATO

Serves 4

Preparation Time: 45 Minutes
Pre-heat oven to 350°

Bass Filet Ingredients:

2 lbs. boniato (yellow Cuban sweet potato)	1 yellow onion, thinly sliced
1 head garlic, roasted	1 cup flour
¼ lb. butter, softened	1 leek, white part only, julienne
½ cup sour cream	¼ cup clarified butter
Salt and pepper to taste	4 striped bass filets, about 8 oz. each
2 cups vegetable oil	

Garnish and Sauce Ingredients:

3 fresh hearts of palm	Salt and pepper to taste
⅓ cup + 2 Tbsps. clarified butter	½ bunch green onions, chopped
4 Tbsps. butter	½ bunch chives, chopped
3 key limes, juiced	
1 cup vegetable stock	

FOR THE BASS FILETS: Peel and cook the sweet potatoes in salted water until tender. Remove and dry. Combine the sweet potatoes with the roasted garlic, softened butter, and sour cream and mash until smooth. Season to taste with salt and pepper.

Heat the oil in a heavy saucepan. Dredge sliced onion in flour seasoned with salt and pepper. Deep fry until crisp and golden brown. Remove from oil, drain and chop finely.

Deep fry the julienne leek, drain and reserve.

In a large, heavy sauté pan, heat clarified butter. Season fish with salt and pepper. Coat the filets on the fleshy presentation side with the fried chopped onion and sauté in the clarified butter for about 2 minutes. Turn the fish over and finish cooking in the oven to desired doneness, about 5 minutes.

FOR THE GARNISH AND SAUCE: While the fish is cooking, slice the hearts of palm on the bias and sauté in 2 Tbsps. clarified butter until golden brown. Remove and reserve.

Using the same pan, melt 4 Tbsps. butter over low heat, browning it slowly. Deglaze with lime juice and vegetable stock, and let reduce by half. Finish with the remaining clarified butter and season with salt and pepper.

Divide the mashed sweet potato mixture evenly among 4 plates, placing fish in the center. Garnish with hearts of palm, green onions, chives and fried leeks. ✳

WINE PAIRING: The use of the vegetable stock, along with the prevalence of the onions suggests the selection of a young Sauvignon Blanc or an aged Chardonnay. Ojai Vineyards makes a Sauvignon Blanc Semillon blend that would be very nice here. Their Chardonnays age nicely as well.

TOWER OF THE ISLANDS
WHITE CHOCOLATE SPICE ICE CREAM WITH GUAVA AND PASSION FRUIT RIPPLE SORBET ON GINGER TUILES

Serves 8

Preparation Time: 1½ Hours (note refrigeration time)

Ice Cream Ingredients:

12 egg yolks	1 cup white chocolate,
1 cup sugar	chopped
2 vanilla beans	¼ tsp. allspice
2 cups half and half	1 qt. heavy cream

Sorbet Ingredients:

1 qt. water	5 guavas, ripened,
2 cinnamon sticks	unpeeled, large dice
2 oranges	or ¾ cup guava purée
1 cup sugar	8 passion fruits or ¾
	cup passion fruit purée

Ginger Tuiles Ingredients:
Pre-heat oven to 350°

¼ lb. fresh ginger,	⅓ cup powdered sugar
grated fine	½ cup cake flour, sifted
2 egg whites	¼ cup melted butter,
	slightly cooled

Vanilla Sauce and Garnish Ingredients:

1 vanilla bean, split	2 oranges
¾ cup light corn syrup	1 ripe mango
1¼ cups simple syrup	8 strawberries,
	de-stemmed, julienne

Caramelized Plantain Ingredients:

1 cup vegetable or	1 Tbsp. brown sugar
peanut oil	1 tsp. lemon juice
1 plantain, peeled,	1 Tbsp. rum
diced into ¼-inch	1 Tbsp. butter
cubes	

FOR THE ICE CREAM: Whisk the egg yolks and sugar over simmering water until the sugar is dissolved and warm to the touch. Scald the vanilla beans in half and half. Add white chocolate and allspice to half and half, and mix with hand mixer until chocolate is melted. Slowly pour the white chocolate mixture into the egg yolks, stirring constantly. Add the heavy cream and churn until frozen.

FOR THE SORBET: Prepare a simple syrup by combining the water, cinnamon sticks, oranges and sugar in a saucepan. Bring the mixture to a boil. Strain when cooled.

If using whole guava fruit, steep the pieces in half of the warm simple syrup to soften and then purée. Pass through a fine mesh strainer. Transfer to an ice cream maker and process. If using guava purée, mix with half of the simple syrup and process in an ice cream maker.

If using whole passion fruits, cut each in half and scoop out pulp and seeds. Steep in other half of the warm simple syrup to soften and then purée. Transfer to an ice cream maker and process. If using passion fruit purée, mix with half of the simple syrup and process in an ice cream maker until frozen.

Chill a medium-size stainless steel bowl in freezer. When both sorbets are frozen, transfer to the chilled bowl and swirl together, taking care not to overmix.

FOR THE GINGER TUILES: Squeeze the ginger through cheesecloth to yield 1 Tbsp. ginger juice. Set aside.

Whip the egg whites with powdered sugar until frothy. Add the flour and ginger juice, mixing until smooth. Fold in the butter.

Line a baking sheet with parchment paper. Using a circular template, 1/16-inch thick and 1 1/2-inches in diameter, spoon 1 Tbsp. batter into a circle. Using a flat metal spatula, spread thinly to create a flat circle of batter. Repeat with the rest of the batter.

Bake at 350° until golden around the edges. Let cool and store in a dry place.

FOR THE VANILLA SAUCE AND GARNISH: Prepare the vanilla sauce by scraping the vanilla seeds into the corn syrup and 1/4 cup simple syrup, blending well.

Prepare the orange compote by removing the orange peel, using a serrated knife. Cut off each end. Stand oranges on end and then slice off the peel and white membrane in strips, slicing end to end and following the curve of the orange. Making a "V" cut between the membranes of each segment, remove the fleshy portion. Remove any seeds. Set aside.

Bring 1/2 cup simple syrup to a boil, add the orange segments and cook. Remove from heat and cool. Set aside.

For the mango purée, peel the mango and cut away from seed. Purée in a blender until smooth. If mixture is too thick, add a little simple syrup to thin. Pass through a fine mesh strainer. Set aside.

FOR THE CARAMELIZED PLANTAINS: In a heavy saucepan, heat the oil and deep fry the plantain. Drain on paper towels.

Melt the brown sugar in a saucepan with the lemon juice. Add the rum and plantain. Add the butter until melted. Set aside.

To assemble, place one ginger tuile in center of plate and top with a small scooped ball of ripple sorbet. Place another ginger tuile on top and press slightly to secure.

Scoop a small ball of white chocolate spice ice cream on top of second tuile and top with a third tuile.

Garnish the top of the tower with a spoonful of the caramelized plantains. Spoon orange compote onto the plate and garnish with julienne strawberries, drizzling vanilla sauce and mango purée over it. ✳

Nancy Silverton

CAMPANILE RESTAURANT • LA BREA BAKERY • LOS ANGELES, CALIFORNIA

Nancy Silverton, pastry chef and owner of Campanile restaurant and baker and owner of La Brea Bakery, began working as a vegetarian cook in her dormitory kitchen at age 18. After apprenticing at a small Northern California restaurant, she attended the Cordon Bleu in London.

The turning point in her career occurred after completing a series of pastry courses at the École Le Notre in Plaiser, France. Soon after, Nancy was appointed head pastry chef at Wolfgang Puck's Spago restaurant, where she was responsible for developing the highly acclaimed desserts.

In 1985, she and her husband, Mark Peel, moved to Manhattan and spent six months revamping Maxwell's Plum. La Brea Bakery was opened in January 1989; Campanile was opened in June 1989.

Nancy has written three successful cookbooks: *Desserts,* and *Mark Peel and Nancy Silverton at Home; Two Chefs Cook for Family and Friends,* and *Nancy Silverton's La Brea Bakery Breads.* Nancy is in the process of writing another book with Mark, and it is likely that she will include the recipe she shares with us here for Rustic Bread.

RUSTIC BREAD

Yield: 2 loaves

Preparation Time: 1¼ Hours (note dough rising time)
Pre-heat the oven to 500° for 1 hour before baking

2⅔ cups 70° lukewarm water	1 Tbsp. sea salt
2 cups + 2 Tbsps. white starter	3 Tbsps. cold milk
½ cake or 1 tsp. packed fresh yeast	3 Tbsps. extra-virgin olive oil
2 lbs. 3 oz. (about 7⅔ cups) bleached white bread flour	Semolina flour for dusting

Place 2⅓ cups water, white starter, yeast and bread flour in the bowl of a mixer and stir with a rubber spatula or wooden spoon just to moisten. Fit the mixer with a dough hook and mix the dough on medium speed for 6 minutes. Turn the mixer off and allow the dough to rest for 20 minutes.

Add salt and mix on medium speed for 2 more minutes, scraping down the sides of the bowl with a rubber spatula as necessary.

Place milk, olive oil and remaining ⅓ cup water in a small bowl and stir together. With the mixer on low speed, very gradually add the liquids to the dough. Don't add the liquids too rapidly or they will slosh out of the bowl. Continue mixing on low until the ingredients are completely incorporated and then beat on high speed for 4 minutes.

Cover the bowl with plastic wrap and allow the dough to ferment at room temperature 2 to 2½ hours, or until it reaches the top of the bowl and doubles in volume. Sprinkle the work surface heavily with flour and pour the dough out to form a rough oval. Sprinkle the top of the dough with flour, cover it with a cloth and allow it to rest for 20 minutes.

Cut 2 pieces of parchment paper approximately 12 x 16-inches and place them side-by-side on the work surface. Sprinkle the papers heavily with semolina, then with bread flour. Uncover the dough and sprinkle the top with more bread flour.

In a single continuous motion, cut the dough with a dough cutter into 2 equal pieces, carefully pulling the dough apart with your free hand as you go. Without pausing, carefully scoop up 1 piece of the dough, using the dough cutter and your free hand to hold each end, and lay the dough on a piece of parchment paper, allowing the dough to stretch as it falls to form an oblong shape approximately 8 x 10-inches in area and 1½-inches thick. It's more important to get the proper thickness than the right width or length. Repeat the procedure with the second piece of dough.

Using your index fingers, dimple each piece of dough at random 2-inch intervals, being sure to press through all the way through to the parchment paper.

Lightly sprinkle the dough tops with bread flour and semolina. Cover each with a cloth and allow them to proof at room temperature for 2 hours. Test for readiness by lightly pressing two fingers into the dough. The dough should feel soft and alive, no longer sticky.

Open the oven door and heavily spritz the oven with water from a spray bottle and quickly close the door. Keeping the parchment paper under the dough, slide the baker's peel under 1 piece of dough. (The baker's peel is a flat, smooth, shovel-like tool used to slide pizzas and yeast breads onto a baking stone or baking sheet in an oven). Open the oven door, slide the dough and the parchment paper onto the baking tile and quickly close the door. Spritz and load the second piece of dough in the same manner as the first. Turn the temperature down to 450°. Spritz the oven with water 2 more times during the next 5 minutes. Refrain from opening the oven door for 15 minutes.

After 15 minutes, slide the peel between the bread and the parchment paper and remove the paper. Return the bread to the baking tiles and rotate if necessary to ensure even baking. Continue baking another 5 minutes. With the peel, flip the bread upside down to allow even browning. Bake another 5 to 8 minutes for a total of 30 to 33 minutes. Remove the loaves from the oven and place them on a cooling rack. When the bread is cooled, dust off excess flour. ✳

RUSTIC OLIVE AND HERB BREAD VARIATION

1 recipe Rustic Bread	20 tufts fresh rosemary
40 Atlanta whole green olives, pitted	

Mix, shape and proof dough as directed for Rustic Bread. Just before baking, press the olives into the dimples of each loaf. Intersperse with small tufts of rosemary inserted about ¼-inch into the dough. Bake as directed for Rustic Bread, but do not invert the bread during the last 5 minutes of baking — the olives would fall off the bread. ✳

TRADE SECRET: *In this recipe you will find all the elements that make sourdough baking worthwhile — crispness in the crust, tartness in the crumb, an open hole structure that mirrors the texture of the starter. It's the one bread I felt I had to perfect before I could open for business as a baker.*

Susan Spicer

BAYONA • NEW ORLEANS, LOUISIANA

Susan Spicer began her cooking career in 1979 as an apprentice in New Orleans. After four years as a chef, she formed a partnership with Regina Keever and, in the spring of 1990, opened Bayona in a beautiful, 200-year-old Creole cottage in the French Quarter. With solid support from local diners and critics, Bayona soon earned national attention and has been featured in numerous publications, including *Food & Wine, Gourmet, Food Arts, Bon Appetit, Travel & Leisure, Restaurant Business, Gault et Millau's Best of New Orleans* and many more.

Susan has been guest chef at the James Beard House, on Cunard's "Sea Goddess," at the Oriental Hotel in Bangkok, on local and national television and for countless charity events in New Orleans and around the country. In 1993, she was the recipient of the James Beard Award for Best Chef, Southeast Region, and in 1995 was chosen for the Mondavi Culinary Excellence Award. Most recently, Bayona was voted #1 Restaurant in New Orleans in a poll of 29,000 readers of *Gourmet* magazine.

We are pleased to feature two recipes that are our personal favorites: Garlic Soup and Vegetable Gratin with Polenta and Smoked Tomato Butter.

GARLIC SOUP

Serves 8

Preparation Time: 1¹/₄ Hours

2 lbs. onions, roughly chopped	¹/₂ loaf French bread, stale, in chunks
1 cup garlic, peeled and chopped	1 pt. half-and-half or cream, heated
2 Tbsps. olive oil	Salt and pepper
2 Tbsps. butter	to taste
2 qts. chicken stock	Toasted croutons
1 bouquet garni: stems of parsley, thyme and 1 bay leaf, tied with string	for garnish

In a saucepan, sauté the onions and garlic in oil and butter, stirring frequently, over low to medium heat until they turn a deep golden color, about 30 minutes. Add the chicken stock, bouquet garni and bread. Simmer 15 to 20 minutes.

Remove bouquet garni. Purée soup in a blender. Add the half-and-half or cream. Season with salt and pepper to taste. Garnish with toasted croutons. ✳

VEGETABLE GRATIN WITH POLENTA AND SMOKED TOMATO BUTTER

Serves 4

Preparation Time: 1 Hour
Pre-heat oven to 350°

Vegetable Gratin with Polenta Ingredients:

1 cup milk	2 cans artichoke hearts,
2 cups water	quartered, drained,
1 cup polenta or	sliced
stone-ground	2 zucchini, sliced
corn meal	lengthwise into
½ tsp. salt	⅛-inch ribbons
2 Tbsps. butter,	2 red peppers, roasted,
softened	peeled, seeded,
Fresh herbs (basil,	cut into strips
rosemary or sage),	2 garlic bulbs, roasted,
chopped	peeled
1 eggplant, peeled, cut	1 bunch fresh spinach,
into ½-inch dice	washed, stemmed
½ lb. mushrooms	½ cup grated Parmesan
	or Fontina cheese

Tomato Butter Ingredients:

2 medium tomatoes	¾ cup (1½ sticks)
2 Tbsps. onion or	unsalted butter,
scallions, finely	softened
chopped	Salt and pepper
1 cup white wine	to taste

FOR THE VEGETABLE GRATIN: In a medium heavy-bottomed pot, bring milk and water to a boil, then sprinkle in the polenta, whisking constantly. Keep whisking or stirring until mixture boils and thickens. Reduce heat and simmer for about 10 to 15 minutes, stirring occasionally. Add the salt, butter and herbs.

Pour into a 8-inch square baking pan brushed with olive oil or butter. Smooth into an even layer about ¼-inch to ½-inch thick. Let cool.

Separately, sauté the eggplant, mushrooms and artichoke hearts, and wilt the spinach, in olive oil.

Alternate layers of the peppers, garlic, eggplant, mushrooms, artichoke hearts, zucchini and spinach, pressing down firmly on each layer and ending with the red peppers.

Top with cheese and bake at 350° for about 30 minutes. Cut into squares and serve.

FOR THE TOMATO BUTTER: Smoke the tomatoes for 10 minutes in a home smoker.

Core and quarter the tomatoes. Purée in a blender. Place the purée in a saucepan with the onions and wine and bring to a boil. Reduce heat and simmer until liquid is reduced to 1 or 2 Tbsps.

Whisk in the butter, one Tbsp. at a time. The sauce should be thick and creamy. Strain, then season with salt and pepper. Serve warm but not hot. ✳

Joachim Splichal

PATINA RESTAURANT • PATINA CATERING • PATINETTE AT MOCA
PINOT BISTRO • CAFÉ PINOT • PINOT HOLLYWOOD • LOS ANGLES, CALIFORNIA
PINOT BLANC • ST. HELENA, CALIFORNIA
PINOT AT THE CHRONICLE • PASADENA, CALIFORNIA

The New York Times describes Splichal's style as "clearly rooted in classic French cuisine, yet he adds a California sensibility that both lightens it and provides visual whimsy. If Mr. Splichal's cooking has a trademark, it might be called the crackerjack factor - there is a little surprise every time."

California's bountiful resources and a receptive business community in Los Angeles have provided Splichal with the perfect environment in which to perfect his playful, yet perfectionist vision. His instincts have helped create a new standard of dining excellence in his adopted city. "I somehow felt that my restaurant concepts would find an appreciative audience here," he remarks, "and I'm gratified by the success I've been able to cultivate in this lively dining culture."

Patina's success enabled Splichal to open Pinot Bistro in Studio City, Patinette at MOCA and Cafe Pinot in downtown L.A., Pinot Hollywood in Hollywood, Pinot Blanc in St. Helena, Napa Valley, and Pinot at the Chronicle in Pasadena; each adopting characteristics unique to their neighborhoods while maintaining Splichal's high standards of cuisine and service. Patina Catering flourishes amid the constant demand for special events and private parties.

His recipe for Sardines "A Day in Nice" is a beautiful addition to this cookbook.

Joachim Splichal is a leading figure in America's evolving food and restaurant industry. Acknowledged as one of the country's premier restaurateurs and master chefs, Splichal, with his wife Christine, opened the famed Patina Restaurant in Los Angeles in 1989, and has since opened four additional restaurants and a catering division. In 1995 he was inducted into the James Beard Foundation Who's Who of Food & Beverage in America, was named "Best California Chef" by them in 1991, and has twice been nominated "Best Chef of the Year," in 1991 and 1994. He was recently named "Treasure of Los Angeles" by the Central City Association.

SARDINES "A DAY IN NICE"

Serves 4

Preparation Time: 45 Minutes

Vegetables Ingredients:

¼ cup extra-virgin olive oil

1 head of fennel, 12 oz., outer layer removed, cut into thin julienne strips, feathery tops reserved for garnish

4 very ripe plum tomatoes, peeled, seeded, diced

⅓ cup Niçoise olives, pitted, halved

1 Tbsp. basil chiffonade

1 medium shallot, finely chopped

½ tsp. coarsely cracked white pepper

Sardines Ingredients:

8 sun-dried tomatoes, softened for 20 minutes in hot water, squeezed dry and halved (if available, use Hollywood roof-dried tomatoes)

8 very fresh sardines, heads, tails and fins removed, carefully fileted to remove all the bones.

Assembly Ingredients:

The reserved fennel, julienne

4 ¼-inch thick slices country-style white bread, toasted until golden

The reserved tomato and olive mixture

The reserved fennel tops, torn into tiny sprigs, for garnish

Small handful of pale inner leaves from a heart of celery, for garnish (optional)

FOR THE VEGETABLES: In a medium sauté pan, heat half the oil over medium heat. Add the fennel and sauté for 5 to 6 minutes, stirring occasionally or until softened. Set aside, covered, until you are ready to assemble the dish.

In a medium mixing bowl, combine the tomatoes, olives, basil, shallot, the remaining 2 Tbsps. of oil and the pepper and toss to mix. Set aside.

FOR THE SARDINES: Lay the 16 sardine filets on the work surface, larger end facing away from you. Place a sun-dried tomato half close to the smaller (tail) end of the filet and roll the filets up tightly, then secure with a toothpick. Bring a saucepan of water to a simmer over medium heat and set a steamer inside it. Steam the sardine rolls, covered, for 4 to 5 minutes, or until just firm. Remove from the heat.

FOR THE ASSEMBLY: Reheat the fennel julienne gently until just heated through. On each of 4 heated appetizer plates, place a crouton and mound ¼ of the fennel over it. Remove the toothpicks from the sardine rolls and balance 4 rolls on top of the fennel on each plate. Spoon a little of the tomato and olive mixture around the fennel, and garnish each plate with 2 or 3 sprigs of fennel and a few celery leaves, if desired. ✳

Cal Stamenov

HIGHLANDS INN • CARMEL, CALIFORNIA

Since joining the staff of Highlands Inn in 1994, Cal has been winning kudos from some of the country's most discriminating culinary critics. After graduation from the California Culinary Academy, Cal began his career at New York's Four Seasons restaurant. Thereafter he acquired experience in the European tradition by working in the most demanding kitchens under some of the world's most prestigious chefs.

Cal describes his style as contemporary regional cuisine, preparing local ingredients with elegant cooking techniques to intensify flavors. "The variety and availability of ingredients in the Monterey Bay area were keys to my accepting this position. I believe that perfection should be found in the flavors of a dish and that the food should be handled minimally and presented naturally."

Stunning examples of Cal's cooking style include Roasted Rack of Lamb with Stuffed Tomatoes and Potato Risotto, Venison Wrapped in Pancetta with Turnips, Butternut Squash, Celery Root and Black Truffles and Fresh Monterey Sardine Filets on Basil Potatoes and Black Olives with Tomato-Rosemary Vinaigrette.

ROASTED RACK OF LAMB WITH STUFFED TOMATOES AND POTATO RISOTTO

Serves 4

Preparation Time: 1¼ Hours (note marinating time)

2 racks of lamb, trimmed of excess fat	1 cup cream
8 garlic cloves, chopped, 1 Tbsp. reserved	1 cup chicken stock
¼ cup rosemary, chopped, 1 Tbsp. reserved	3 oz. Parmesan cheese
1 sprig thyme, chopped	3 oz. goat cheese
½ cup olive oil	Salt and pepper to taste
6 small tomatoes	Additional sprigs of fresh thyme
2 large potatoes, chopped fine	Additional extra-virgin olive oil

Marinate the lamb overnight or longer with garlic, herbs and olive oil. Refrigerate.

Blanch the tomatoes in salted boiling water for 30 seconds. Place in ice water bath. Remove outer skin and cut off top ½-inch of each tomato. Reserve tops. Remove insides to form a cup.

Place potatoes in a small pan over low heat and cook with cream, reserved garlic and rosemary until thickened. Add the chicken stock, Parmesan cheese and goat cheese. Stir for 45 minutes or until potatoes are "al dente." Stuff into tomatoes. Replace top. Set aside. Preheat oven to 500°.

Remove lamb from the marinade and season with salt and pepper. Place on a hot grill. When it is well-seared, move the lamb to a cooler part of the grill and cook slowly for approximately 15 minutes at 350°. Place all thyme sprigs in fire while grilling, for flavor.

Heat the tomatoes in a 500° oven, drizzle with the olive oil and serve with the grilled lamb. ✳

VENISON WRAPPED IN PANCETTA WITH TURNIPS, BUTTERNUT SQUASH, CELERY ROOT AND BLACK TRUFFLES

Serves 4

Preparation Time: 1½ Hours
Pre-heat oven to 350°

2 Cervena Venison tenderloins	1 onion, chopped
⅓ lb. pancetta, frozen	1 leek, white part only, sliced
1 sweet potato	5 oz. black truffles, cut into ¼-inch cubes
1 yam	
1 Tbsp. butter, softened	1 bottle (750 ml.) Merlot or Petite Sirah
Olive oil for sautéing	
1 butternut squash, cut into ¼-inch cubes	1 cup brown chicken stock
	1 cup veal stock
1 turnip, cut into ¼-inch cubes	Salt and pepper to taste
1 celery root, cut into ¼-inch cubes	2 Tbsps. clarified butter
2 lbs. fava beans	1 Tbsp. sweet butter
½ carrot, chopped	Fresh chopped herbs

Trim all the silver skin from the tenderloins and reserve scraps for sauce. Place cleaned tenderloins side by side with large end against small end so you have an even thickness of about 2-inches in diameter.

Slice frozen pancetta with an electric slicer set at ^{1}/$_{32}$-inch approximately (thin as possible but keeps even shape). You'll probably need 20 to 25 slices. Lay each slice on a cutting board working away from you, forming a strip of pancetta 10-inches by 2-inches and so on. Eventually you will want a strip of pancetta 10-inches x 12-inches so that you can lay the two tenderloins at one end and roll the pancetta around the venison to overlap by 1-inch. Reserve the pancetta scraps for sauce.

Roll in plastic wrap to form tight cylinder and freeze 20 minutes. Slice crosswise, remove plastic and tie with string one time around. Cut portions 1^1/$_2$-inches thick and reserve until later.

In a 350° oven, bake sweet potato and orange yam until tender. (Sweet potato is firmer and more starchy; orange yam is sweeter, has better color but has a looser consistency.) Remove and purée with softened butter. Hold warm.

Sauté the squash, turnip and celery root individually, season well and reserve. Clean and blanch fava beans and reserve.

For the sauce, sauté the carrot, onion and leek with the pancetta scraps and cook until sweet.

Roast venison scraps to caramelize, then add to sauce vegetables. Add the bottle of wine and reduce until almost dry. Add the brown chicken stock and veal stock and reduce to sauce consistency. Adjust the seasonings and add half the chopped truffles. Set aside.

Season the venison medallions well with salt and pepper. Heat clarified butter in a large, heavy skillet and sear venison over high heat, so meat browns nicely. Cook to medium rare.

In another pan, heat remaining butter, then add the squash, turnip and celery root and remaining truffles. Adjust seasoning. Add the fresh herbs and glaze with a little of the sauce. Add the fava beans and heat through.

To serve, spoon vegetables onto a hot serving plate. Place the venison (don't forget to cut string!) on top, then pipe sweet potato purée on the side of the venison. Drizzle the sauce over the meat and garnish with thyme sprigs.✳

FRESH MONTEREY SARDINE FILETS ON BASIL POTATOES AND BLACK OLIVES WITH TOMATO-ROSEMARY VINAIGRETTE

Serves 6

Preparation Time: 45 Minutes

6 fresh sardines
Salt and pepper to taste
1 cup olive oil
1 medium onion, sliced thin
1 bunch thyme
2 potatoes
½ cup extra-virgin olive oil
2 bunches basil
2 shallots, finely chopped
1 Tbsp. sherry wine vinegar

1 bunch chives, finely chopped
10 oil-cured black olives, finely chopped
10 sprigs rosemary, finely chopped
2 medium tomatoes, finely diced
Additional sherry wine vinegar and olive oil to taste
Rosemary sprigs for garnish

Filet the sardines using a sharp knife by cutting off head and running knife down both sides of backbone (or have fish market filet and clean). You should have 12 filets of semi-boneless fish (most remaining bones are very small and you cannot tell they are there). Place on a sheet pan, skin side down and season lightly with salt and pepper.

Pour ⅛ cup of the olive oil into a sauté pan, and place the sardine filets in it side by side, skin side up, and cook over medium heat until just cooked through, approximately 2 minutes. Carefully remove from pan with a spatula and place cooked filets back on clean sheet pan, skin side up. Cool in refrigerator.

Layer onion and thyme sprigs in a glass casserole dish large enough to fit the sardines in one layer. Place the cooked sardine filets on top of onion and thyme mixture and cover with olive oil to preserve. (Keeps up to one week in refrigerator.)

Peel and quarter potatoes and cook in salted water until tender. Drain well and purée with ¼ cup of the remaining olive oil. Use the rest of the olive oil to purée the basil.

When the potatoes are cool, fold in the puréed basil, 1 Tbsp. of the chopped shallots and 1 Tbsp. vinegar. (This resembles a potato salad with basil.)

Serve on individual plates. Pipe out basil potatoes the length of sardine filets and lay the filets on top of basil potatoes, 2 per plate. Sprinkle with chives, black olives, rosemary, and diced tomatoes and finish with a drizzle of sherry wine vinegar and olive oil. Garnish with rosemary sprigs. ✳

WINE PAIRING: Didier Dagueneau is one of the finest producers of Pouilly Fumé, a perfect match for this dish. While it is crisp and fresh on the palate, its grassy, smoky, aromatic qualities complement the multitude of flavors found here. ✳ Other choices might be Sauvignon Blancs from Spottswoode Vineyard, Napa Valley; Rochioli Vineyard Russian River Estate; and Gainey Vineyards Limited Selection, Santa Ynez Valley.

Alessandro Stratta

THE PHOENICIAN • SCOTTSDALE, ARIZONA

Alessandro Stratta joined The Phoenician as chef de cuisine of Mary Elaine's in November, 1989. During his tenure at the resort, he has also been the driving force behind the Italian cuisine at The Terrace Dining Room.

Stratta's northern Italian family has been in the hotel and restaurant business for four generations. As a child, while his father was president of Princess Hotels International, Stratta lived in the world's finest hotels in Italy, France, Singapore, Pakistan and the United States. That worldwide experience has provided Stratta with an impressive culinary and cultural background. We are delighted to share his recipe for Braised Leeks with Black Truffles and Balsamic Vinaigrette.

BRAISED LEEKS WITH BLACK TRUFFLES AND BALSAMIC VINAIGRETTE

Serves 4

Preparation Time: 1 Hour

4 large leeks, white part only, quartered	2 tsps. extra-virgin olive oil
2 cups chicken bouillon	Salt and pepper to taste
Fresh whole chives	1 tsp. fresh chives, chopped
2 Tbsps. black truffles, julienne	Shaved black truffles
1 Tbsp. black truffle juice	Fresh chervil sprigs
1 tsp. balsamic vinegar	

In a covered saucepan, braise the leeks in the chicken bouillon over medium heat until tender, approximately 30 to 45 minutes. Remove the leeks and reduce the bouillon by ¾.

Lightly steam a few of the chives and tie around the leeks. Reserve at room temperature.

Add the black truffles, the truffle juice, balsamic vinegar and the olive oil to the bouillon. Warm the leeks in the vinaigrette and season with salt and pepper. Finish with chopped chives and shaved black truffles and garnish with chervil. Serve warm. ✳

Jeremiah Tower

STARS RESTAURANT • SAN FRANCISCO, CALIFORNIA

Jeremiah Tower is internationally recognized as one of America's most influential chefs and restaurateurs. Tower has been greatly responsible for revolutionizing American cuisine — the way people think about dining out and cooking at home — since his start in 1972. His time-honored, traditional recipes are prepared with innovative techniques and the freshest ingredients possible. Tower is currently at work on his second book, a 25-year retrospective of his career and influence on the restaurant industry and a look at the future of cooking in America.

Born in the United States and educated in England, Tower obtained a Bachelor of Arts degree from Harvard University and a Master of Architecture degree from the Harvard Graduate School of Design.

Recognized by countless organizations, societies and industry publications for excellence, Tower was named 1996 Farberware Millennium Outstanding Chef of the Year by The James Beard Awards Foundation in New York. His accolades also include Chef of the Year and Regional Best Chef, California, both awarded by the James Beard Awards Foundation and USA Chef of the Year, to name a few.

We are delighted to include his imaginative recipes for Grilled Duck Leg with Endive Salad and Pecan Puff Pastry with Chocolate Sauce and Sabayon.

GRILLED DUCK LEG WITH ENDIVE SALAD

Serves 4

Preparation Time: 45 Minutes
Pre-heat oven to 325°

4 duck legs
2 duck livers
  Salt and freshly
  ground pepper
2 Tbsps. butter
2 Tbsps. Madeira or
  dry sherry
16 small slices bread
  for croutons
3 Tbsps. tomato
  concassé

1 Tbsp. chopped
  fresh parsley
2 Tbsps. fresh
  lemon juice
¼ cup hazelnut or
  walnut oil
1 large curly endive,
  picked, washed,
  spun-dried
½ cup hazelnuts,
  toasted, skinned
4 Tbsps. duck
  cracklings

Turn the legs skin side down. Cut along each thigh bone and remove it.

Remove the sinews from the duck livers. Season and then sauté over high heat in the butter for 3 minutes. Pour in the Madeira or sherry and cook another minute. Purée the liver and juices in a food processor or press through a food mill until smooth; then set aside.

Bake the bread for 10 minutes and then let cool.

Heat the grill or broiler. Season the duck legs and grill or broil for 5 minutes on the flesh side and 8 minutes on the skin side.

Spread the liver purée on the croutons, put ½ tsp. of the tomato concassé on each crouton, and sprinkle with chopped parsley.

Dissolve salt and pepper in the lemon juice and whisk in the oil. Toss the endive and hazelnuts in the dressing. Place the salad on warm plates, a duck leg on top of each salad, the liver croutons around the salads, and the cracklings on top of the endive. ✳

TRADE SECRET: *Use whatever bitter greens you have on hand, mixing them, if you like. The richness of the duck is best balanced with the clean, biting taste of curly endive, Belgian endive, radicchio, escarole, watercress, rocket (arugula), and the like. The combination of nut oils like hazelnut or walnut with the various forms of endive is very special and works well with duck.*

PECAN PUFF PASTRY WITH CHOCOLATE SAUCE AND SABAYON

Serves 4

Preparation Time: 45 Minutes (note refrigeration time)
Pre-heat oven to 350°

Sabayon Mousseline Sauce Ingredients:
Yields 2 to 3 cups

6 egg yolks	1 cup champagne
½ cup sugar	or white wine
Pinch salt	1 cup heavy cream

Pecan Puff Pastry and Chocolate Sauce Ingredients:

4 rectangles	¾ cup water
puff pastry,	½ cup sugar
4 x 2¼-inches	3 Tbsps. butter
1 cup pecan pieces	1 Tbsp. whipping
½ cup light sugar	cream
syrup	1½ cups sabayon
Salt to taste	mousseline sauce
5 Tbsps. Dutch-	
process cocoa	

FOR THE SABAYON MOUSSELINE SAUCE:

Prepare an ice bath and keep it by the stove. Boil a pot of water that is large enough to hold the mixing bowl so that it sits half way down in the pot.

Combine the yolks, sugar, and salt in a stainless steel mixing bowl. Mix well and add the champagne or wine. Over barely simmering water, whisk the mixture vigorously until it is thick and pale yellow, about 10 minutes. Put the mixing bowl immediately into the ice bath and whisk vigorously again until the sabayon is cold. Keep chilled. When you want to use the sauce, whip the cream and fold it into the sabayon.

FOR THE PASTRY AND CHOCOLATE SAUCE:

Place the cold puff pastry pieces on a wet baking sheet and bake for 20 minutes. Let cool. Slice the pieces horizontally in half. Scoop any uncooked pastry from the centers. Put the pieces on a tray and reserve.

Toast the pecans on a tray in the oven for 10 minutes. Let cool. Then put them in a food processor and grind them. Add the syrup and salt and purée until smooth.

To make the chocolate sauce, mix 4 Tbsps. cocoa with just enough of the water to make a smooth paste. Bring the sugar and remaining water to a boil and stir into the cocoa. Whisk until smooth and return to the saucepan. Simmer for 15 minutes, stirring constantly. Let cool a bit. When the mixture is still warm, stir in the butter and then the cream. Keep warm.

Warm the pecan purée in a double boiler.

Spoon the chocolate sauce on warm plates. Put the bottom pieces of the pastry in the center and spoon the pecan purée onto the pastry. Put the tops on, spoon some sabayon over, and sprinkle with the remaining cocoa. ✳

 TRADE SECRET: *I invented this dish for a 1982 dinner at San Francisco's Clift Hotel. It was such a success that I used it again at the now legendary inaugural dinner, at the Stanford Court, of the American Institute of Wine and Food, the dinner being prepared by chefs from all over the United States. It is a superb combination of flavors and is very easy once you master puff pastry, a discipline that I have always thought was best left to other people.*

Norman Van Aken

NORMAN'S • CORAL GABLES, MIAMI

From his pioneering work in Key West in the early 1980s, Chef Van Aken is acknowledged as the originator of South Florida's vibrant "New World Cuisine." His culinary philosophy is "to create a marriage of the raw and rustic with the classic and intellectual in a celebration of the various places we live."

Although Van Aken is self-taught, he holds an honorary doctorate from Johnson and Wales University. He has cooked, consulted and lectured on "New World Cuisine" internationally. His restaurant and cuisine have been applauded by The James Beard Foundation, *Bon Appetit* magazine and *Condé Nast,* to name a few.

We are fortunate to feature several of his unique recipes: Rhum and Pepper Painted Fish with Habañero-Mango Mojo, Key Lime Natilla en Tortilla, Caramelized Plantain Mash en Relleno, and Cuban Bread Brûlée with Añejo Espresso Caramel.

RHUM AND PEPPER PAINTED FISH WITH HABAÑERO-MANGO MOJO

Serves 4

Preparation Time: 45 Minutes
© Norman Van Aken's New World Cuisine

Paint Ingredients:

2½ Tbsps. whole black peppercorns	¾ cup light rhum
12 whole cloves	2½ Tbsps. grated lemon zest
½ cup sugar	2 Tbsps. lemon juice
¾ cup soy sauce	

Mojo Ingredients:

1 ripe, juicy mango, peeled and cut away from the stone	½ fresh habañero, scotch bonnet or other hot chile, seeds removed, minced
¼ cup Chardonnay	
½ orange, juiced, about 2 Tbsps.	

Fish Ingredients:

4 black grouper skinless filets or other fresh fish, 7 to 8 oz. each	1 Tbsp. canola or peanut oil
	Lime wedges, garnish

FOR THE PAINT: Toast the black peppercorns and the cloves together in a dry skillet over moderately high heat until you see puffs of smoke, about 1 minute. Grind them together in an electric spice grinder. Transfer them to a heavy saucepan. Add the remaining ingredients and heat over medium heat. The mixture will begin to foam as it reduces. When it has reduced by approximately half, about 25 to 35 minutes, strain it through a fine-meshed strainer into a bowl. Reserve until needed. This may be made up to 1 month ahead and kept refrigerated until needed.

If the "paint" seems a little too thin to you, return it to a saucepan and reduce it a bit more on low heat. Don't worry that you've already strained it. The flavor will be fine.

FOR THE MOJO: Blend the mango, Chardonnay and orange juice in a blender. Add the minced chile and reserve.

FOR THE FISH: Just before serving, preheat an oven to 450°; paint the fish liberally on one side only. Warm the mojo in a small saucepan until just barely hot.

Heat a large skillet until almost smoking hot. Add the canola oil and carefully add the fish, paint side down. Shake the pan to avoid sticking. When the fish is quite dark on the painted side flip it over, de-grease the pan if necessary and place the pan into the preheated oven.

Bake the fish 7 to 9 minutes.

Ladle about ½ cup mango sauce onto each serving plate. Remove the fish from the pan and place it on top of the sauce. Serve with a wedge of lime. ✳

KEY LIME NATILLA EN TORTILLA

Serves 4

Preparation Time: 1¼ Hours (note refrigeration time)
Pre-heat oven to 350°
© Norman Van Aken's New World Cuisine

Natilla Ingredients:

2 eggs	½ cup (1 stick) butter,
2 egg yolks	cut into small
⅔ cup + 1 Tbsp. sugar	squares, softened
½ cup key lime juice	1 cup heavy cream or
	less if you prefer it
	more tart

Tortilla Ingredients:

4 sheets phyllo	6 Tbsps. granulated
¼ cup melted butter	sugar
	Cayenne pepper
	to taste

FOR THE NATILLA: Combine whole eggs, yolks, sugar and juice in large mixing bowl. Whisk vigorously and constantly over double boiler until the mixture is thick and pale in color. Remove from the heat and whisk in the softened butter. Scrape down sides of bowl and cover with plastic wrap.

Whip cream until stiff. Whisk approximately ¼ of the cream into the key lime mixture to lighten it. Carefully fold in the remaining cream with a rubber spatula. Cover and refrigerate from 2 hours to overnight.

FOR THE TORTILLAS: Brush 1 sheet phyllo liberally with melted butter. Sprinkle on a thin even layer of sugar. Repeat with each sheet, stacking as you go and sprinkling cayenne on the second sheet. This may be done to taste. Refrigerate the stacked phyllo to chill butter and ease handling.

Remove from refrigerator and cut into 5-inch diameter circles. Cut each of these in half. Place on a parchment-lined sheet pan. Top with another sheet of parchment and place a sheet pan on top of that.

Bake at 350° until sugar caramelizes, about 15 to 20 minutes. Let cool. May be kept in airtight container up to 2 days.

Tropical Fruit Salsa Ingredients:

½ cup sugar	1 papaya
½ cup water	½ pineapple
2 mangoes	

Cilantro Syrup Ingredients:

1 sprig of cilantro	½ cup water
½ cup sugar	

FOR THE FRUIT SALSA: Prepare a simple syrup by combining the sugar and water in a saucepan. Bring the mixture to a boil. Strain when cooled.

Purée 1 of the mangoes with enough simple syrup to obtain a smooth sauce-like consistency. The ratio is about 2 parts mango and 1 part simple syrup.

Dice the papaya, pineapple and remaining mango into very small pieces and stir them into the mango purée. Adjust with more fruit or purée until you achieve a salsa-like consistency. Refrigerate until ready to use.

FOR THE CILANTRO SYRUP: Blanch the cilantro in boiling water for about 20 seconds. Immediately plunge into ice water. This will intensify the flavor and color of the cilantro.

Prepare a simple syrup by combining the sugar and water in a saucepan. Bring the mixture to a boil. Strain when cooled.

Place the cilantro in an electric blender and purée with enough syrup to obtain a smooth consistency. Refrigerate.

To assemble, place half-moon of phyllo on plate. Spoon key lime mixture on and top with another half moon. Spoon salsa around the "tortilla" and streak with cilantro syrup. ✳

CARAMELIZED PLANTAIN MASH EN RELLENO

Serves 4

Preparation Time: 45 Minutes
Pre-heat oven to 350˚
© *Norman Van Aken's New World Cuisine*

Vegetable oil for deep frying the chiles

2 poblano chiles, stems left on

Peanut oil for frying the plaintains

2 very ripe (maduro) plantains, peeled, cut into ½-inch thick slices

2 Tbsps. butter

Salt and pepper to taste

Heat oil in a French fryer or a deep, heavy pot to 365˚ and then lower the chiles in. Ideally, there should be enough oil to submerge the chiles but you can get the job done in less oil if you turn the chiles on all sides from time to time. You can gently put something non-reactive on them to keep them submerged or turn them occasionally until evenly blistered all over if you are using a deep fryer.

Place them in a large bowl with absorbent toweling in the bottom and cover the bowl tightly with plastic wrap. Allow to steam about 5 minutes Now, (protecting your hands with rubber gloves!) remove the chiles. Using your fingers or a knife, delicately pull off the skins.

Take the fried, peeled chiles and split them in half lengthwise. Try to carefully split the stem so that each half has a neat half of a stem.

Heat a large skillet and add some peanut oil. When the oil is quite hot, carefully add the plantains and cook to a dark golden color. Turn them over and brown the other side. Remove the plantains to absorbent toweling for a moment. Scoop the cooked plantains into a bowl and mash like mashing potatoes. Add the butter, salt and pepper.

Pack the plantain mixture into each of the 6 chile cavities. Turn each chile over and re-shape it to its original curvy self. To serve, warm in a oven until they are hot in the center, approximately 10 minutes.

 TRADE SECRET: *Chiles have a thinner skin than bell peppers. Roasting bell peppers on a fiery grill is not too difficult because their "meaty" walls don't quickly break down like the very thin walls of the poblano chile do. So we shock them (and other chiles) out of their skins by using the preceding method. You can make the rellenos up to a day or 2 ahead, wrapping and chilling them, if desired. If they are refrigerated they will naturally take a little longer to warm through. Other cooked mashed tubers — for example, sweet potatoes or boniato — can be substituted. I also have been known to take some small bits of foie gras, sear them and stir them into the mix for a very interesting plantain mash.*

CUBAN BREAD BRÛLÉE WITH AÑEJO ESPRESSO CARAMEL

Serves 6

Preparation Time: 1¹/₂ Hours
(note soaking and refrigeration time)
Pre-heat oven to 350°

Cuban Bread Ingredients:

1 qt. heavy cream	10 egg yolks
1 vanilla bean, split, scraped	6 Tbsps. raisins, soaked in ¹/₄ cup light rum overnight
1 whole nutmeg, ground	2 cups Cuban bread (or plain baguette), cubed and allowed to become slightly stale
1 cinnamon stick, ground	
1 cup granulated sugar	

Añejo-Espresso Caramel Ingredients:

Yields ¹/₂ cup

2 Tbsps. water	¹/₄ cup freshly brewed espresso
¹/₂ cup sugar	4 Tbsps. granulated sugar
5 Tbsps. hot water	
¹/₂ tsp. lemon juice	
2 tsps. aged "Añejo" rum	

FOR THE CUBAN BREAD: Bring a couple quarts of water to boil in a kettle.

Combine the cream with the vanilla bean, nutmeg, cinnamon and ¹/₂ cup of the sugar. Place over medium heat and bring to just under a boil. Set aside and let steep for approximately 20 minutes.

Whisk together yolks and rest of sugar. Temper yolk mixture by slowly whisking in some of the hot cream. Add yolk mixture to the rest of the cream and whisk until smooth. Pass through a fine chinois.

Strain rum off raisins, reserving rum. Sprinkle raisins in the bottom of the six 8-ounce ramekins. Place 4 to 5 cubes of bread in each. Sprinkle reserved rum over the bread cubes. Now pour 1 cup of the custard over each and let sit 15 to 20 minutes.

Place ramekins into a pan big enough to hold them and pour boiling water around them, coming about halfway up the sides. Cover pan loosely with aluminum foil to protect tops. Bake until set, but still slightly jiggly, approximately 40 to 60 minutes. Remove from water bath and chill well.

FOR THE CARAMEL: Combine water and sugar in a heavy saucepan. Cook over medium high heat, stirring occasionally until it gets golden brown. Carefully whisk in the hot water. Be careful, this will splatter.

Add the lemon juice, rum and espresso and bring back to a boil. Remove from heat.

To serve the brûlée, sprinkle ramekin tops with about 1¹/₂ tsps. of sugar and place them under a very hot broiler until just beginning to smoke and caramelize. Remove and allow to harden for a minute. Serve with the añejo-espresso caramel in a side bowl. ✳

Brian Whitmer
CONSULTANT • SAN FRANCISCO, CALIFORNIA

Brian Whitmer entered a new phase of his dynamic culinary career as managing partner and chef in his newest restaurant, Montrio. Whitmer's exceptional talents elevated the regional cuisine of Highlands Inn's Pacific's Edge restaurant to the forefront of contemporary dining during his six-year tenure. In creating seasonal menus, Whitmer consistently garnered critical acclaim for his innovative and contemporary cooking style, influenced by classic European methods and the region's extensive harvest.

At Montrio, he continued his style of creative use of varied ingredients in extracting robust flavors. Whitmer has also broadened his scope by incorporating breakthrough products and new culinary influences. His culinary talents have been recognized nationally by such publications as *Bon Appetit, Gourmet, Chocolatier, Food & Wine* and *The Wine Spectator.*

He has been generous in giving us a sampling of recipes: Cannelloni of Lamb and Eggplant, Pacific Salmon with Pencil Asparagus and Morels, Curried Sea Scallops with Dungeness Crab Wontons and Tabbouleh of Maine Lobster with Cilantro Pesto.

CANNELLONI OF LAMB AND EGGPLANT

Serves 8

Preparation Time: 1½ Hours
Pre-heat oven to 400°

Jus Ingredients:

2½ lbs. lamb bones	2 qts. water
1 medium Spanish onion, skin on	1½ celery ribs, chopped
2 garlic bulbs, cut in half	1 medium carrot, chopped
1 Tbsp. tomato paste	1 bay leaf

Cannelloni Ingredients:

Pre-heat oven to 375°

3 medium eggplants	¾ lb. ground lean lamb shoulder
6 Tbsps. olive oil	
2 medium onions, peeled, sliced thin	2 oz. goat cheese, crumbled
2 garlic cloves, peeled, sliced thin	2 small pear tomatoes, diced
2 medium tomatoes	Thyme sprigs, garnish
3 sprigs fresh thyme	

FOR THE JUS: Combine the lamb bones and unpeeled Spanish onion and garlic bulbs. Add tomato paste and roast in a large roasting pan in a 400° oven for 15 minutes, or until dark brown, but not burnt.

Remove bones from pan and pour 2 qts. water into roasting pan to loosen flavorful food particles from bottom. Transfer into a saucepan and add the celery and carrot along with cracked bay leaf. Bring liquid to a boil. Skim foamy impurities from top of stock with a ladle and lower heat to a slow but steady boil. Reduce until approximately 2 cups remain.

FOR THE CANNELLONI: Cut one eggplant in half, lengthwise, and score both sides with a knife. Drizzle with 1 Tbsp. olive oil and place on a baking sheet. Bake for 20 minutes. The pulp should be soft and mushy. Using a large spoon, scoop the pulp out and transfer to a mixing bowl.

In a heavy saucepan with 3 Tbsps. of the olive oil, slowly cook the onions and garlic for 15 minutes over low heat. Stir frequently. Onions should caramelize, turning a brownish color.

Skin the 2 tomatoes by scoring their tops, removing the bottoms, coring with a paring knife and submerging in boiling water for 20 seconds.

Peel skin off, smash tomatoes in your hands and combine with the onion-garlic mixture. Add thyme sprigs and stew ingredients for 30 minutes over low heat. Mixture should be almost paste-like, with all the water from the tomatoes cooked out. Let mixture cool to room temperature and combine with eggplant.

In a skillet, cook ground lamb shoulder until just done, about 5 minutes. Cool and add to tomato-eggplant mixture.

Peel the skin off the two remaining eggplants on a slicing machine or with a very sharp knife; then slice lengthwise, 1/8-inch thick. Season with salt and pepper. Using a 10-inch skillet, sauté the slices in 2 Tbsps. olive oil, until both sides are golden, about 1 minute each side. Remove from the skillet and place on paper towels to absorb oil. You will need 16 slices.

To assemble cannellonis, lay a slice of eggplant out flat on a smooth surface. On the wide end, spread about 3 Tbsps. filling. Sprinkle with goat cheese. Roll cannelloni so mixture is securely wrapped by eggplant slice. Repeat.

Reduce oven heat to 350°. Reheat the cannellonis on a baking sheet, uncovered, for 15 minutes. Warm lamb *jus* and add diced pear tomatoes for garnish. Arrange two cannellonis in a V-shape on plate and drizzle lamb *jus* on and around the entree. Garnish with a sprig of fresh thyme. ✳

WINE PAIRING: This particular dish requires a full-bodied, earthy red wine from a ripe vintage with the richness of fruit to stand up to the sweet flavors of the caramelized onions: Brunello di Montalcino or Vino Nobile di Montelpuciano, both from Tuscany. A California Zinfandel, such as one from the A. Rafanelli Winery in the Dry Creek region of Sonoma, would also work nicely.

PACIFIC SALMON WITH PENCIL ASPARAGUS AND MORELS

Serves 8

Preparation Time: 30 Minutes
Pre-heat oven to 450°

24 pencil asparagus	Salt and pepper
10 oz. salmon filet	to taste
2 Tbsps. olive oil	3/4 cup vermouth
12 medium-size fresh	1/2 lb. butter
morels, cut in half	1 bunch chervil
1 medium shallot,	
minced	

Trim the woody ends of the asparagus. Peel as necessary. Cook by submerging in salted, boiling water for 3 minutes and then transferring to ice water.

Clean the salmon filet of any small bones. With a sharp knife, slice very thin 2 1/2-oz. portions of salmon and place each between two sheets of plastic wrap, yielding four portions. With a mallet, or the back of a knife, lightly pound salmon so it is transparently thin. Remove from plastic wrap and line the bottom of a 10-inch plate with thin sheets of fish.

Heat olive oil in a skillet until just smoking. Add the morels and sauté for 1 minute. Add the shallot, asparagus, salt and pepper and stir thoroughly.

In a small saucepan over low heat, reduce the vermouth to 2 Tbsps. Whisk in butter to form a butter sauce. Set aside.

Place salmon in oven for 3 minutes. Remove when fish is warm. Place some mushroom-asparagus mixture in a mound in the center of each plate, drizzle plate with butter sauce and sprinkle with sprigs of chervil. ✳

CURRIED SEA SCALLOPS WITH DUNGENESS CRAB WONTONS

Serves 6

Preparation Time: 2¹/₂ Hours

Carrot Purée Ingredients:

1 lb. young carrots
with tops, peeled,
chopped
4 Tbsps. cream

¹/₄ lb. butter, softened
Salt and white
pepper to taste

Vegetable Nage Ingredients:

3 qts. water
2 carrots, peeled,
cut in 1-inch pieces
1 leek, cut in 1-inch
pieces
¹/₂ onion, quartered
4 ribs celery, cut in
1-inch pieces

3 bay leaves, broken
1 Tbsp. black
peppercorns
1 cup tomatoes,
diced, canned
¹/₂ head romaine lettuce
1 Tbsp. salt
³/₄ cup butter

Wonton Ingredients:

2 ribs celery, cut in fine
julienne, blanched
2 medium carrots, cut
in fine julienne,
blanched
1 leek, cut in fine
julienne, blanched
1 bulb fennel, cut in
fine julienne,
blanched
3 Tbsps. butter

1 shallot, peeled,
minced
1 clove garlic, peeled,
minced
³/₄ tsp. curry powder
9 oz. Dungeness crab
meat, cleaned and
picked
Salt and freshly
ground white pepper
12 wonton wrappers
2 egg yolks, beaten

Cilantro Purée Ingredients:

3 bunches cilantro

2 Tbsps. olive oil

Assembly Ingredients:

12 large sea scallops
¹/₄ cup flour combined
with ¹/₄ cup curry
powder
Pinch of salt and
pepper
¹/₄ cup olive oil

Oil for deep frying
12 wontons
Carrot purée
Vegetable nage
3 Tbsps. cilantro
purée
1 Tbsp. lime juice

FOR THE CARROT PURÉE: Steam the carrots until cooked through. Blend in a food processor with cream and butter to form a smooth purée. Season with salt and pepper. Store in a covered bowl in a warm place.

FOR THE VEGETABLE NAGE: Place all ingredients, except the butter, in a stock pot and bring to a boil. Cook at low simmer for approximately 1½ hours. Strain out vegetables, pressing them to extract all the flavors. Liquid yield must be approximately 1½ to 5 cups. With hand mixer, incorporate butter while liquid is hot. Adjust seasoning as desired.

FOR THE WONTONS: Sauté the vegetable julienne in butter with shallot, garlic and curry powder over medium heat for 5 minutes or until vegetables are just limp. Remove from heat, transfer to a mixing bowl and fold in the crab meat. Season with salt and pepper.

Lay out wonton wrappers on a flat surface. Place in the middle of each wrapper a small mound of the crab mixture, and with a brush, moisten the outer rim with the egg wash. Fold each wrapper over in a half-moon shape and press edges firmly to seal. Reserve, covered with a kitchen towel.

FOR THE CILANTRO PURÉE: Clean cilantro leaves and remove stems. Purée in a blender with olive oil.

FOR THE ASSEMBLY: Lightly toss the sea scallops in the mixture of flour, curry powder and salt and pepper.

Sauté scallops in hot olive oil for 3 minutes on each side or until scallops are golden on the outside, yet still slightly underdone in the middle. Remove from skillet and transfer onto paper towels.

In a deep, heavy saucepans, deep fry the wontons until crispy. Transfer onto towels. Place a small mound of the carrot purée in the middle of each plate. Tuck 2 scallops slightly into the purée across from each other. In between the scallops tuck into the purée 2 wontons facing upright. Reheat nage and add cilantro purée and lime juice. Incorporate and adjust seasoning. Sauce plates liberally and serve. ✳

WINE PAIRING: The curry suggests the selection of a Gewürztraminer. One of the great producers of Alsace comes to mind — Domaine Ostertag. Their outstanding Gewürztraminer from Epfig is dry, often to austerity, spicy and refreshing. Another choice is a Domaine Zind-Humbrecht Tokay Pinot Gris from Clos Windsbuhl, a massive white wine with intense flavors that could be fun with this particular dish.

TABBOULEH OF MAINE LOBSTER WITH CILANTRO PESTO

Serves 8

Preparation Time: 1 Hour

Cilantro Pesto Ingredients:

½ cup olive oil	2 bunches cilantro, leaves only

Pesto Vinaigrette Ingredients:

6 Tbsps. virgin olive oil	3 Tbsps. lime juice
	1 Tbsp. cilantro pesto
	Salt and pepper

Lobster Ingredients:

1 Maine lobster, approximately 1¼ lb.	2 ribs celery, cut in ¼-inch dice
Pinch of salt	3 tangerines, peeled, sectioned, diced
4 Tbsps. butter	3 plum tomatoes, diced (reserving ⅓ for garnish)
½ medium onion, finely chopped	
1 Tbsp. garlic, peeled, chopped	¼ cup cilantro pesto
1½ cups couscous	Pesto vinaigrette
¼ cup chicken stock	Cilantro leaves, garnish

FOR THE CILANTRO PESTO: In a blender, pour in olive oil, cover, and start blade on slow speed. Carefully lift off the lid and slowly add the cilantro leaves until a smooth purée is formed. Transfer to a container and reserve.

FOR THE PESTO VINAIGRETTE: Whisk together the olive oil, lime juice and pesto. Season to taste and set aside.

FOR THE LOBSTER: Whisk together the olive oil, lime juice and pesto. Season to taste and set aside. In a medium-size stockpot, bring 2 qts. of water to a boil with a pinch of salt. Cook lobster for 6 minutes. Cool and remove all meat. Cut into coarse pieces, about ¾ inch thick. Set aside.

Melt 2 Tbsps. of the butter in small casserole. Add onion and garlic and cook over medium heat for approximately 5 minutes until translucent. Add couscous and chicken stock; stir for 3 minutes. Turn off heat and cover for 10 minutes.

Remove the couscous from the casserole by running it through your fingers, loosening any clumps.

In a small saucepan, heat the remaining butter and cook the celery slightly.

Combine the couscous with the celery, tangerines, tomatoes and cilantro pesto.

Firmly press couscous mix into the bottom halves of four 3-oz. timbale molds. Add ¼ of the chopped lobster to each mold, and pack more couscous over, filling to the top.

Shake each mold carefully and invert onto plate. Drizzle pesto vinaigrette around plate. Garnish with reserved diced tomato and cilantro leaves. Serve at room temperature. ✳

Roy Yamaguchi

ROY'S RESTAURANT • HONOLULU, HAWAII

The Hawaii connection goes back to Yamaguchi's grandfather, who owned a tavern in the '40s in Wailuku, Maui, and who was also a pioneer of sorts in the local supermarket industry. Roy attributes his earliest appreciation of food to his father, a career military man born and raised on Maui, and to his Okinawan-born mother. Brought up in a fluent bilingual environment in Tokyo, Roy recalls that he has always loved to cook, be it fried Portuguese sausage and eggs for breakfast or a full-on Thanksgiving dinner in home economics class. So even before graduating from high school in 1974, Roy knew what he had to do: he immediately traveled clear across the Pacific to the Culinary Institute of America in New York, where he received his training in classical traditions.

Recently, Yamaguchi described his approach to food as simply "a wonderful way to preserve personal creativity."

He illustrates his point well and deliciously with Seared Shrimp Salad with Feta Cheese and Candied Garlic, Seared Ahi with Island-Style Passion Fruit Shrimp Salsa, and Seared Ulua and Szechuan-Style Shrimp with Chinese Peas and Green Onions.

One of the earliest assessments of Roy Yamaguchi's first restaurant in the Hawaiian Islands — called, simply, Roy's Restaurant — was that "Yamaguchi may very well become a pivotal figure in the creation of a true contemporary Hawaii cuisine — that blend of East and West and Polynesia that's been long expected and slow arriving."

SEARED SHRIMP SALAD WITH FETA CHEESE AND CANDIED GARLIC

Serves 4

Preparation Time: 30 Minutes

Candied Garlic Ingredients:

⅓ cup garlic cloves, peeled	½ cup sugar
1 cup white wine	2 Tbsps. butter, unsalted

Salad Ingredients:

½ cup radicchio lettuce, torn	Salt and ground white pepper to taste
½ cup escarole lettuce, torn	2 Tbsps. peanut oil
¼ cup red leaf lettuce, torn	1 tsp. sherry vinegar
	2 Tbsps. olive oil
¼ cup Boston lettuce, torn	1 tsp. salt
16 shrimps, peeled and deveined	½ tsp. ground white pepper
	2 oz. feta cheese, crumbled
	16 Niçoise olives
	Candied garlic

FOR THE CANDIED GARLIC: Place all ingredients into a 5-inch saucepan and cook down slowly until liquid becomes syrupy.

The object is to cook the garlic completely without getting it mushy and allowing the liquid to turn syrupy. Reserve in a double boiler.

FOR THE SALAD: Wash the lettuces thoroughly and tear into bite-size pieces. Toss in a large salad bowl.

Salt and pepper the shrimps and coat them with peanut oil. Sear shrimp in a sauté pan until cooked through. Set aside.

In a small bowl, combine the sherry vinegar, olive oil, salt and white pepper. Toss with the lettuces, gently adding the crumbled feta.

Place the salad in four salad bowls. Top with four shrimps each, along with four Niçoise olives each and some candied garlic. ✳

SEARED AHI WITH ISLAND-STYLE PASSION FRUIT SHRIMP SALSA

Serves 4

Preparation Time: 30 Minutes

Salsa Ingredients:

1 passion fruit	1 Tbsp. cilantro,
¼ cup Maui onion,	minced fine
finely minced	¼ lb. shrimp, cooked,
1 tsp. Tabasco sauce	chopped
½ cup tomato, peeled,	2 Tbsps. green onion,
seeded and diced	minced fine
fine	Salt and pepper
	to taste

Ahi Ingredients:

4 pieces ahi,	2 Tbsps. peanut oil
4 oz. each	Salt and ground
	pepper to taste

FOR THE SALSA: Scoop out the pulp from the passion fruit and press through a fine sieve, reserving juice.

Combine the passion fruit juice with the minced onion, Tabasco, diced tomato, cilantro, shrimp and green onion. Season with salt and pepper.

FOR THE AHI: Coat the ahi steaks with peanut oil and season with salt and pepper. Sear to desired doneness.

Arrange the ahi steaks onto four plates. Spoon the passion fruit shrimp salsa over each steak before serving. ✳

SEARED ULUA AND SZECHUAN-STYLE SHRIMP WITH CHINESE PEAS AND GREEN ONIONS

Serves 4

Preparation Time: 45 Minutes

Shrimp Ingredients:

15 shrimp, 16/20 size, peeled, deveined and chopped

½ tsp. Chinese garlic chile paste

½ cup mushroom soy sauce

Sauce Ingredients:

½ cup white wine

1 Tbsp. white vinegar

1 shallot, minced

2 Tbsps. heavy cream

1½ cups unsalted butter (3 sticks), room temperature

2½ red bell peppers, diced

2½ green bell peppers, diced

2½ yellow bell peppers, diced

2¼ green onions, diced

1¼ onions, diced

1¾ cups Chinese peas

4 Ulua filets, 7 oz. each

1 oz. peanut oil

1 Tbsp. vegetable oil

1 tsp. sesame seed oil

Salt and ground white pepper to taste

FOR THE SHRIMP: Combine chopped shrimp with garlic chile paste and mushroom soy sauce. Set aside.

FOR THE SAUCE: Prepare the white butter sauce by simmering the wine, vinegar and shallot in a heavy, medium-sized saucepan over low heat. Reduce to about 1 tsp. of liquid. Add the cream and reduce by half. Add the butter slowly and whisk. Hold warm.

Mix together all the peppers and onions. Set aside.

In a medium-size saucepan, blanch the peas in boiling water for a few seconds and immediately shock in ice water. Drain and reserve.

Season the filets with salt and pepper. Heat the peanut oil in a heavy iron skillet and sear the fish to desired doneness.

In a large sauté pan, heat the vegetable oil and sesame oil to the smoking point. Quickly stir-fry Chinese peas and distribute among 4 heated plates. Quickly add the bell pepper-onion mixture and sauté for 30 seconds. Then add marinated shrimps. Stir over extremely high heat for about 15 seconds and remove from heat.

To serve, pour the white butter sauce around the Chinese peas, place some bell pepper-shrimp mixture over the peas, then top each plate with a filet. ✳

Babcock Vineyards

LOMPOC, CALIFORNIA

"I had no idea if I could make good wine," the young winemaker admits. Although Bryan Babcock had studied at the school of viticulture and enology at University of California at Davis, the responsibility of making premium wines using grapes from a new vineyard was an awesome task.

Now, looking over rows of oak barrels and gleaming metal fermentation tanks that line the inside of the winery, Bryan can step back and take a deep breath. In the winery's short history, he has consistently produced award-winning wines.

Probably the best known wines are the *Eleven Oaks* Sauvignon Blanc (named by *Bon Appétit* magazine as one of the Best Wines of the year, three years in a row) and the *Grand Cuvée* Chardonnay, which has been described as "the closest thing to truly fine white Burgundy yet to be made in California" (Norm Roby, *Wine Spectator*). As for Bryan himself, *Los Angeles Times* wine writer Dan Berger named Bryan one of the "Ten Best Winemakers of the Year" in 1989 and one year later designated him "Most Courageous Winemaker of the Year." In 1995, Bryan was chosen as one of the "Top Ten Small Production Winemakers in the World" at a James Beard Foundation event in New York City. He was the only American awarded this honor.

Babcock Vineyards is located in the Santa Ynez Valley Wine Appellation District in Santa Barbara County, nine miles west of Buellton. Here the mountains run east and west, creating a marvelous coastal climate that draws cool ocean air into the valleys. The cool ocean influence, coupled with good soils and gentle slopes, make for an ideal vineyard site.

"It was the scariest time of my life," Bryan Babcock says, remembering the 1984 harvest and the day he crushed the first five tons of grapes at his parent's fledgling winery — Babcock Vineyards.

Bernardus Winery

CARMEL VALLEY, CALIFORNIA

Combine the daring of a Le Mans race car driver, the creativity of an entrepreneur, the sophistication of a world traveler and the acumen of an international businessman and you get a pretty good idea of the spirit behind Carmel Valley's Bernardus Winery.

Owner Ben Pon could have chosen anywhere in the world to plant vines; he chose the Carmel Valley. Since the early 1970s, there has been a growing awareness of the potential for great Bordeaux varieties from this area. The soils and climates of the Carmel Valley are similar to the Bordeaux region in France. The centerpiece of the Bernardus story is formed by the Carmel Valley Bordeaux-style red, Monterey Chardonnay, Bordeaux-style white Sauvignon Blanc and a limited production of Bernardus Pinot Noir.

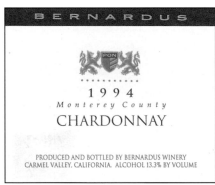

Bernardus Winery was constructed to create traditional wines aged in oak barrels specially crafted in the French regions of Bordeaux and Burgundy. Oak is purchased from six to seven coopers in France to allow for blending of different flavors. The diverse soils and climates have been complemented by differentiations in row directions, orientations, spacing and vertical trellising. Two fruiting wires and up to three sets of mobile wires are used to hold foliage upright.

Winemaker Don Blackburn's early impressions about wine came from his education and apprenticeship in France. In the vineyards and cellars of famous Bordeaux and Burgundy wine estates, he absorbed the practical laws of winemaking. At Bernardus, "the textural element — the mouth feel — is

the most important expression of the wine," says Don. "We want to make a wine that has a supple mouthful and bright flavors." For sampling wines, Bernardus has a visitor's facility in Carmel Valley Village, 800-223-2533.

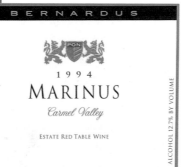

Bonny Doon Vineyard

Santa Cruz, California

Randall Grahm is the proprietor-winemaker of Bonny Doon Vineyard, which he started near Santa Cruz in 1983. Often called a renegade, a maverick and the best winemaker in the United States, Grahm has acquired the nickname as the swaggering Rhône Ranger.

The name refers to the grapes that have made Grahm's career. He began Bonny Doon hoping to produce a perfect Burgundian Pinot Noir. But when his vineyard proved unsuitable for producing good Pinot, Grahm looked to France's Rhône Valley for inspiration, bottling his first Syrah in 1983.

One of his biggest successes has been *Le Cigare Volant* (French for "flying saucer" — literally, "flying cigar" — which refers to an actual law that prohibits flying saucers from landing in vineyards in the southern Rhône). Randall has become ideologically committed to the prospects of popularizing Rhône varieties in California.

In 1989, Randall was initiated into Who's Who of Cooking in America by *Cook's Magazine* for "lifetime achievement and leadership in the improvement and development of American cuisine." He was also nominated for Wine and Spirits Professional of the Year by the James Beard Foundation in 1991 and 1993, and in 1994 he finally walked off with the award.

Poire
PEAR EAU DE VIE

Nectarine
NECTARINE EAU DE VIE

California Pink Wine
Alc. 20% by vol.

Ca' del Solo
Grappa

di Moscato

PRODUCED & BOTTLED BY CA' DEL SOLO
SANTA CRUZ, CA USA
375 ML   ALC. 42.91% BY VOL.

PRODOTTO DEGLI STATI UNITI
Ca' del Solo

Prunus

FRUIT BRANDY FROM
APRICOT, CHERRY AND PLUM
(APRICOT 67%, CHERRY 11.5%, PLUM 21.5%)

PRODUCED & BOTTLED BY CA' DEL SOLO
SANTA CRUZ, CA USA
375 ML   ALC. 40.95% BY VOL.

Ca' del Solo
Big House Red
1995 CALIFORNIA RED WINE

Caymus Vineyard

RUTHERFORD, CALIFORNIA

The Wagner family began farming Napa Valley in 1906, growing grapes in 1941 and making wines in Rutherford, California, in 1972. Chuck Wagner, winemaker/grower at Caymus Vineyards, practices winemaking techniques unique to the California wine industry. Having developed his own definitive style over the past decade, Wagner attributes much of his *Special Selections'* success to the small vineyard from which the fruit is harvested and the singular vinification techniques used in the making of the wine.

Harvested from vines planted in the mid-1960s, the *Caymus Vineyards Special Selection Cabernet Sauvignon* originates from the same 14-acre Rutherford appellation vineyard every year. Growing on low-yielding, gravelly loam, the vines produce fewer clusters than the average vine, thus producing more intensely flavored berries. One-hundred percent Cabernet Sauvignon, the Special Selection has become known for its consistency and distinct characteristics.

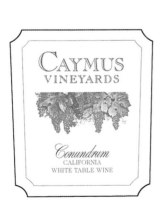

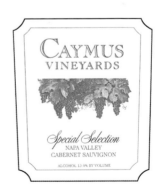

Chalone Vineyard

SOLEDAD, CALIFORNIA

The hills where the vines are planted and the winery now stands are situated in an extremely dry climate. The shallow soil is marbled with limestone with poor organic content, and the area receives as little as 7 inches of rainfall in a calendar year. Temperatures can vary up to 60° in one day, with summer months ranging from 40° at night to 100° at midday.

Chalone Vineyard is named for a tribe of Costanoan Indians who once inhabited the remote area of the Gavilan Mountains to the east of the Salinas Valley in Monterey County, California. Dick Graff fell in love with the beauty and isolation of the land in the 1960s, but his main reasons for choosing this site were the topsoil and the climate — the "terroir." The original vineyard was planted in 1919 by a Frenchman looking for a site that resembled the soil in his native country. There were additional plantings in 1946, and the first commercial wines were produced by Philip Togni in 1960.

The adverse farming conditions produce fruit characterized by intense, concentrated flavors and, in turn, wines of extraordinary depth, flavor and varietal characteristics, with layers of complexity that express themselves more fully the more mature the wines become.

Winemaking techniques are based on traditional Burgundian methods and have been adapted, through careful experimentation, to the climate and soil conditions unique to the Chalone appellation. All the white wines are fermented in French oak barrels in underground cellars. The Pinot Noir is aged in French oak for 14 to 16 months.

Chappellet Vineyard

ST. HELENA, CALIFORNIA

Donn and Molly Chappellet established Chappellet Vineyard in 1967 — the second new winery built in the Napa Valley since Prohibition and one of the earliest to actively pursue hillside farming.

Located on the eastern slopes of the Napa Valley above Lake Hennessey, the winery and vineyard are nestled in a natural amphitheater on Pritchard Hill. "The volcanic soils and warm dry temperatures contribute both force and finesse, the essence of truly great wine," says Chappellet. Today, 110 acres of the 640-acre property are planted as estate vineyards of Cabernet, Chardonnay, Chenin Blanc and Merlot at altitudes of 800 to 1,800 feet. The soil varies

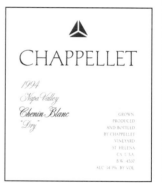

from rocky to sandy loam. The vineyards feature cover crops and terracing with approximately 50% dryfarmed. The fruit is intensely concentrated with firm acidity and balanced structure.

The Chappellet brand logo, a pyramid-shaped section of a tetrahedron used on all labels, represents the spectacular geometric winery, which was designed by the family. With its reddish steel roof, the building harmonizes with the natural environment by reflecting the colors of the surrounding volcanic soils.

Chateau Montelena Winery

CALISTOGA, CALIFORNIA

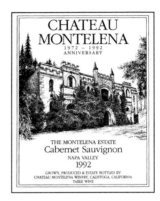

Chateau Montelena's rich history began on a chilly fall morning in January of 1882 when Alfred L. Tubbs spaded over and inspected soil where he hoped to plant estate vineyards. He struck a deal with the property owner, and so the San Francisco entrepreneur became the owner of 254 acres of rugged land just two miles north of Calistoga. It took less than a decade to turn his dream into reality when Chateau Montelena was christened the seventh largest winery in Napa Valley.

Under the leadership of James Barrett, the Montelena Estate vineyard was replanted and the Chateau outfitted with modern winemaking equipment. The philosophy at Chateau Montelena is simple: make the best. Period. To that end, Jim Barrett found talented winemakers and grew or contracted for the highest-quality grapes in Napa Valley.

Then in 1976, Chateau Montelena put California in the forefront of world-class winemaking. That year, connoisseurs of the French wine and food community gathered for a tasting in Paris. Four each of white Burgundies and Bordeaux were tasted against six California Chardonnays and six California Cabernet Sauvignons. When the scores were tallied, French judges were convinced the top-ranking white wine was one of their own white Burgundies. But, in fact, it was Chateau Montelena's 1973 Chardonnay, rated above all other wines.

A treat for wine lovers seeking excellence, the setting is one of the most peaceful in the Napa Valley — a stone castle carved into a hillside that overlooks a Chinese garden and a lake. The hospitality room, located on the top floor of the Chateau, is where visitors may sample and purchase wines, including library releases.

VENISON CHOPS MONTELENA

Serves 4

Preparation Time: 45 Minutes
Pre-heat oven to 350°

4 Tbsps. dried porcini
   mushrooms
2 cups beef or
   chicken stock, hot
2 shallots, minced
1½ Tbsps. olive oil
2 Tbsps. oil-cured
   olives, pitted,
   chopped

1 Tbsp. each fresh
   oregano and
   marjoram, finely
   chopped
1 Tbsp. unsalted
   butter, optional
4 venison chops
   Salt and pepper
   to taste

Crumble mushrooms in a non-metallic bowl and cover with hot stock.

In a small heavy-duty saucepan, sauté the shallots in 1 Tbsp. olive oil until lightly caramelized. Add the mushroom stock, straining through a fine sieve. Add olives and herbs and reduce to a sauce consistency, adding butter at the end for body. Set aside and keep warm.

Season the venison chops with salt and pepper. In a heavy skillet, add the remaining olive oil and sear chops on both sides over medium-high heat. Finish cooking in oven to desired doneness.

Place the chops on plates and pour sauce in a broad band across them. Distribute the olives and mushrooms evenly on and around each chop. Serve immediately. ✻

WINE PAIRING: Given the heartiness of this dish, one should look for a ripe vintage Chateau Montelena, like a 1985, 1987 or 1990. This winery offers bigger, rounder flavors than are found elsewhere in the northern part of Napa Valley. Another wine that would also work well would be an Amarone from Veneto in Northern Italy.

Cuvaison Winery

CALISTOGA, CALIFORNIA

The vineyards of Cuvaison consist of 284 planted acres of vines on a 400-acre estate in the Carneros district, located in southern Napa Valley. This famed grape-growing district is noted for its early-ripening varieties of Chardonnay, Pinot Noir and Merlot.

The Schmidheiny family of Switzerland purchased the vineyard property in 1979, believing that, over the years, this location would prove to be the basis for the production of superb wines. Great care and study went into the cloning of specific varietals to specific locales within the vineyard.

The winery's name, "Cuvaison" (Koó-vay-sawn), is French for the fermentation of wine on the grape skins. Situated on the historic Silverado Trail in picturesque Calistoga, the unique tasting room is open daily.

ROSEMARY SOURDOUGH FLATBREAD

Serves 4

Preparation Time: 1 Hour (note rising time)

Starter Ingredients:

6 cups bread flour	4 cups warm water

Sponge Ingredients:

⅓ cup fresh yeast	4 cups bread flour
2 cups warm water	

Dough Ingredients:

1 cup warm water	8 cups bread flour
3 Tbsps. kosher salt	Cornmeal for
½ cup rosemary,	dusting
chopped	Rosemary-infused
1 Tbsp. black pepper	olive oil

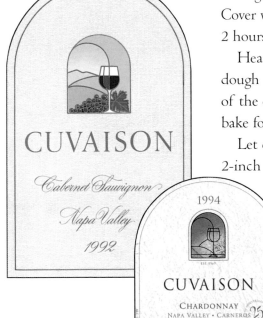

FOR THE STARTER: In a large ceramic bowl, combine the flour with the water, stirring to blend, and cover with cheesecloth. Leave in a warm area for at least one week.

FOR THE SPONGE: In a large mixing bowl, combine the yeast and the water. Mix until dissolved. Slowly add the bread flour and knead for 10 minutes. Cover and let rest for 8 hours.

FOR THE DOUGH: In a large bowl, mix the water, salt, rosemary and black pepper. Add this to the starter and then to the sponge. Knead for 1 minute, then slowly add the 8 cups bread flour. Knead for an additional 10 minutes. Cover with a damp cloth and let rest for 4 hours.

Divide the dough into 4 equal portions and shape into flat loaves, stretching them across a baking sheet that has been dusted with cornmeal. Cover with a damp cloth and let rise for at least 2 hours or until double in height.

Heat oven to 375°. Press your fingers into the dough to form dimples across the entire surface of the dough. Brush with rosemary olive oil and bake for 35 minutes.

Let cool completely before cutting into 2-inch squares. ✳

Duckhorn Vineyards

ST. HELENA, CALIFORNIA

This winery is located on a 10-acre parcel along the Silverado Trail just north of St. Helena, California, in the Napa Valley. However, Duckhorn Vineyards owns more than 100 acres of prime vineyard land.

The grapes come from the great appellations of Howell Mountain and Carneros as well as some elevated benchlands throughout the Napa Valley. All the grapes are hand-picked and hand-sorted before crushing. The wines are then fermented and barrel-aged in 100% French oak barrels separately by vineyard lot until the final blends are created.

Duckhorn produces 45,000 cases with an emphasis on Merlot; however, they also produce Cabernet Sauvignon and Sauvignon Blanc. Cabernet Franc and Sémillon are also crushed and used for blending.

Georis Winery

CARMEL VALLEY, CALIFORNIA

It seems as if destiny decreed that Walter Georis would become a winemaker. He was born in a wine cellar in Malmedy, Belgium, near the front where the Battle of the Bulge was being waged. His wine label reflects the symbol of his home town — a dragon inside the sun. An accompanying inscription in Latin is taken from a old Walloon saying: "When the sun shines, it shines for everyone."

One of driving forces behind such successful California restaurants as La Boheme, Casanova and Fandango, Georis is part of a large extended family that eventually settled on the Monterey Peninsula, after immigrating from Belgium in the 1950s.

Owing to the microclimate of Carmel Valley and the clay and sandy loam soils, Georis Winery produces only reds. All the aging is done in French oak chateau barrels where the wine rests from 16 to 19 months.

Grace Family Vineyards

ST. HELENA, CALIFORNIA

The Grace family wine adventure started serendipitously in the spring of 1976 when the family purchased a 100-year-old Victorian home in St. Helena and moved to the Napa Valley, deciding that the one-acre parcel in front of their new home would make a fine vineyard. In 1976, they prepared the land, planted root stock and budded to the Bosche clone of Cabernet Sauvignon.

Grace Family Vineyards was among the first Napa owners to adopt the European practice of closely spacing the vines as well as hand hoeing the vineyards for weed control, not relying on either pesticides or herbicides. The winery uses organic farming techniques, supports pristine vineyard conditions and employs all-new Sequin Moreau oak barrels. In 1985, a second acre adjoining the home was planted.

Grace Family wine is sold only through a mailing list of approximately 480 clients, each of whom is allowed to purchase four 750-ml bottles and one magnum. The Grace Family Vineyards waiting list is currently in excess of 1,200. Information can be obtained at 1210 Rockland Road, St. Helena, CA 94574 (707) 963-0808.

"Wine as a catalyst toward healing our planet" has become the winery's mission statement. By raising money at charity wine auctions, Grace Family Vineyards has contributed to charities that help people in need.

Heitz Wine Cellars

St. Helena, California

When Heitz Wine Cellars opened in 1961, Napa Valley had fewer than 20 wineries. Today there are more than 200. The original winery on St. Helena Highway is still open to the public as a sales and tasting room, and it offers a glimpse into the origins of Heitz Cellars.

At Heitz, growth has always been slow and calculated, with quality and consistency of utmost importance. Today the winery accommodates an annual production of 40,000 cases, from 140 acres of prime vineyards situated in the heart of Napa Valley. From 1985 onward these vineyards have produced most of the grapes for Heitz wines, the exceptions being the two legendary vineyard-designated Cabernet Sauvignons from "Martha's Vineyard" and "Bella Oaks Vineyard."

Although Cabernet Sauvignon and Heitz Cellars have come to be almost synonymous, the original fame of the label rested with Chardonnays. The hallmarks of Heitz Chardonnay then and now are a fullness of flavor and a texture in a dry traditional style.

J Wine Company

HEALDSBURG, CALIFORNIA

The J bottle itself is unique. Specialized through a labor-intensive process, this bottle is elegant and artistic with its long neck and body. The individual signature and character of the glass reflect the hand-crafted art of each bottle.

J Wine Company was founded in 1986 to create a wine that, while faithfully reflecting the finest traditions of Champagne, would exploit the possibilities of California vines. The initial aromas are suggestive of flowers, figs, pears, melons and fresh lychee nuts. As the wine "opens up" in the glass, the yeast aromas reveal themselves: light, doughy and toasty nuances interlaced with vanilla and butterscotch.

Headed by the father-daughter team of Tom and Judy Jordan, the company is located in Sonoma County with an impressive staff of professionals, state-of-the-art equipment and superb fruit from Sonoma County. The company is confident that J Sparkling Wine, its sole product, will bring pleasure to its clientele.

At J, wine is viewed as an integral component of a meal and is in fact a food in itself. J Winery Chef de Cuisine Thomas Oden's enviable task is to harmoniously pair food with J's world-class wines in a manner that enhances flavors on many levels.

Sparkling wine can easily grace an entire meal: starting with classic hors d'oeuvres and appetizers like caviar and oysters, through savory courses featuring rich seafood or mushroom concoctions, on to lightly smoked fish, fowl and cheeses, and finally embracing lightly sweetened creamy desserts perfumed with lemon rind.

STAR-ANISE-CURED SALMON WITH ARUGULA

Serves 4

Yields 16 hors d'oeuvres, or serves 4 as a first course
Preparation Time: 30 Minutes (note marinating time)

½ cup light brown
  sugar, packed firmly
½ cup fine sea salt
1 tsp. finely ground
  black and white
  peppercorns
¼ tsp. ground allspice
½ tsp. ground star
  anise
2 lbs. fresh salmon
  filet, center cut,
  deboned

½ cup J Sparkling
  Wine
1 bunch arugula
2 small fennel bulbs,
  halved, then
  julienned thinly
1 Meyer lemon,
  zested in ⅟₁₆ inch
  strips with no
  white membrane
2 to 3 Tbsps.
  extra-virgin olive oil

In a mixing bowl combine the sugar, salt and spices. Place the salmon, skin side down, in a glass dish and completely cover it with the sugar mixture. Sprinkle with the wine. Refrigerate for 36 to 72 hours.

Rinse the salmon quickly with cold water, dry with paper towels and refrigerate, uncovered, on a rack, for an additional 24 hours or until a thin skin develops on the surface of the fish. Slice the salmon on a slight diagonal angle, as thinly as possible.

Place several arugula leaves, a slice of fennel and a strip of lemon zest on each slice of salmon. Roll into small bundles. Cover and refrigerate.

Just before serving, drizzle with olive oil. Place 4 bundles on a plate to serve as a first course, or individually on a round of toasted bread as an hors d'oeuvre. ✳

SMOKED STEELHEAD WITH FENNEL AND GREEN OLIVE TAPENADE

Yields 40 appetizers

Preparation Time: 45 Minutes

2 lbs. white fennel bulb,
  green stalks and leafy
  fronds reserved
6 Tbsps. olive oil
6 cloves garlic, peeled
1 tsp. kosher salt
¼ cup J Sparkling Wine
  Black pepper to taste
10 green olives, chopped
½ tsp. red chile pepper
  flakes

2 to 3 tsps. lemon juice
2 Tbsps. parsley,
  chopped
2 to 4 Tbsps. yogurt
1 baguette, sliced into
  40 ovals about ⅜-
  inch thick, brushed
  with olive oil, toasted
1 side smoked steel-
  head or salmon,
  approximately 4 lbs.,
  cut into 40 slices

Split fennel bulb in two and cut each half through the core into two or three wedges. In a saucepan, brown them in 2 Tbsps. of olive oil with garlic and salt, caramelizing slowly. Add the wine and black pepper. Braise for 30 minutes until tender.

Finely chop one cup of stalks and place in a bowl with the olives, pepper flakes and lemon juice. Finely chop the leafy fronds of the fennel, add them to the chopped Italian parsley and set aside.

When the fennel bulbs are done, finely chop them and the garlic cloves. Purée with the braising liquid until smooth. Slowly drizzle in the remaining olive oil. Combine the purée with the mixture and the yogurt. Season to taste.

Place a thin smear of the tapenade on the crostini. Add a slice of the smoked steelhead, twisted into a cone on top of the tapenade. Spoon tapenade inside the steelhead cone. ✳

RAVIOLI FILLED WITH
ROCK SHRIMP AND SCALLOPS

Serves 4

Preparation Time: 1¹/₂ Hours

Rock Shrimp and Scallop Ingredients:

Salt and freshly
ground white pepper

¹/₂ lb. rock shrimp,
peeled, deveined

¹/₂ lb. bay scallops,
muscle removed

3 Tbsps. extra-virgin
olive oil

1 clove garlic, chopped

1 leek, white portion
only, cut into thick
coins

1 small fennel bulb,
core and green
stalk removed,
medium-dice

¹/₄ cup J Sparkling
Wine

¹/₂ tsp. fresh thyme,
chopped

¹/₂ cup heavy cream

Rind of ¹/₄ lemon

1 small radicchio,
core removed, cut
in julienne strips

1 ear white corn,
cut from the cob

Pasta Ingredients:

6 egg yolks

1 tsp. olive oil

1 tsp. water

Pinch of salt

1¹/₄ cups all-purpose
flour

Sauce Ingredients:

2 shallots, finely
chopped

1 Tbsp. butter

¹/₂ cup J Sparkling Wine

¹/₂ cup cream

Parsley, fennel or
thyme, chopped,
for garnish

FOR THE ROCK SHRIMP AND SCALLOPS:
Salt and pepper the rock shrimp and the scallops
and toss them separately with 1 Tbsp. each of the
olive oil.

Heat a heavy skillet over high heat. When hot,
throw in rock shrimp, tossing them vigorously in
the pan for 30 seconds. Scrape them back into
the bowl and repeat with the scallops.

Add last Tbsp. of olive oil to pan and heat.
Add the garlic, leek and fennel, moving them
continuously in the pan. When they turn golden,
add the wine and the fresh thyme and continue
to cook over high heat until the liquid is nearly
evaporated. Add the cream and lemon rind, reduce
the heat to medium and cook until very thick.
Remove from the stove, add the radicchio and
corn, mixing them well. Allow this mixture to cool.

At the same time, drain the seafood, saving the
liquid, and coarsely chop it to the size of the corn
kernels. Mix it with the cooled vegetable mixture.
Add more salt and pepper to taste. The pasta
filling needs to be somewhat highly seasoned so
that it doesn't become bland in the second
cooking in boiling water. ✳

FOR THE PASTA: To mix by hand, combine the egg yolks, olive oil, water and salt in a mixing bowl. Slowly, stir in the flour. Mix into a dough ball that is moist but not sticky, adding more flour if necessary.

To mix with a food processor, add the flour to the liquid mixture and process, adding more flour, if necessary, until the dough mass pulls away cleanly from the sides of the bowl.

Roll out the dough into sheets with a pasta machine to the thinnest setting. Make large ravioli 4 to 5 inches in diameter. The ravioli can be cut either with a large cookie cutter or by hand, using a saucer as a template. Put ½ cup of filling between 2 sheets of pasta, moistening the edges with a wet finger before sealing.

Place the finished ravioli on a cookie sheet spread with an even layer of semolina on the bottom, and refrigerate until ready to cook. If they are to be held for more than a few hours, freeze them until hard on the cookie sheets and transfer them to sealed freezer bags.

FOR THE SAUCE: In a small saucepan, sauté the shallots in butter. After 30 seconds add the wine and reduce to ¼ cup over medium heat. Add the cream and bring to a boil. Add the reserved seafood liquid and bring back to a boil.

At the same time, cook the ravioli in salted boiling water until tender on the edges, about 4 minutes. If they've been frozen, place them directly from the freezer into the boiling water without defrosting. They may need a minute more to cook. Drain them, arrange on plates, and top with 2 Tbsps. of the sauce. Garnish with chopped parsley, fennel, thyme or any combination of the and serve immediately. ✳

Joullian Vineyards

CARMEL VALLEY, CALIFORNIA

One of the advantages of owning an estate winery is the ability to create wines for special family occasions and custom tailor others to suit family members' taste. 1993 saw the creation of a *Family Reserve Sauvignon Blanc* and a *Family Reserve Chardonnay* for two very special occasions: the marriages of Marion Joullian Story and Alice Sias Pippin.

After tasting these first wines at the winery, members of the wine trade persuaded the family to go public with subsequent vintages of their unique blends of "ten finest barrels in the cellar."

For the *Family Reserve Chardonnay*, Joullian Vineyards selected the richest and most deeply fruited Sleepy Hollow and La Reina Vineyard wines, fermented and aged in medium to heavily toasted, tight-grain French oak. These wines were combined with the more elegant, citrine Joullian Estate Chardonnay out of mostly new Voges and Troncais Forest Barrels. The result is a wine with voluptuous fruit and texture, supported by an elegant toasty oak framework.

The Sauvignon Blanc is a 100% barrel-fermented estate blend of nine barrels of "musquet" clone of Sauvignon Blanc and one barrel of Semillon. The unique barrel blend of French-coopered American oak plus light-toasted French oak perfumes the wine, while malolactic fermentation and five months "surlie" aging enhance the opulent melon and light herbal flavors.

Matanzas Creek Winery

SANTA ROSA, CALIFORNIA

Elegance, complexity, balance and consistency are the words that have come to describe the wines of Matanzas Creek Winery. Founded in 1978, the winery produces some of the world's most coveted wines. This accomplishment is the result of nothing less than always making quality the first concern.

Matanzas Creek's winemakers, Bill Parker and Susan Reed, produce Chardonnay, Merlot and Sauvignon Blanc, along with the rare Journey wines. An ongoing program of intense research and experimentation assures that the wines are always improving. This constant drive to create nothing but the best led Jim Laube of the Wine Spectator to give *Matanzas Creek* a rare five-star rating.

Matanzas Creek encourages visits to the winery as much for the gardens as for the wine. A self-guided garden tour acquaints visitors with the entire property and features some 4,500 lavender plants that produce well over 2 million high-quality stems each year. Signs at stops along the way point out certain elements of landscape theory, as well as unique plants and settings, and offer tips on how visitors might improve their own home gardens.

LAVENDER ROASTED LAMB

Serves 4

Preparation Time: 10 Minutes
(note marinating and cooking times)

¼ cup dried lavender flowers	¼ cup virgin olive oil
½ cup garlic cloves, crushed	1 de-boned leg of lamb, or 4 frenched racks of lamb
½ cup fresh thyme	Salt and pepper to taste
½ cup fresh marjoram	
½ cup fresh rosemary	

MATANZAS CREEK WINERY

1994
SONOMA COUNTY
SAUVIGNON BLANC

PRODUCED AND BOTTLED BY MATANZAS CREEK WINERY·
SANTA ROSA, CA ALCOHOL 13.7% BY VOLUME

Combine the lavender, garlic, thyme, marjoram, rosemary and olive oil in a large mixing bowl. Apply the mixture to the lamb and allow to marinate overnight. Do not marinate for more than 24 hours.

While waiting for grill to heat, remove lamb from marinade. Season lamb well with salt and pepper. Grill until lamb reaches desired temperature. When the lamb begins to emit small pearls of pink juice, it has reached medium-rare. ✳

Serve with *Matanzas Creek Sonoma Valley Merlot.*

Morgan Winery

SALINAS, CALIFORNIA

Since establishing their winery in 1982, Daniel Morgan Lee and his wife Donna have produced exquisite Monterey County Chardonnays and Pinot Noirs. A recent Chardonnay tasting "of some of the best" by *Wine Enthusiast* magazine places Morgan's 1994 Monterey Chardonnay at the top of the list with the following verdict: "this beauty epitomizes what Monterey fruit can offer."

In the spring of 1996, Daniel and Donna saw the last element of their original dream fall into place: to provide the winery with a continual source of top-quality fruit, they purchased 67 acres of prime vineyard land along the base of the Santa Lucia Highlands.

The emphasis was and still is on quality and not quantity. The winemaking philosophy is a simple one: obtain the best possible grape, and let the fruit determine the production techniques to enhance the natural flavors and quality of the fruit rather than overpower it. Total production is 35,000 cases annually.

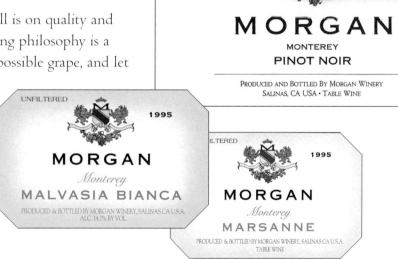

Mount Eden Vineyards

SARATOGA, CALIFORNIA

High atop the Santa Cruz Mountains, the vineyards of this small historic wine estate dot the vertical terrain of a 2,000-foot mountain about 15 miles from the Pacific Ocean. "The reason for the existence of the world's great wines has to do in large part with great locales, and we are fortunate to have one of them," says winemaker and winegrower Jeffrey Patterson.

First planted in 1942 by Martin Ray, Mount Eden is recognized as the original "boutique" California wine property, focusing on small lots of Pinot Noir, Chardonnay and Cabernet Sauvignon. Growing in austere and infertile Franciscan shale, some of the original vines are over 50 years old.

Patterson's gentleness and naturalness in handling the grapes have created a lineage of rich and complex wines. He knows winemaking is a reflection of the "ecology" of the mountain — the soil, the rainfall, the temperature. He views himself as a facilitator, bringing out the best qualities nature offers each year. "I am continually in awe of the mysteries of nature and fine wine, and I thank my good fortune to be the tender of such special mountain vineyards."

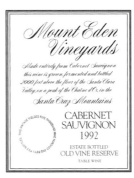

Nalle

HEALDSBURG, CALIFORNIA

Winemaker Doug Nalle and his four grape growers in Dry Creek Valley, California, work closely to produce the highest quality grapes. Old Zinfandel vines, some planted before 1900 on low-yielding benchland soils, include Petite Sirah, Carignane, Syrah, Alicante Bouchet and Gamay.

Nalle Zinfandel is produced with methods used world wide for fine red wines — hand-sorted grapes and open-top tank fermentation, French oak cooperage, frequent racking and egg white fining.

The goal is to express, in the wine's youth, the intrinsic "zinberry" fruit and elegance of *Dry Creek Valley Zinfandel* and, with bottle age, the complex characteristics that define all world-class wines.

Ojai Vineyard

OAKVIEW, CALIFORNIA

Helen and Adam Tolmach established their winery in 1983, producing Syrah, Sauvignon Blanc/Semillon, Chardonnay, Pinot Noir and Viognier from select vineyard sites in Ojai (Ventura County, northern Santa Barbara County) and Arroyo Grande Valley.

Total production is about 5,000 cases, divided between 11 separate bottlings.

Steadfastly refusing to delegate the craft of producing their wines to others, the Tolmachs are involved in every step from grape to bottle. They believe that this hands-on approach is essential in making distinctive, individualistic wines with strong character.

Pahlmeyer

NAPA, CALIFORNIA

When Demi Moore sets out to seduce Michael Douglas in the hit film *Disclosure*, she starts with wine. "The '91 Pahlmeyer," he exclaims happily. "How did you know about that?" "I want all the boys under me to be happy," she replies.

Jason Pahlmeyer, a lawyer-turned-winemaker, began developing a 25-acre vineyard at Coombsville, in the early 1980s. Situated as far south as the cool Carneros District, the vineyard is laid out on terraced hillsides at an elevation of 500 feet.

The distinctive elements of close vine spacing, new and different clones and rootstock, and climate and elevation meld into a unique viticultural foundation for exceptional wine.

The winery has produced consistently rich vintages of red table wines all noted for their complexity and longevity. In exceptional vintage years, Pahlmeyer also releases small quantities of Chardonnay and 100% varietal Merlot.

RED TABLE WINE RISOTTO

Serves 4

Preparation Time: 45 Minutes

5 cups lamb or
chicken broth

2 Tbsps. olive oil

1 large red onion,
chopped

1½ cups Arborio rice

1½ cups Pahlmeyer red
table wine

Salt and pepper
to taste

2 Tbsps. butter

¼ cup Italian parsley,
chopped

16 oil-cured black
olives

Parmesan or
Romano cheese,
freshly grated

In a medium saucepan, bring the broth to a simmer.

In a heavy saucepan, heat 2 Tbsps. of olive oil. Add the onion and rice and sauté for 2 to 3 minutes. Pour in ½ cup of red wine. When absorbed, add the simmering broth, ½ cup at a time, stirring frequently, until ½ cup of broth is left.

Add the next ½ cup of red wine and stir until incorporated, followed by the final ½ cup of wine. Cook for 2 to 3 minutes while continuing to stir.

Add the final ½ cup of simmering broth and cook briefly, leaving enough liquid so that the risotto has a consistency similar to a thick, rich soup.

Season with salt and pepper to taste.

Remove from heat and add 2 Tbsps. of butter and the chopped parsley. Spoon or ladle into bowls and add olives for garnish. Offer Parmesan or Romano cheese as a topping. ✳

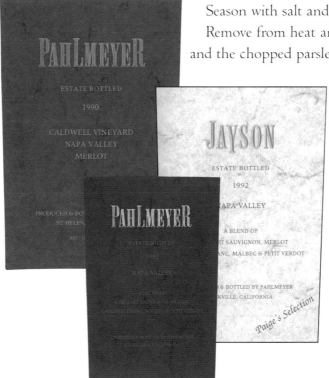

WINE PAIRING: Cabernet Sauvignon, Cabernet Franc, or Merlot- based wines would all be appropriate, along with the obvious — enjoying the rest of the bottle of cooking wine.

Peter Michael Winery

CALISTOGA, CALIFORNIA

The label on the back of each bottle of Peter Michael wine simply says "Mountain Vineyards, classical wine making, limited production." Each of these three elements is essential to the final product, but it is the mountain vineyards that take first place.

The views from these mountainous vineyards perched 2,000 feet above sea level on the western face of Mount St. Helena are breathtaking. Only the hardy and sure-footed can navigate these slopes, whose vine rows plunge straight down the mountainside.

The vineyard's volcanic-origin rhyolitic soils are extremely rocky and well drained, which keeps yields low. The soils are also high in potassium, which boosts photosynthesis, thereby imparting deep color and flavor to the grapes. Extremely rare in winegrowing regions, rhyolitic soils are one of the most prized of all wine-growing soils. Their rare mineral composition gives grapes exceptionally distinctive flavors and aromas.

To ensure intensity of flavor, winemaker Mark Aubert keeps the densely planted vine canopies small and growth in check. He call this "bonsai-ing" the vines. Each vineyard site was chosen following extensive research of the soil, climate and grape variety. The cost of planting and farming the mountain vineyards here is at least twice that of valley-floor sites, and, of course, hand picking is the rule: no machines can navigate these steep slopes.

The estate Chardonnay vineyards are planted at the highest and coolest elevation on the property, nearly 2,000 feet above sea level. Peter Michael's *Les Pavots* vineyard is planted with Cabernet Sauvignon, Merlot and Cabernet Franc just below the Chardonnay vineyards, at around the 1,500-foot level, in extremely rocky volcanic soils.

ROASTED QUAIL WITH DRIED CHERRY HERB STUFFING

Serves 6

Preparation Time: 45 Minutes

Quail Ingredients:

2 loaves fresh herb bread

12 boned quail, 5 oz. each

2 large shallots, coarsely chopped

3 leeks, large, whites only, sliced in ⅛-inch half moons

2 Tbsps. olive oil

1 tsp. garlic, chopped

2½ cups chicken stock

1½ cup dried cherries

½ cup Italian parsley, chopped

¼ cup fresh marjoram, chopped

Salt and pepper to taste

Sauce Ingredients:

3¾ cups chicken stock, unsalted

2 oz. dried cherries

1 tsp. balsamic vinegar

2 oz. Cassis liqueur, optional

Salt to taste

2 Tbsps. unsalted butter

Fresh ground pepper

Reserved fresh herbs

FOR THE QUAIL: Cut the loaves of herb bread into ½-inch cubes. Place on a baking sheet and lightly toast under the broiler on the lower shelf. While the bread is toasting, rinse the quail in cold water, lay them on a baking sheet and pat dry. Remove the croutons when done and turn the oven to 400°.

In a large, heavy skillet, sauté the shallots and leeks in 1 Tbsp. of the olive oil over low heat until soft and translucent. Add the garlic, sauté for a minute, then add chicken stock. Simmer for 5 minutes.

Coarsely chop the dried cherries. Reserve 1 Tbsp. each of the parsley and marjoram for garnish. Combine the rest in a large bowl with the bread and cherries. Add the leeks, shallots and chicken stock to the stuffing. Season with salt and pepper to taste.

Gently stuff each quail and pin the legs together with a toothpick. Rub the outside skin with the remaining olive oil and salt lightly. All the steps to this point can be done ahead of time. Place the remaining stuffing in a baking dish.

Roast the quail, placing the quail on the top shelf and the stuffing below, covered with foil. Remove the foil for the last 5 minutes of cooking. Depending on the size of the quail, the roasting time is approximately 15 to 20 minutes.

FOR THE SAUCE: In a small saucepan, combine the chicken stock and dried cherries. Reduce the stock by half, or until it lightly coats a spoon. Add the balsamic vinegar and Cassis. Season with salt to taste. Keep warm on low heat until ready to serve. Whisk in the butter and half the reserved fresh herbs just before serving.

When the quail are finished, turn them breast side down while you prepare the plates, allowing juices to moisten and flavor the breast meat.

Serve the quail on a small bed of stuffing and drizzle sauce on each bird and around the stuffing. Finish with fresh ground pepper and a dusting of the remaining herbs. ✳

Ridge Vineyards

CUPERTINO, CALIFORNIA

In 1959, three Stanford Research Institute engineers and their families bought the William Short vineyard, situated at an elevation of 2,300 feet on Monte Bello Ridge in the Santa Cruz Mountains. They never dreamed that their weekend retreat with its spectacular view of the San Francisco Bay Area, its vines and cluster of old buildings, would achieve the renown it has today as Ridge Vineyards.

Ridge now produces between 50,000 and 60,000 cases per year. Cabernet, Merlot and Zinfandel make up most of the production; Petite Sirah and Mataro account for a small percentage. Though known primarily for its red wines, Ridge makes limited amounts of Santa Cruz Mountains Chardonnay, one of the most complex and regionally distinctive white wines in California.

The winemaking approach at Ridge continues to be straightforward: begin with the most flavorful, intense grapes, intrude as little as possible on the natural process and draw all the richness from the fruit into the wine. All wines are watched over continually and tasted regularly throughout their barrel times. These ongoing assessments determine when to rack, what — if any — varietal blending will be done and when bottling will take place. One, if not the most, crucial criterion of greatness in red wine is its ability to age — to develop in quality, and to achieve exceptional complexity.

RIDGE 1993 CALIFORNIA MONTE BELLO®

86% CABERNET, 7% MERLOT, 7% PETIT VERDOT
SANTA CRUZ MOUNTAINS   ALCOHOL 12.9% BY VOLUME
GROWN, PRODUCED AND BOTTLED BY RIDGE VINEYARDS BW 4488
17100 MONTE BELLO RD, BOX 1810, CUPERTINO, CALIFORNIA 95015

MESQUITE GRILLED PORK LOIN

Serves 6

Preparation Time: 45 Minutes (note marinating time)

½ cup garlic black
   bean sauce
¾ cup hoisin sauce*
½ cup dark brown
   sugar, packed
½ cup molasses
¼ cup sesame oil
½ cup peanut oil
¾ cup soy sauce
½ cup rice wine
   vinegar, unseasoned
1 tsp. wasabi paste**
¼ cup tomato paste

2 Tbsps. fresh ginger,
   grated
1 jalapeño, diced
2 lemons, sliced
½ bunch fresh
   cilantro, chopped
1 medium yellow
   onion, sliced
Ground black
   pepper to taste
1 pork loin, cleaned,
   about 4 lbs.

In a medium-size bowl, blend all the marinade ingredients well. Place marinade on and around pork loin. Cover and refrigerate for 6 to 8 hours, or overnight.

Remove loin from refrigerator and let sit for 1 hour before grilling. Using mesquite wood, prepare grill.

Grill and periodically baste with extra marinade. Cook until done, 160° internal temperature. Let meat rest for 5 to 10 minutes. Slice and serve with mahogany rice and accompany with grilled vegetables. ✳

Hoisin sauce, also called Peking sauce, is a thick, reddish-brown sauce that is sweet and spicy.

**Wasabi paste, which comes from the root of an Asian plant, is the Japanese version of horseradish.*

MAHOGANY RICE

Serves 6

Preparation Time: 45 Minutes

2 cups Lundberg
   Farms japonica
   rice*
4 cups water
¼ cup sesame oil,
   toasted
4 carrots, julienned
1 red bell pepper,
   julienned
1 yellow bell pepper,
   julienned

1 bunch scallions,
   sliced
½ bunch Italian
   parsley, finely
   chopped
2 Tbsps. plum
   vinegar
Salt and pepper
   to taste
2 fresh plums,
   sliced

Place the rice and water in a large stockpot. Bring to a boil, then lower the heat and cover.

Cook the rice until the water evaporates, about 15 to 20 minutes.

Heat 2 Tbsps. of the sesame oil in a sauté pan over medium-high heat and sauté the carrots and bell pepper. Turn off the heat and add the scallions and parsley.

Add the vegetables, the remaining sesame oil, and the plum vinegar to the rice. If you wish, you can increase the amount of vinegar to taste.

Toss and season with salt and pepper. Garnish with sliced plums. ✳

Japonica rice is a field blend of short-grain black rice and medium-grain mahogany rice. It provides interesting taste appeal with nutty mushroom like muskiness coupled with an exotic, subtly sweet spiciness.

Rochioli Vineyard and Winery

HEALDSBURG, CALIFORNIA

The Rochioli family has been growing grapes at their 130-acre ranch since the 1930s. The ranch is located in the Russian River Valley, bordered by the Russian River to the east and the Pacific Ocean to the west, where the climate is cool, with fog insulating the ranch from scorching summer temperatures.

The soils range from deep, rich and well-drained loam near the river to rocky clay soil on the rolling hills above the valley floor. It is an area ideal for the cultivation of Rochioli's cool-climate varieties such as Pinot Noir, Sauvignon Blanc, and Chardonnay.

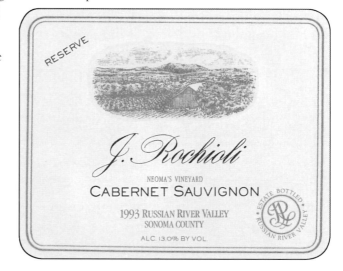

"The thing about this business is that I'm not making a style of wine for the masses but for a certain type of wine-knowledgeable person," says Tom Rochioli. His small production also means that he can practice labor-intensive winemaking techniques that produce good results. He punches down the cap of his Pinot Noir instead of pumping over, thus extracting maximum spice and richness from his grapes. He barrel ferments and ages his Chardonnay, stirring weekly to create a silky richness in the wine. "The less you manipulate the wines, the more concentration and flavors are retained," Tom states.

Tom Rochioli also has been experimenting with different oak for aging his Chardonnay and Pinot Noir. "At the moment, I really prefer the perfumed vanilla taste of the Troncais forest," he says. To this end, he uses French Troncais and Alliers oak barels for Chardonnay and Pinot Noir and mixed forest for Sauvignon Blanc and Cabernet Sauvignon.

Sarah's Vineyard

GILROY, CALIFORNIA

Located in Santa Clara County, California, the winery comprises 13 acres of Chardonnay and Pinot Noir grapes. Production has remained small, with the largest harvest at about 2,000 cases.

The purpose of Sarah's Vineyard has been, from the beginning, to concentrate on small volumes of production and to emphasize quality and elegance. The winemaker, Marilyn Clark, has worked with a variety of grapes, determining her favorites, those that allow her to express herself, much as a jewelry artisan might choose gold or silver.

Sarah's Vineyard

SANTA CLARA COUNTY
CHARDONNAY

LOT II
1992

ESTATE

Alcohol 13.0%
By Volume

GRILLED RABBIT WITH MUSTARD SAUCE

Serves 6

Preparation Time: 40 Minutes (note marinating time)

2 rabbits, about 3 lbs. each, cut into serving pieces	1 cup olive oil
2 Tbsps. green peppercorns, mashed	2½ Tbsps. stone ground mustard
2 Tbsps. lemon juice	2½ Tbsps. Dijon mustard
5 cloves garlic, finely chopped	1 tsp. fresh thyme, chopped
	1 cup heavy cream

Pat the rabbit dry and place in a large bowl.

In a small bowl, combine the peppercorns, lemon juice and garlic and slowly whisk in the olive oil. Pour over the rabbit pieces and marinate overnight or for several hours. Grill over white mesquite coals between 15 to 20 minutes, turning only once until cooked through. Take care not to overcook.

Meanwhile, combine the mustards, thyme and cream and heat in a small pan until just bubbly.

To serve, place the rabbit on a warm plate and drizzle sauce over it. ✳

HALIBUT WITH AVOCADO BUTTER

Serves 6

Preparation Time: 45 Minutes (note marinating time)

Avocado Butter Ingredients:

⅓ cup butter, softened	1 tsp. shallot, finely chopped
⅓ cup ripe avocado, mashed	1 tsp. garlic, finely chopped
1½ tsps. lime juice	½ tsp. salt
3 Tbsps. parsley, chopped	

Halibut Ingredients:

⅓ cup soy sauce	¾ cup of olive oil
1 Tbsp. Dijon mustard	6 halibut filets, 6 oz. each (Other fish, such as sea bass or monkfish can be substituted)
1 tsp. grated lemon peel	
½ cup lemon juice	
1 Tbsp. garlic, finely chopped	

FOR THE AVOCADO BUTTER: Blend the butter, avocado and lime juice. Add the parsley, shallot, garlic and salt. Either fill a small ramekin or dish, or shape the butter into a log about 1½-inches in diameter on a piece of waxed paper. Wrap the paper around the log and refrigerate until hard.

FOR THE HALIBUT: Whisk the soy sauce, mustard, lemon peel, lemon juice and garlic in a small bowl. Gradually whisk in the olive oil. Pour marinade over fish in a glass dish and refrigerate 2 to 3 hours.

Prepare the barbecue grill and, over hot coals, grill fish approximately 5 minutes on each side. Brush with marinade when turning. The fish is done when it has just turned opaque. Pass the avocado butter separately, or place one slice of the avocado butter log on each piece of fish and serve. ✳

Silver Oak Cellars

GEYSERVILLE AND OAKVILLE, CALIFORNIA

The Napa Valley winery was established in 1972 and is located in Oakville on the site of the old Oakville Dairy.

The success of Silver Oak Cellars is due in part to Justin Meyer's persistent dedication to making the finest Cabernet Sauvignon in California each year. His formula is simple: pick very ripe fruit, age it almost 30 months in mostly new American oak barrels and bottle the wine without stripping out its perfume and flavor. All the Silver Oak Cabernets are produced in a similar manner, regardless of vintage or appellation. They are notable for their well-developed bouquet, complexity and finesse.

The main building is a huge barrel cellar, with a hospitality room and office in the center. Winery visitors and personnel are literally surrounded by 2,500 barrels of aging Silver Oak Cabernet. A crushing, fermenting and bottling building is located off to the side.

In the fall of 1992, Silver Oak Cellars purchased an existing winery in the Alexander Valley. The grapes are processed from the 200+ acres of Alexander Valley vineyards in a state-of-the-art facility. The cellars hold 2,500 American oak barrels, in which the Alexander Valley Cabernet Sauvignon is aged.

Visitors to both wineries will find a warm reception and the special opportunity to purchase older vintages and large bottles.

ROMAINE, GORGONZOLA, WALNUT SALAD WITH GARLIC CROUTONS AND MUSTARD-GARLIC DRESSING

Serves 6

Preparation Time: 30 Minutes

Mustard-Garlic Dressing Ingredients:

4 Tbsps. vinegar	4 Tbsps. Dijon
1 tsp. salt	mustard
4 cloves garlic, peeled	2 cups olive oil
1 tsp. pepper	

Salad Ingredients:

Pre-heat oven to 400°

2 small baguettes, cut into cubes	1 large head romaine lettuce, torn into bite-size pieces
½ cup butter	
½ cup olive oil	1 cup Gorgonzola cheese
4 cloves garlic, peeled	
Salt and pepper to taste	1 cup walnuts, toasted

FOR THE DRESSING: Allow the vinegar and salt to stand in a blender for a few minutes. Add the garlic, pepper and mustard. Turn on the blender and slowly add the olive oil. Blend until all the ingredients are thoroughly mixed.

FOR THE SALAD: Place the croutons on a sheet pan and toast in oven.

Heat a large frying pan and add the butter and oil, garlic and bread, tossing frequently over medium heat until golden brown. Season to taste with salt and pepper.

Toss the croutons together with the lettuce, cheese and walnuts. Pour ¼ cup dressing over all, tossing together. Taste and add more dressing, if necessary. ✳

Simi Winery

HEALDSBURG, CALIFORNIA

At Simi, the most important objectives are refinement and finesse. A third objective is flavor concentration — that is, full and persistent flavors in the mouth. A fourth is complexity, a diversity of aromas and flavors that is pleasing to the palate.

In 1876, two Italian brothers, Giuseppe and Pietro Simi, brought their winemaking heritage to Northern California. The moderate climate of Sonoma County reminded them of their native Tuscany and in 1890 they completed construction of their own cellars in the little town of Healdsburg.

For nearly 100 years, these cellars housed the crushing, pressing, fermenting, and aging of all the wines. Today, these massive, historic cellars are still at the heart of the winemaking activities that produce 150,000 cases annually.

Simi's vineyard comprises 175 acres in Alexander Valley, planted primarily with red Bordeaux varietals, and 100 acres in the Russian River Valley, planted with Chardonnay grapes. The beautiful picnic area and tasting room in Healdsburg, surrounded by towering redwood trees, is available daily for tours, food and wine pairings, and reserve wine tastings.

Spottswoode Vineyard & Winery

ST. HELENA, CALIFORNIA

Spottswoode is a family-owned grape-growing and wine-making estate located on the western edge of St. Helena in the Napa Valley.

The 46-acre estate, which was established in 1882 by George Schonewald, is distinguished by the historic Victorian home depicted on labels. Classic formal gardens grace the entrance to the house while the 40-acre vineyard, planted primarily with Cabernet Sauvignon, stretches behind it to the Mayacamas mountains.

The vineyard is hand-tended and treated with the utmost reverence and care. Organic farming practices have been employed sine 1985.

Spottswoode produces only two wines — Cabernet Sauvignon and Sauvignon Blanc. To ensure the highest possible quality, each is produced in limited quantities, and no effort is spared in the growing of the grapes or in the crafting of the wines. The goal is to produce classic wines that faithfully reflect their grape origins in a distinct, refined style — in short, wines that are worthy to stand among those of the world's great wine estates.

SPOTTSWOODE

1995
SAUVIGNON BLANC
Napa Valley

CELLARED IN ST. HELENA, CA • BOTTLED IN RUTHERFORD, CA
BY SPOTTSWOODE VINEYARD & WINERY • TABLE WINE • USA

TOMATO AND RED PEPPER SOUP

Yields 1 to 2 gallons

Preparation Time: 1 Hour

3 cans Italian peeled tomatoes, 28 oz. each, drained	½ tsp. dried thyme
	1 Tbsp. sugar, optional
10 red bell peppers, about 4 lbs., cut into 2-inch pieces	1 cup heavy cream
	Salt and freshly ground black pepper to taste
10 garlic cloves, halved	
1 bottle (750 ml.) dry white wine, preferably Sauvignon Blanc	¼ cup goat cheese, crumbled
	5 sun-dried tomato halves, packed in oil, drained, diced
3 cups chicken stock	
½ cup fresh basil, coarsely chopped	5 fresh basil leaves, shredded

In a large stockpot, combine the tomatoes, bell peppers, garlic, wine, stock, basil and thyme. Bring to a boil over high heat. Cover and simmer over moderately low heat, stirring occasionally until the peppers are tender, about 45 minutes.

Purée the soup in a blender. Pass the purée through a food mill or coarse strainer.

Return the soup to the pan and add the sugar if it is too tart. Stir in the cream. Bring to a simmer over moderate heat and season with salt and pepper.

To serve, ladle the soup into serving dishes. Garnish with the crumbled goat cheese, sun-dried tomatoes and shredded basil and serve hot. This soup pairs very well with Spottswoode Vineyard Sauvignon Blanc. ✴

GRILLED MARINATED LEG OF LAMB

Serves 6

Preparation Time: 45 Minutes (note marinating time)

1 bottle (750 ml.) red wine, preferably Zinfandel	10 fresh mint leaves
	10 fresh basil leaves
1 cup olive oil	9 lb. leg of lamb, boned, butterflied and trimmed of excess fat
5 garlic cloves, chopped	
2 fresh rosemary sprigs	Salt and freshly ground pepper

In a large mixing bowl, combine the wine, olive oil, garlic, rosemary leaves, mint and basil. Mix well.

Place the lamb in a dish large enough for it to lie flat or in a strong plastic bag. Pour the marinade over the lamb and refrigerate for at least 6 hours, or overnight.

Bring the lamb to room temperature. Before grilling, season the meat with salt and pepper.

Grill over hot coals, turning once, until medium-rare. Because of varying thickness of the meat, different parts will cook to different temperatures.

Remove from the grill and allow to sit for approximately 10 minutes covered with foil.

Slice and serve, accompanied by a bottle of Spottswoode Cabernet Sauvignon. ✴

Robert Talbott Vineyards

CARMEL VALLEY, CALIFORNIA

Most men with a family business as successful as the Talbott Tie Company would be reluctant to leave this security for the risky business of producing wine. But the risk added to the attraction for Robert Talbott of Talbott Vineyards & Winery.

Today, his high standards as a vintner are well-known through his acclaimed Talbott Chardonnay. The Diamond T Estate Vineyard, now in the third generation of the Talbott family, comprises 22 acres situated 1,200 feet above the valley floor and 8 miles from Carmel Bay. The closely spaced rows of vines face the south in a climate moderated by cool fog in the mornings and evenings. The mountaintop is shale filled with fossils and granite, the soil having long since washed away. Chardonnay grown in an area such as this reflects the character of the rocky soil.

Talbott's first Pinot Noir has recently been released under the Logan label, named after his son. His second Pinot Noir is named *Case*, after his oldest daughter. Talbott also offers two other new releases as well: a second label of *Rosewood Monterey Chardonnay* and *Talbott Cuvée Cynthia Chardonnay*, named for his wife.

At harvest time, usually in early October, the grapes are hand-picked and then given a long, cool fermentation in French oak barrels. Production continues to be small because of to the low yields from the grapevines and the difficult growing conditions on the rocky mountaintop.

Bollinger

CHAMPAGNE REGION, FRANCE

Bollinger has been rooted in France's Champagne region since the 15th century, when the de Villermont family — granted nobility in 1359 by King John the Good of France for service in the 100 Years War against the English — owned vineyards in Cuis.

This attachment to the land has stood Bollinger in good stead over the past five centuries — and more so today than ever before. In a region where 70% of Champagne firm sales are handled by three conglomerates and the best grapes are difficult to buy, it is imperative to the Bollinger style that the house have access to Champagne's finest grapes. Bollinger today owns 346 vineyard acres, 60% in grands crus, 30% in premiers crus and 10% in Vallée de la Marne — with an overall 98% rating — that account for 70% of its production needs.

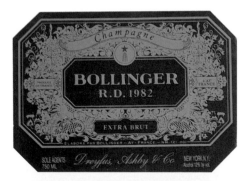

For more than 160 years Bollinger has produced classic, rich, full-bodied, extra-aged and complex Champagnes. Each is named for a specific characteristic that expresses an aspect of the greatness that Champagne can achieve.

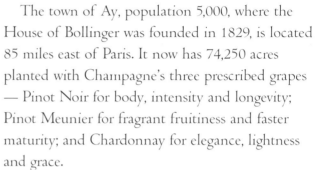

The town of Ay, population 5,000, where the House of Bollinger was founded in 1829, is located 85 miles east of Paris. It now has 74,250 acres planted with Champagne's three prescribed grapes — Pinot Noir for body, intensity and longevity; Pinot Meunier for fragrant fruitiness and faster maturity; and Chardonnay for elegance, lightness and grace.

The harvest, based on grape maturity, is usually in mid-October. Picking is still done by hand, into baskets called paniers. All Bollinger Champagnes come from the same rich, full-bodied vins clairs, or base wines, rather than from allocating different crus to different cuvées, as do most houses. Champagnes are then bottled and aged on their lees for a minimum of $2^{1}/_{2}$ to 10 years before release. The aging takes place in Bollinger's cellars 30 feet below street level, at around 50°F.

Bollinger maintains a remarkably large inventory of stocks — $7^{1}/_{2}$ million bottles, equal to five years of sales.

Champagne Taittinger

REIMS, FRANCE

The Estate de la Marquetterie, built in the 18th century in Pierry, close to Epernay, is now the heart of the House. It stands in the middle of vineyards of alternating Chardonnay and Pinot Noir, which, during the weeks preceding grape harvesting, give the surrounding hills the appearance of a huge checker-board; hence the name Marquetterie.

The history of the legendary House of Taittinger is inextricably entwined with that of the Champagne region. Not only did the House of Taittinger contribute significantly to the prosperity of a unique wine growing region, it also helped bring forth the finest example of that wine to the world, creating international awareness, prestige and respect.

SCEAU DE THIBAUD IV   COMTE DE CHAMPAGNE

CHAMPAGNE

TAITTINGER

Anciennes Maisons Fourneaux Forest et Succ.

FONDÉE   *France*   EN 1734

A REIMS

BRUT   LA FRANÇAISE

APPELLATION D'ORIGINE CONTRÔLÉE – ÉLABORÉ PAR TAITTINGER, REIMS FRANCE

ALC. 12% BY VOL   IMPORTED BY KOBRAND CORPORATION NEW YORK, N.Y.   PRODUCE OF FRANCE 375 ML

SOLE UNITED STATES IMPORTERS

It is impossible to tour the vast holdings of the House of Taittinger and not relive the history they span. Within its wine cellars alone are seventeen centuries of Reims history, from the Gallo-Roman chalk pits of the 2nd century to the 12th and 13th-century ruins of the once-prominent, Champagne-producing Saint-Nicaise monastery, to present-day innovations. Within the walls of the venerable 13th-century Counts of Champagne residence, now part of the Taittinger domain, lived Count Thibaud IV, who played a major role in Champagne history by bringing back the first Chardonnay grapes from Cyprus. And in Pierry, the parish of Brother Oudart, one of the founding fathers of Champagne, Taittinger has lovingly preserved the stunning 18th-century Chateau de la Marquetterie.

Pierre Taittinger was a noted gastronome, whose culinary philosophy foretold the trend toward light, natural cuisine so strongly favored today. Turning from the heavy, liquorous style of Champagnes prevalent at that time, he infused his winemaking with the visionary principles of his gastronomy. He set the standard for lightness and delicacy that was to become the distinctive style of the house of Taittinger, producing only brut Champagnes requiring the highest quality wines, with an elegance demanding a proportionately higher use of the costly Chardonnay grape. In 1956 Champagne Taittinger achieved the most perfect expression of that style in the creation of *Comtes de Champagne Blanc de Blancs*, a Champagne made exclusively from the Chardonnay grape, which became Taittinger's *tête de cuvée*.

Champagne Taittinger today is the last privately held Champagne house of its size, a family empire of impressive holdings. In tribute to its founder, the firm sponsors the annual Prix Culinaire International Pierre Taittinger, the most exacting culinary competition of its kind. Mr. Claude Taittinger, son of Pierre and Président-Directeur-Général of Champagne Taittinger, oversees the firm's operations in France and in more than 120 export markets where Champagne Taittinger is distributed.

LOBSTER IN ROSÉ CHAMPAGNE ASPIC

Serves 2

Preparation Time: 1 Hour

2 live spiny lobsters
  or Maine lobsters,
  1 to 1¼ lbs. each
½ cup dry white wine
1 onion, coarsely
  chopped
1 celery stalk, coarsely
  chopped
1 carrot, coarsely
  chopped
3 sprigs parsley

3 sprigs thyme
½ bay leaf
1 tsp. unflavored
  gelatin
1 bottle rosé
  Champagne, chilled
Salt and freshly
  ground pepper
  to taste
3 oz. Beluga caviar

In a 5-qt. stockpot, heat 2 qts. water to boiling. Add the lobsters; return to boiling. Boil 5 minutes. Drain. Remove lobster meat from shells; reserve meat and shells separately.

In a 3-qt. saucepan, combine reserved shells with white wine, onion, celery, carrot, parsley, thyme, bay leaf and enough water to cover; heat to boiling. Reduce heat to low and simmer 30 minutes. Strain liquid through fine sieve into clean saucepan. Reduce to ¾ cup.

Meanwhile, sprinkle gelatin over 2 Tbsps. cold water. Let stand 5 minutes. Add gelatin mixture to hot lobster broth and stir until completely dissolved. Stir in ¾ cup rosé Champagne. Season with salt and pepper to taste. Set aside.

Cut each lobster tail into 5 medallions and arrange in two shallow soup bowls (reserve any remaining lobster meat for another use). Pour the warm lobster aspic on top. Spoon a bit of caviar onto each medallion. Refrigerate 15 minutes. The bowls must not get too cold — this would diminish the flavor of the lobster. ✳

Champagne Veuve Clicquot

REIMS, FRANCE

The House of Veuve Clicquot, founded in 1772, continually strives to uphold the standards set by Madame Clicquot, whose insistence on quality was and remains the foundation of the success of Champagne Veuve Clicquot.

Today the House of Clicquot is among the most prestigious Champagne firms. Its extensive vineyard holdings, many originally purchased by Madame Clicquot, stretch throughout the top-rated areas of the Champagne region and are unparalleled in size and quality. As in Mme. Clicquot's day, bottles age in the House's vast, vaulted cellar in Reims, a portion of which were constructed some 2,000 years ago by the Romans.

The remarkable Madame Clicquot (1777—1866) is often considered the first businesswoman of the modern era. Widowed in 1805 at the age of 27, Mme. Veuve Clicquot (veuve means "widow" in French) defied every convention of the day and took the helm of her late husband's small Champagne house. She enlisted help wisely, took astute risks and made important technological innovations (including the invention of remuage, or riddling), leading the House to world reknown. One of her most significant triumphs was sending a secret shipment of her Champagne to Russia in 1814 in defiance of the Napoleonic blockage — a great success!

The Champagnes of Veuve Clicquot are full-flavored, with elegance, crispness and a lingering aftertaste.

The House of Clicquot is best known for its "Yellow Label" brut non-vintage Champagne, which was a best-seller in America before Prohibition. Veuve Clicquot also produces a Vintage Réserve, a Rosé Réserve and a Demi-Sec. The firm's most prestigious Champagne, La Grande Dame, is named after the Widow Clicquot and is made exclusively from the finest Pinot Noir and Chardonnay grapes picked from vineyards she purchased in the early 1800s.

Chateau Pichon Longueville

PAUILLAC, FRANCE

Succeeding her father, May-Eliane de Lencquesaing has owned this paradise since 1978, devoting herself to the renovation and update of technology at Château Pichon Longueville. An investment plan of $10 million ensured such a renaissance.

This vineyard has always been family-owned. The Château, enhanced by its tower and very elegant circular staircase, reflects the taste of its architect (Duphot, 1840).

The variety of the land plots, due to soil make-up and vine varieties, explains the complex personalities of Pichon wines. Vineyard plots encircle the Château, close to the river and alongside Château Latour, the famous Premier Grand Cru. The 185 acres of vines traverse the heights of Saint-Julien

to reach close to the Léoville plateau before stretching away on the large Pichon Longueville plateau to the south of the Pauillac appellation.

The exceptional richness of the Pauillac appellation is due to the poor and miserly soil. The hills are made of gravel on clay, which leads to excellent drainage. The Pauillac region enjoys a microclimate and relative dryness that aid concentration of the grapes.

FILET MIGNON IN PASTRY

Serves 6

Preparation Time: 45 Minutes
Pre-heat oven to 400°

1 large truffle, halved	4 oz. pâté mousse
1 center-cut filet of beef, trimmed, about 2 lbs.	1 sheet puff pastry dough, 12" long x 10" wide x ¼" thick, chilled
Salt and pepper	
1 Tbsp. clarified butter	1 egg yolk beaten with 1 Tbsp. water
½ cup Port	

Cut half of the truffle into slivers and shred the other half finely. Insert the slivers into small cuts in the filet, made with the sharp tip of a knife, as if they were garlic. Season with salt and pepper. Heat the clarified butter in a large sauté pan over high heat. Sear the filet on all sides, browning evenly. Deglaze with the port, allowing to evaporate. Let cool.

Spread half of the pâté mousse down the center of the puff pastry sheet. Place the rest of the finely shredded truffles over the pâté. Place filet on top of truffles and cover with the rest of the pâté.

With a pastry brush, spread the egg wash down both sides and ends of the exposed pastry. Trim pastry if necessary to form a neat package, gathering it up around the filet and pinching seams together to seal. Brush outside of pastry with egg wash, decorating with pastry scraps if desired.

Place seam side down on sheet pan and bake in oven to desired doneness, about 20 minutes for medium-rare. ✳

 TRADE SECRET: *Any vegetables can accompany this dish — in particular, small new potatoes garnished with Mornay sauce.*

WINE PAIRING: The earthiness of Bordeaux and truffle are a marriage made in heaven. Pick a good vintage, such as *Chateau Pichon Longueville Comtesse de Lalande 1985*, and you have created a memorable meal.

Les Domaines Barons de Rothschild

PAUILLAC, FRANCE

For the Chateau Lafite-Rothschild, it is the earth at Lafite which makes the property unique. Nature performed a miracle when it created the perfect combination of soil, subsoil, exposure, plus that certain "je ne sais quoi" which makes the wines of Lafite incomparable. Already recognized as outstanding in the London markets of the 16th century, Lafite received recognition at the Court of Louis IV, when Alexandre de Ségur, introduced the wines to the king.

The vineyard divides itself into three separate areas. The soil is gravelly, well drained and planted with the three classical grapes of the Médoc: Cabernet Sauvignon (70%), Cabernet Franc (10%) and Merlot (20%). The methods of cultivating are traditional: a small amount of manure and hard pruning allow the vines to reach old age, up to 80 years. Harvesting is done by hand.

Nowadays the vinifaction is done with all the sophisticated instruments of modern oenology, however, it is still the Maître de Chais, Robert Revelle, whose palate determines the length of the fermentation. The wines are aged in new oak barrels which are made on the spot, in order to control the quality of the wood and its aging.

The wines are then bottled at the château after 18 to 24 months in these barrels. During this time, the wine is racked 7 times and is fined with the whites of 6 eggs per barrel. Only certain vats are kept to make Lafite. The others are used to make the second wine of Lafite, the "moulin des Carruades".

Domaine de la Romanée-Conti

BURGUNDY, FRANCE

The scarcest, most expensive — and frequently the best — wine in the world is the Romanée-Conti from the aptly-named Domaine de la Romanée-Conti. If you can access a case — and it is a big if — you would have to pay £5000 or more for a young vintage — double or triple that for a wine in its prime.

The vineyard is tiny and consists of 4½ acres with an average production of 7,500 bottles (625 cases) a year. As a grand cru, it is entitled to appellation contrôlée in its own right and is one of the smallest appellations in France.

An interesting aspect in the making of these wines is the fashion of the harvest. By allowing the tight clusters of Pinot Noir to remain on the vine well into mid-October, each grape can collect the best elements nature provides. A late harvest, carefully picked by hand, will yield full tannic juice rich in natural sugar and spices.

Then, according to the old Burgundian tradition, a very long fermentation takes place before the wine is racked and placed in small 60-gallon barrels, where it will develop and mature for the next two years. New French oak barrels are used every year because the fresh wood releases certain essential extracts into the newly made wine.

Before leaving the Domaine to find its new home in a connoisseur's private wine cellar, each bottle is carefully labeled by hand and given a registration number.

Domaine Zind Humbrecht

ALSACE, FRANCE

The annual production varies between 14,000 and 21,000 cases of wine, of which 75% is exported, with only 25% being sold in France to private customers and restaurants.

The Domaine Zind Humbrecht was created in 1959 by the union of the family-owned properties of Zenon Humbrecht, winegrower at Gueberschwihr and of Emile Zind, winegrower in Wintzenheim. Before this date, each of the families was producing and selling wines under their own names.

After many years of experience, it was possible to consecrate certain Alsace grape varieties to certain specific soil types and micro-climates. The different single-vineyards and Grand Crus vineyards are located in five different villages in the Haut-Rhin, consisting of Thann, Hunawihr, Gueberschwihr, Wintzenheim and Turckheim.

Hine

JARNAC, FRANCE

Since the day Thomas Hine released his first casks, the connoisseurs of the world — oenologists, cellarmen and sommeliers — have distinguished Hine cognac for its unique, consistent style, its outstanding personality. Six generations later, as direct descendants of Thomas Hine, Bernard and Jacques Hine keep this heritage alive, maintaining the same qualities of the original cognac in defiance of changing fashions.

A venerable Grande Champagne from the Hine family's private reserves is proudly and sparingly released in a strictly limited number of bottles each year to be enjoyed by connoisseurs of truly exceptional cognacs.

Coming exclusively from the Grande Champagne district, Triomphe is over 40 years old. On the nose, Triomphe shows finesse and elegance as well as subtle nuances of fungus, flowers and tobacco. The palate will delight in the characteristic roundness, sustained flavor and distinction.

Georg Breuer

RÜDESHEIM AND RAUENTHAL, GERMANY

Breuer wines are synonymous with authenticity in Germany. The wines are distinguished by their precise balance of high extract, flavor intensity and racy aromatic elegance from slate soil, disciplined harvesting and minuscule yields. Clarification and stabilization are achieved delicately through natural settling in seasoned cooperage in Breuer's underground cellars.

Weingut Georg Breuer was founded in 1880, and currently owns 54 acres of vines in the famous Rheingau communes of Rüdesheim and Rauenthal. The Rieslings are classical and meant for the serious table. They are ageworthy, investment-quality wines of the highest order, regarded with considerable awe by the European trade and press.

Weingut Gunderloch

RHINE RIVER, GERMANY

Since its foundation, the estate has remained in the same family, now in its fifth generation with Friz and Agnes Hasselbach. The principal grape variety is Riesling, which finds its most powerful expression in the Nackenheimer Rothenberg vineyard. Annual production is 7,000 cases.

The Gunderloch estate in Nackenheim, just south of Mainz on the Rhine River, was founded in 1890 by banker Carl Gunderloch. From the beginning, the estate was run with a strict commitment to quality. Carl bought top vineyard sites, including a large part of the great Nackenheimer Rothenberg, and was one of the pioneers of high-quality wine production on the Rhine. Along with contemporary developments such as the introduction of vineyard-designated wines and improvements in viticulture, Carl developed a strong belief in natural wine production with full fermentation.

Rothenberg means red mountain, a name that comes from the band of red slate that runs along the Rhine. The red soil drains well, is rich in minerals, and is very good at collecting and retaining the sun's energy. The combination of its steepness, exposure, soil structure and proximity to the Rhine gives the Rothenberg vineyard the optimum micro-climate for ripening Riesling.

All of the vineyards of the Gunderloch estate are cultivated using methods that respect their ecology. No chemical fertilizers have been used for many years. The objective is to pick grapes with concentrated fruit and good acidity, resulting in wines that complement food as well as exhibiting a long aging potential.

Dr. Loosen

MOSEL, GERMANY

The individuality of the Riesling wines is the hallmark of the best estates on the steeply-sloping slate-covered vineyards of the Mosel. Across Dr. Loosen's 20 acres of vines, there are so many variations in microclimate that they produce some 30 different bottlings a year with an average size of just 200 dozen bottles each. Riesling is the preferred vine, and covers over 90% of his vineyards.

The estate of Dr. Loosen in Germany's Middle Mosel goes back some 200 years, so it seems a little strange to consider it among the fastest-rising stars in Germany. Because of his father's declining health, Ernst Loosen was summoned home to look after the 1985 vintage. His return brought with it not just a new family face to a long-established scene, but a change to "hands-on" managements.

Ernst introduced revolutionary ideas such as vertical pruning, long fermentation's of his wines and the use of organic fertilizers. The results are wines characterized by very clean, fresh fruit, usually with good length and elegance, with some complexity developing even in the youngest wines.

DR. LOOSEN

1995
Wehlener Sonnenuhr
Riesling Kabinett trocken

QUALITÄTSWEIN MIT PRÄDIKAT · PRODUCE OF GERMANY
GUTSABFÜLLUNG WEINGUT DR. LOOSEN · D-54470 BERNKASTEL/MOSEL
A.P.NR. 2 576 162 33 96

alc. 10.5% by Vol Mosel·Saar·Ruwer e 750 ml

Marchesi Antinori

TUSCANY, ITALY

Twenty-six generations of the Marchesi Antinori family have produced wine for six centuries. Quoting from Civiltà del Bere, Italy's wine magazine, "Antinori arrives first, paves new roads, not only facing the risks of the unknown but opening up spaces and opportunities for others to follow."

In Florence, Antinori properties include 15th century Palazzo Antinori with La Cantinetta, an informal wine-bar and restaurant. In Chianti's northwestern corner of the Classico region are situated a winery and cellars in San Casciano Val di Pesa and three vineyards or farm estates. Antinori also owns Castello della Sala, a 14th century castle in Umbria, near Ficulle south of Orvieto, and on the Tuscan seacoast in Maremma, Tenuta Belvedere. More recently, the family purchased Le Maestrelle, an estate in the Montepulciano-Cortona area.

Antinori continually experiments in its vineyards and winery with clonal selection of indigenous and international grape varieties, cultivation, vineyard altitudes, fermentation methods and temperatures, traditional and modern vinification techniques, wood barrel types, sizes and ages, and varying lengths of bottle age.

Since the 1960s, Antinori has employed a highly complex system of aging for its red wines called the Mosaic System, which allows each wine to receive the exact amount and type of wood aging required to maximize its flavors and style while providing an opportunity to experiment with aging in barrels of different types of oak, size, and age. The cellars also include a laboratory with the latest equipment, including machines to measure aromas and determine potential cork mold.

Blandy's Madeira

Funchal, Madeira

Many generations of the family have nurtured and developed Blandy's into one of the most highly respected Madeira houses. The current generation of the family still lives on the island and is closely involved with all aspects of the company, thus upholding the traditions and prestige given root by their forefathers.

Born in Dorchester, John Blandy first set foot on Madeira in 1807. He was a 23-year-old soldier, posted to the island with a British Army garrison under the command of General Beresford, and sent to help the Portuguese thwart any invasion attempt by Napoleon's navy. As a quartermaster, young John Blandy inevitably came into contact with local wine merchants and it was from here that his interest in wine burgeoned. He was to return in 1811 to found the company that still bears his name.

The remote sub-tropical island of Madeira is set far out in the Atlantic Ocean some 372 miles due west of the Moroccan coast and 527 miles to the southwest of its parent Portugal. Had it not been for the island's strategic position on the Atlantic shipping lanes, which made it a regular port of call, Madeira would probably never have become the widely known and much appreciated wine it remains to this day. Madeira wine was used to toast the Declaration of Independence and the inauguration of George Washington, who it is said, "drank a pint of Madeira at dinner daily".

There are four fundamental styles of Madeira — dry, medium dry, medium rich and rich. These wines are matured in casks for periods ranging from 3 to 15 years. The very best Madeiras will become Vintages or Soeras.

Graham's Port

VILLA NOVA DE GAIA, PORTUGAL

Graham's Vintage Ports are sweet and elegant, with highly concentrated fruit and a strong backbone of tannins. These are wines built for long-term aging. Quinta do Malvedos forms the backbone of the Graham's Vintage Ports. The Quinta is at the confluence of the Tua and Douro rivers. Graham's declared Vintage Port will include wines from other outstanding vineyard sites in the Upper Douro blended in with the best casks selected from the Malvedos vineyard site.

The firm of W&J Graham has its roots in a Glascow-based textile concern. During the early nineteenth century, an office of this trading company was established in Oporto. In 1820, the brothers William and John Graham, who were then managing the office, accepted 27 pipes of Port wine in settlement of a bad debt. This Port was shipped to the parent company in Glascow which initially reprimanded the brothers for not sending cash. Fortunately, after it was sold, the Port turned out to be very popular and soon William and John were being urged by their parent company to acquire and ship more of this finest of fortified wines. Within the next few years, Graham's reputation grew as a shipper of fine Port, first to Scotland and gradually all over the Port-drinking world. By the late 19th century Graham's was firmly established as a prominent Port shipper.

CHOCOLATE CAKE

Serves 8

Preparation Time: 45 Minutes
Pre-heat oven to 325°

Butter for
greasing pan
Flour and cocoa
powder for dusting
4 oz. bittersweet
chocolate, chopped
½ cup butter, unsalted

½ cup *Graham's*
Six Grapes or
10-year *Tawny Port*
1 cup sugar
3 eggs, separated
¾ cup flour
⅛ tsp. salt
Powdered sugar,
garnish

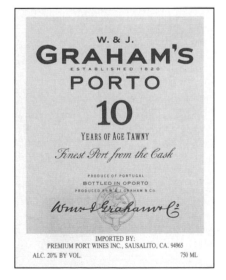

Butter a 10-inch springform pan and sprinkle with a mixture of flour and cocoa powder.

In a heavy saucepan, melt the chocolate and butter with the Port over low heat. In a mixing bowl, beat all but 2 Tbsps. of the sugar with the egg yolks at high speed for 5 minutes. Add the melted chocolate mixture to the eggs and mix until smooth. Beat in the flour.

In a separate mixing bowl, beat the 3 egg whites with the salt until soft peaks form. Gradually add the remaining 2 Tbsps. sugar and continue mixing at high speed until the whites hold stiff peaks.

Fold ⅓ of the chocolate mixture into the whites. Gently fold in the remaining chocolate until it is just blended with the whites. Pour into a prepared pan.

Bake 30 minutes at 325°. Cool on a rack for 5 minutes, then run a knife around the edge of the pan to loosen. Remove from the pan and let cool. Sprinkle the top with powdered sugar before serving. ✳

WINE PAIRING: When this cake is made with *Graham's Six Grapes Port, Graham's LBV* or *Vintage Ports* are perfect matches to the rich flavors of fresh fruit from the *Six Grapes* and the chocolate. If the cake is made with the *Tawny Port*, serve a Graham's 20- or 30-year *Tawny Port* and you will taste darker flavors of molasses, nuts and coffee, which harmonize perfectly with the bittersweet chocolate.

Recipe Index